MW00476979

YO CHING

ANCIENT KNOWLEDGE FOR STREETS TODAY

Printed in the United States of America
First Printing, 2015
ISBN 978-09964625-0-1
True Player
www.yoching.net

Cover Art and Wrexagrams copyright © 2015 by True Player

Cover art and Wrexagram design by Brendan Miller,
works.bkm@gmail.com

Book design by Maureen Cutajar,
www.gopublished.com

Produced by Hugh Gallagher,
www.hughgallagher.net

FOREWORD
by
Hugh Gallagher

Living in Asia had been a lifelong dream. During the economic stagnation of 2010, when life in America had little to offer, it seemed a reasonable reality. Traveling alone, I landed in Bangkok on a one way ticket, with two bags and three thousand dollars. With dumb luck and smart hustle, I lived for several years in South East Asia. It proved to be a pivotal adventure. Based in Bangkok, I traveled throughout Thailand, enjoyed significant forays through Laos as well as Cambodia, and learned languages, cultures and histories I had never before explored. Along the way I met lots of people, many characters, and one True Player.

I'd like very much to share his real name, but my collaborator wishes to remain anonymous. Foreigners hold a delicate place in the fiercely intricate hierarchy of Asian business. Prospering quietly is preferred. Such demands limit us to broad profile. True Player is a black man from the Bronx, born in the late 1960s. His business in Asia started in 1989, when a hip-hop tour he was with finished in Tokyo. Choosing to remain in Japan, True Player began as a party promoter and later expanded into other ventures throughout Asia. These were obviously lucrative, as judged by his tailored slacks, high end cologne, bespoke white silk shirts, jade cuff links, and top-shelf female companionship. We met when one of these stunning Thai women spilled my drink at The Cosmos.

The Cosmos is an old Bangkok bar, famous as a CIA watering hole during the Viet Nam war. The dim, darkly stained place is filled with carved wooden Thai statues and haunted with shadows. It's easy to see why the sleazy elegance was favored by Company men during the war. It remains popular with expats today. Greeted by Thai women with chilled wet hand towels, men wipe off the sweat from Bangkok's blazing heat and soak up the atmosphere, chatting over whiskey sodas. When mine was spilled by True Player's date on the night we met, he insisted on buying another. Generously upgrading me to Johnny Walker Black, the large, well groomed man toasted cheers and we fell into chatting.

New York City formed an easy, instant bond between us. I had spent most of my life there. True Player had been born in The Bronx. Half a life in Asia had done little to change his uptown roots. His profanity laced speech was blunt, rhythmic and straightforward; kind of like a boxer punching you. But when his ultra slim gold phone rang, he flipped effortlessly into Japanese or Thai. True Player was the epitome of international gentleman cool. I was happy to find him. Having just recently landed in Bangkok, still fumbling with the adjustment to international living, I welcomed a fellow New Yorkers' casual tutelage.

While meeting as regulars at The Cosmos, True Player shared perhaps the broadest base of bar room knowledge I have ever encountered. Beyond tips to living well in Thailand, his riffs covered everything from market shares to political *coups*, Burmese border disputes, Vietnamese factory riots, the way Laotian women orgasm, Khmer Rouge history, the films of Edward G Robinson, salacious hip hop gossip, gravy recipes, Japanese yakuza tales, Louie Rankin lyrics, detailed historical anecdotes about Julius Caesar, ruminations on the Rothschild family, Chinese real estate, pancakes, and everything in between. Framed in a gallery of "motherfucker" "bitches" and "shit", his jewels of wisdom were both hilarious and limitless. So one night when True Player brought up the *I Ching*, which he claimed to have memorized, I wasn't too surprised.

I had learned of this classic Chinese book while a student at New York University, in a survey course on ancient Asian literature. The *I Ching* is one of the oldest books in the world, dating back to BC China. The original author remains lost in the mists of time. But the cryptic text has since puzzled scholars, mystics, and seekers of truth for more than 3000 years. A myriad of minds, from Confucius to Jung, have meditated on the *I Ching*, trying to decipher the meaning of its 64 different "hexagrams". Dividing the book into chapters, these cryptic lines are filled with Princes and Inferiors, armies and kingdoms, jackals, arrows, rivers, stars and seasons, all providing metaphoric images reflecting profound Chinese wisdom. The *I Ching* has been described by Terence McKenna as a "Periodic Table of Time". Like the Western Periodic Table defines the elements of matter, the Eastern *I Ching* defines the temporal elements which generate life situations. But people are not meant to digest this wisdom by reading the *I Ching* straight through. This text is used as a tool. Randomly accessing various chapters, followers of the *I Ching* believe the spirit of the book presents precisely what they need to know, about whatever situation they are seeking guidance on, without their conscious choice.

That the vastly and randomly informed True Player was familiar with this cornerstone of Asian thought did not, as mentioned previously, surprise me. He was widely read, and half his life had been spent on that part of the planet. But when he began reciting from memory various passages—translated into "motherfucker"-thick Bronx patois, I was intrigued. Player's profound and casual take on the *I Ching*—which he called *Yo Ching*—was totally profane and utterly wise. His disregard for propriety opened new dimensions within the work. Throughout history, many learned sages have applied themselves to translations of this classic world text. But none of them, to my knowledge, have utilized phrases like "crab ass",

"bitch slap", and references to "roll on motherfuckers cross town".
Impressed, I proposed to preserve it for posterity. He would talk,
and I would write. We shook hands on that arrangement, and late
that night in a Bangkok bar, *Yo Ching* was born.

For the next two years, off and on, months at times passing be-
tween meetings, I sat with True Player in The Cosmos and
transcribed *Yo Ching*. Translating ancient Chinese knowledge to
modern Bronx street talk was an incredible talent of Player's. He
had an innate ability to break down the most arcane and obscure
elements of this puzzling Chinese classic into plain, straightfor-
ward, profane simplicity. But the task of capturing this was far
from simple. Because my publicity shunning partner forbade any
form of recording him, I was forced to scribble shorthand. My jag-
ged scrawl filled at first pages, then entire notebooks. The steady
stream of whiskey sodas True Player supplied me with further
blurred my hasty handwriting, as did frequent, not entirely un-
pleasant interruptions by Thai women working the bar. Despite
these hurdles, or perhaps enriched by them, *Yo Ching* eventually
took form in four large spiral bound notebooks; splashed with so-
da, stained with whiskey, and steeped in knowledge.

These were all rather hastily packed with my belongings when an
unexpected business offer brought me back to the United States in
2014. Given mere days to move, I missed the chance to bid fare-
well to True Player, who was attending to his own business in
China. Regretfully, I left a quickly written note at The Cosmos,
providing contact information and my solemn promise to bring *Yo
Ching* to life. But back home, I found that the promise I had
blithely scribbled on the back of a Thai bar tab was no simple one
to keep. Culture shocked by my return to America, thrust into a
high pressure, fast moving commercial writing project, I had very
little time for reflection. Spare days were spent trying to find a
home, re-establish friendships, attend to tax matters, and the oth-
er time consuming minutiae a re-patriot faces. It was nearly a year

before I revisited my notebooks from The Cosmos. Leafing through the scribbled, bar stained pages, I was not entirely surprised to find that writing which had seemed illuminated in the dark glow of a Bangkok bar now seemed erratic and fragmented. Nevertheless, I remembered my promise to True Player, and setting Saturdays aside, began the work.

As I commenced editing this treasure trove of Chinese born, Bronx slanted wisdom, I found myself gradually falling back into the rhythm of True Player's speech. I took to speaking the notes aloud, which helped me both remember my friend warmly, and make the text much more clear. (It is a technique I would suggest for all readers of this volume. *Yo Ching* is most alive when spoken aloud.) Over the course of the next half year, my misgivings vanished and the transcription proceeded smoothly, if slower than I would have liked. But what I myself wanted seemed to matter very little in this process. During my entire experience with *Yo Ching*, I felt my place to be little more than secretary. First, desperately scribbling as True Player expounded in a Bangkok bar, and later in America, where I felt *Yo Ching* practically writing itself, finding form in the pages you read now.

This final product is both transcendent and brutally practical. The depth of wisdom that has enticed *I Ching* scholars of all schools, through many generations, is evident within every "Wrexagram" of *Yo Ching*. But the blunt brilliance of the Bronx brings these lessons to modern heights. Both savvy and sage, profane and noble, True Player's *Yo Ching* reflects the disjointed contradictions of our time. We have inherited an era of instant information and endless confusion. But there is a rhythm to things. The *I Ching* has shared that lesson for thousands of years. Finding our place within that rhythm is life's central task. True Player shows the way through limitless paths. Following them helps us individually, and preserves us collectively. Like environmental conservation, *Yo Ching* provides mental conservation. Instead of slashing down people and burning the competition, readers of *Yo Ching* learn to perceive reality, blend their intentions, measure results, and refine efforts to realize highest potentials. Such personal realization in turn enriches us all.

The riches held in the pages you now possess are impossible to measure. It is a book about many things. Perhaps everything. Or one thing in particular, which I learned the night *Yo Ching* began. Opening my first notebook in the shadows of The Cosmos, I had asked True Player what it was all about. From that dark bar halfway around the planet, his reply remains clear.

"Harmony, yo."

Hugh Gallagher
2015

INTRODUCTION
by
True Player

Through ancient Chinese symbols and strategies, *Yo Ching* taps into hidden powers of the universe. Brother rolling with *Yo Ching* flows with timeless forces. He follows cosmic patterns for maximum success. Streets today don't have time for theoretical bullshit. *Yo Ching* helps players pop off. Puts brothers in the rhythm of things. Motherfuckers in the wrong place work real hard without shit happening. Players in the right place flex real light, for just the right minute, and have large effects in the game. *Yo Ching* shows how. *Yo Ching* changes a brother. Time don't work against him no more. World spins with him. Like he's floating down the river instead of trying to crawl up some waterfall. That's *Yo Ching* power.

Yo Ching knowledge started in China, three thousand years back. While Europeans were living in caves, Chinese brothers were thinking on some advanced shit. Trying to understand how Time works in The Heavens, and the life of ordinary motherfuckers. Chinese brothers learned that planets, stars, oceans, and seasons all move in rhythm. That rhythm moved through people's reality. Shit was linked. Same power running The Heavens ran them streets. Recognizing that rhythm and learning to flow with it let players run high level game. Put brothers on top of changes, instead of getting played by them.

This shit was written down in the deepest book ever. It showed how reality works. Every situation in life was broken down. Brothers called that book *I Ching: Book of Changes*.

I Ching is the oldest book on the planet still being read today. True Player picked it up in China, during years running business in Asia. Shit is different out there. Motherfuckers roll real long game. Chinese brothers step into business and political situations thinking: *Yo, what's our 150 year plan here?* Thai brothers believe in reincarnation. Treat a bad life the way motherfuckers might look at a bad job: just some shit to deal with, next one around be better. Looking at time like that changes the game. Visitors pick that shit up or get shaken out. Lucky for True Player, some Chinese brothers shared that *I Ching*. Told True Player to do some learning if he planned on living that side of the planet.

Chinese people have a saying. *If a brother wants to understand life, he shouldn't read a whole mess of books. He should read one book, over and over, until he understand that shit.* Only certain books a brother can spend his lifetime reading. *I Ching* is one of them. True Player got deep into that joint. Read about the rhythm of reality, and how shit changes. Learned to flow with those hidden forces. Business picked up. Plays popped off. *I Ching* lead the way. True Player started thinking: *Yo, there's some knowledge here brothers back home should be rolling with.* But True Player know his people. Motherfuckers from around the way ain't having shit to do with no three thousand year old book from China. So what True Player did was break down them ancient Chinese formulas to make sense for streets today. That's **Yo Ching: Ancient Knowledge for Streets Today**.

True Player from the Bronx. Been all over Asia, but never forgot them streets. Shit is real clear uptown. The reality of power, and how it works, breaks down crisp. So True Player used street situations to teach *Yo Ching* lessons. That don't mean *Yo Ching* is just for brothers rolling deep. *Yo Ching* should be interpreted. Like people read the Bible. Christians deep in scripture ain't trying to walk on water. They try to understand the meaning behind them words. That's how to roll with *Yo Ching*. Situations are metaphors in this joint. Brothers should trip out. *Yo Ching* shows higher reality. But it ain't religion. *Yo Ching* is for them streets, and everybody on them streets, believing whatever. Christian, Jewish, Islamic, Buddhist, and all them other religions out there can roll here. *Yo Ching* respects The Heavens. Whatever a brother worship in The Heavens is his business. Brothers who don't really believe in shit ain't have no problem neither. Whatever make them stars shine a billion miles away, holds the planets in orbit, brings seasons round and rolls waves through the ocean is powerful shit. A motherfucker don't have to believe somebody's handling that power if he really ain't feeling it. But that power is real. It's large. It's running things.

Running things is what *Yo Ching* is about. First it helps a brother run his life. Once a brother set his life straight through *Yo Ching* knowledge, he's a Player. Reliable motherfucker rising in the game, putting plays together and making solid moves. Shit will start shaking out for him. If Player moves to the next level, he becomes a True Player. That takes years of maintaining crisp, respecting The Heavens, and running shit right. True Player is an elevated brother who Bring It. True Players set streets straight. They roll right, wherever they maintain. True Players might be running a corporation or driving a bus. Maybe making records or making salami sandwiches at the motherfucking bodega. Don't matter. True Player is about power. Where he feels that power, and what type of power he handles is always different. But he always handle it crisp. True Players might have Legendary runs, or be handling Ill Shit. Either way, they read streets right. True Players don't try to Pop Off when it's time to Maintain. Don't Pull Back when it's time to Get Over. That's because True Players are masters of reality. *Yo Ching* helps brothers master their reality.

Personally, this here True Player feels that more True Players will help the game. World needs brothers living right, rolling right, finding their place in the rhythm of things. Just a few brothers doing that will help bring people higher. **Yo Ching: Ancient Knowledge For Streets Today** is for everybody. It ain't about one brother on top saying: *Look at me, motherfuckers. I got over.* It's about a bunch of brothers rising up saying: *Follow us, motherfuckers. Let's all get over.*

Shit changes. Change it for the better. *Yo Ching* is here.

True Player
2015

HOW TO THROW THE YO

Using the Yo Ching[*]

Yo Ching is more than a book. It's an interactive system offering advice and guidance. Players ask *Yo Ching* questions, and *Yo Ching* answers with a **Wrexagram**. *Yo Ching* is made of **64 Wrexagrams**. These ancient Chinese symbols share hidden knowledge. Brothers unlock *Yo Ching* Wrexagrams through a process called **Throwing The Yo**. Once a player learn how to Throw The Yo, he ain't alone in the game no more. *Yo Ching* gives him answers and advice, like his own personal *consigliere*. But *Yo Ching* don't give 'yes' or 'no' answers. *Yo Ching* don't tell Players what to do. *Yo Ching* shares insight, helping Players make the right decisions for themselves. But to make the right decisions, a player Throwing The Yo have to ask the right questions.

The right *Yo Ching* questions don't lead to yes/no answers. Like maybe Player have questions about some job offer. To Throw The Yo, Player don't say: *Yo Ching, should I take this job?* That would lead to a yes/no answer. Player keeps the question open, asking: *Yo Ching, please tell me what will happen if I take this job?* Or: *Yo Ching, please tell me helpful insight about this job offer?* That style of question lets *Yo Ching* offer advice, without telling a brother what to do.

---

[*] *Players without time to spare can still roll with Yo Ching. Whatever page they open have deep wisdom. For digital brothers, Yo Ching app is on the way. Check yoching.net to find out when it pops off.*

The word *please* shows respect. Think of *Yo Ching* like an old Chinese master from a Kung Fu movie, living in the mountains. Brothers in Kung Fu movies show mad respect to old masters like that. Treat *Yo Ching* like your own Kung Fu master in the mountains. *Please* is the proper way to show respect. If a player Throw The Yo with respect, *Yo Ching* throws real wisdom back his way. But if a motherfucker just mess around, *Yo Ching* throw bullshit right back at him. And players should never ask the same question twice. That shit is disrespectful. One Throw for a question. That's it. If Player don't like the answer, tough shit. *Yo Ching* tells a brother what's real. Sometimes, *Yo Ching* will answer with a Wrexagram that don't make sense. That's **Yo Ching Override**. It happens when a brother is asking one question, but some other shit on his mind. Maybe he Throw The Yo about work. Meanwhile, his girl just got pregnant and he's tripping on that. *Yo Ching* will know. So Player should focus when he's Throwing the Yo. Nothing should be on Player's mind but one single question. He asks that with respect, then Throw The Yo.

That's done with a *Yo Ching*, three coins, a pen, and some paper. Coins can be from anywhere. Just need a clear heads/tails marking. Player takes them three coins in his hands, shakes them up like dice. Then he throws them down, all together at once, on the floor or table. The three coins will land showing heads or tails. Player picks up his pen to record how the coins landed. He does that by drawing lines:

TWO HEADS AND ONE TAILS = STRONG LINE

TWO TAILS AND ONE HEADS = SPLIT LINE

THREE HEADS = STRONG LINE WITH A BREAK

THREE TAILS = SPLIT LINE WITH A BREAK

He draws one line at the bottom of his paper to record how the three coins landed. Then Player picks up the three coins. Shakes them like dice, and throws them all down together on the table again. He records how they landed by drawing another line. (Strong Line, Split Line, Split Line with a Break, or Strong Line with a Break). This second line should be drawn right above the first, like a ladder going up. He does this six different times, drawing each line right above the last one. When he's finished, Player will have six lines, stacked one on top of the other. That's his **Wrexagram**. It might look like this:

Once Player have his Wrexagram, he picks up his *Yo Ching to* look at the Wrexagram Chart. He checks every Wrexagrams in the chart, until he finds the one that matches what he wrote down. The Wrexagram above is **Wrexagram 58: HAPPY.**

WREXAGRAM 58
HAPPY

There's a break on the four. (Remember: Wrexagram lines are written and read from the bottom up.) So Player here opens *Yo Ching* to the chapter for **Wrexagram 58: HAPPY.** Each Wrexagram has a Feel, a Look, and six Breaks. Player here would read the Feel and Look of Wrexagram 58. And since this throw has a break on the four, Player would read the fourth break. Sometimes Wrexagrams have breaks, sometimes they don't. No breaks in a Wrexagram means the situation really ain't changing much, and general advice will do. If Player throws a Wrexagram with lots of breaks, he's in some shit that's really changing. Breaks give specific focus to issues involved.

Player can Throw The Yo for himself, or ask questions for his people. Throwing The Yo with the crew is a good look. Grab some brews and kick knowledge. Different heads thinking on Wrexagrams find different angles. Brothers been having real deep *Yo Ching* raps for thousands of years. That's because this wisdom runs deep. Wrexagrams are filled with different situations, images, and characters to trip on. *Yo Ching* got Big Dogs, Players, True Players, Ordinary Brothers, Crab Asses, Ill Brothers, Shorty, Slim Thing, whatever. **WORD: Yo Ching Glossary** is in the back of this book, where Players can learn definitions of words and terms. A brother will learn how to roll and relate. Maybe some situations he feel like the Big Dog. Other times, he might be the True Player. That's his decision. *Yo Ching* helps a person think. It don't think for him. But *Yo Ching* will talk to a Player, once he learn to Throw The Yo.

It ain't difficult. Paper, pen, three coins and a brother's rolling. Here's the important shit to remember:

- **Don't ask questions that need yes/no answers. Keep them open.**

- **Be respectful, say please, and don't ask the same question twice.**

- **Throw three coins at once. Do that six times in a row. Record each of these six Throws with a line.**

- **Write the lines from the bottom first, stacking them on top of each other.**

- **Find the Wrexagram in the chart that matches, and read that section in Yo Ching.**

- **Check WORD: Yo Ching Glossary in the back of *Yo Ching* for definitions of terms and words in the Wrexagrams.**

That's it. Five minutes of learning for a life time of knowledge. Throw The Yo and flow.

THE WREXAGRAMS

33		PULL BACK	49		THROW SHIT OFF
34		REAL POWER	50		THE POT
35		RISING	51		BOOM
36		DARK OUT	52		STAYING CHILL
37		FAMILY	53		PUSH IT ALONG
38		UP IN YOUR FACE	54		SLIM THING
39		SOME BULLSHIT	55		LEGENDARY
40		BAILED OUT	56		BOUNCING
41		LOSING WEIGHT	57		LIGHT TOUCH
42		BUMP UP	58		HAPPY
43		BREAKTHROUGH	59		BREAK IT UP
44		SAYING WHAT UP	60		LIMITS
45		BRING IT TOGETHER	61		FOR REAL
46		GETTING OVER	62		LITTLE PLAYS
47		PLAYED	63		AFTER SHIT FINISH
48		WATER FOUNTAIN	64		RIGHT AROUND THE CORNER

BRING IT

BRING IT is the power that makes everything happen. Runs The Heavens and them streets. Let There Be Light was the first BRING IT movement. The Lord BRING IT through time and space to light shit up. When a True Player shows up with power to change the game, brothers say he BRING IT.

THE FEEL

Bring It paid rolling low key.
Pushing the game by maintaining.

The brother who BRING IT to the game is called the True Player. When True Player BRING IT, he's rolling with power from The Heavens. BRING IT runs reality. With that force behind his moves, True Player don't miss a beat. But he only BRING IT to the game by living correct. True Player maintains health and harmony. Stays real with brothers. Rolls right all the time. No bullshit, shady plays or crab asses in his game, ever.

True Player sees life clear. He's real with how shit works. He understands the rhythm of things. That lets him roll deeper than ordinary motherfuckers. But he's down with brothers. True Player stays good with them streets. He looks up to The Heavens. Respect for what's right puts power behind his moves. Time don't work against True Players who BRING IT. Every minute working for these brothers. World spins their way. True Players flow with the universal forces running our reality.

Brothers like this set the game straight. True Players are larger than ordinary brothers and always handle shit right. True Players organize motherfuckers and set them rolling on plays. Put people paid. True Player ain't never ill. When he have to break it down, True Player is fair. He have mad love for them streets. Down with every brother from Manhattan Avenue to Malaysia. True Player don't see difference. One blood, yo.

Streets are happy when a True Player BRING IT. Brothers are down with the plays True Player puts them on. They like where his moves lead. That's because True Player don't play the game for himself. When he BRING IT, True Player helps every mother-fucker reach their highest reality. He steps into the game to reminds brothers what's real. He shows them what's good. When a True Players BRING IT, brothers live life like The Heavens planned. Everybody gets over together.

THE LOOK

Heavens rolls with power.
True Player stays strong.
Never tired.

Heaven don't stop making days. The biggest Big Dog on the motherfucking planet won't stop time. Them days just roll. The forces of BRING IT maintain power through time, forever.

True Player learns his game by thinking deep on how the forces of BRING IT roll. He maintains power through time by making himself strong. Throws shit out of his life that wastes time. TV, liquor, drugs, porno, chasing slim things, drama, crab asses, bullshit parties, whatever. Living crisp helps True Player focus. He ain't some motherfucker trying to be everything. True Player puts limits on himself. Picks his plays, chooses his angles, runs them right. All other shit he just let go. Focus like that makes him real powerful.

THE BREAKS

Break on the one means:
Hidden power. Chill.

BRING IT moves power through the world in seasons. Winter time, power chills underground in the earth. Then all that shit bust right out in spring. Power hits the peak in summer time. Real hot days, thunder and lightning storms, all that. Then power rolls back underground in the fall, so it don't burn out. Winter time, power's chilling inside the planet again.

Right here, nobody recognize True Player. Life is like winter for him. Low key and chill. That don't matter to True Player. Whether he's recognized or not don't change his game. True Player rolls right whatever happening. When streets go cold, he lays up like power in the winter. Lets shit play out a minute. True Player don't try and pop off when timing ain't right. A brother who forces shit just burns through his money and connects. That's bullshit.

Break on the two means:
Player in the House.
Let a brother know.

A True Player just been pulled into the crew. He hasn't rolled on a major play yet. But he handles business real powerful. A brother should say what up now. Show he's down. Then brother's in tight when True Player BRING IT down the line.

Break on the three means:
Player making hits. Mind on money all night.
Watch the step. Good look.

True Player throws down his first hit. Straight up BRING IT. Hype blows up. Shit is bananas. Business rolling, females trying to meet him, brothers all up in his face, crab asses climbing in the crew, all that. But True Player maintains his flow. He knows the first step up is the slippery one. Lots of Players made one hit, tripped, and fell right the fuck off. So True Player misses that party bullshit, chills on the bitches, just handles business, and stays focused. Real good look, there.

Break on the four means:
Whatever way he roll.
All good.

True Player BRING IT for real. Gets over, 100%. Ain't no problem with finance no more. He makes the call from here. Blow up large or chill. Fly with that fame or maintain his investments and chill on the islands. Whatever True Player's feeling is the right move. It's all good.

Break on the five means:
Crazy fame.
People see him and freak.

True Player is highly recognized. His style runs the world. His business changes the game. The Heavens have his back. Player flows through a legendary run of hits on the chart, money in the bank, and love in them streets. When True Player steps off, his name will stay up there forever. Even the most crab ass must admit this. People just see True Player and freak. Like, "Oh My God!"

Break at the top means:
Brother check himself or wreck himself.

Brothers who lose touch with reality fall off. When Player is blinded by power, the run plays out. This break is a heads up. Player ain't God. Motherfuckers who try flying to The Heavens fall. Hit streets real hard. Bust ass.

WREXAGRAM 2
WITH IT

When True Player Bring It, WITH IT is down.

WITH IT rolls with the power. He don't bring the power. He's down with it. Every True Player needs somebody WITH IT. They run together and make plays. But if WITH IT step to True Player's face, or try and pop off, that's bullshit. A brother shouldn't try to bring it when he's WITH IT.

THE FEEL

With It gets over low key.
Flowing with the movement.
If Player tries to lead, shit falls off.
But if Player flows With It, he finds his place.
Good look to find brothers with heart and soul.
Let go them flash and fashion motherfuckers.
Maintaining low key puts people paid.

WITH IT rolls low key. He's down with brothers and them streets. People respect. If WITH IT busts off on his own shit, he falls off. But if he rolls with how shit is shaking out, he finds himself in the flow.

WITH IT feels the rhythm of things and follows. Maybe he's rolling with a True Player. Maybe he's letting The Heavens lead him. Either way, he's feeling the power, and rolling WITH IT.

But WITH IT ain't no bitch. He handle his business and maintain tight game. When the crew rolls on a play, he push shit forward by being WITH IT. When True Player is making moves, WITH IT brings weight to the play by following. Both brothers elevate off this set-up. While True Player is flowing on high level shit, WITH IT hits them streets. Saying what up to brothers, he pushes Player's status.

If WITH IT tried to get over by himself, his shit would fall off. But if he rolls with True Player or follows The Heavens, shit shakes out. WITH IT have to be 100% down with his job. He feels what's right and flows with it. That adds power to the movement and helps brothers get over.

But trying to get over is no joke. So after WITH IT handle his side of things, this brother have to chill. WITH IT should pull back sometimes to be down with his own head. Roll up to the country, fly out to the islands. Just lay back a minute.

THE LOOK

Streets have a place for every motherfucker, good or bad.
True Player the same.
Handle everybody.

WITH IT handles VIP scenarios smooth. But also feels them streets. Only a real brother can roll right in both places. That's WITH IT. Nobody ever talk shit about this brother. Handles whatever thrown his way. Right there on it. True Player never BRING IT without a brother who's WITH IT.

THE BREAKS

Break on the one means:
Sniff that shit today,
Smoking it tomorrow.

Bad habits creep up. Brother dust a little here, sniff a little there, he picks up the habit. If not them drugs, might be them party bitches. Or shady business on the side. This break is a heads up: shit gets frosty before it turn to ice. Then it's too late and a brother's slipping. If there's ill shit and a brother's WITH IT, stop that nonsense now.

Break on the two means:
Just rolling.
Good look.

Ain't important to stress the objective right here. Brother shouldn't have plans. Whatever pops up, roll WITH IT. Shit will shake out this way.

Break on the three means:
Don't flash.
Handle business.

WITH IT ain't trying to pop off and blow up. Fame is stressful shit. He plays the game without flashing. Learns moves from watching. Understands how things work. Down the line if he want to bump up a level, WITH IT have the moves. But right now, he don't mind other brothers shining. WITH IT still gets paid. He just wants the right shit to get over.

Break on the four means:
True bad boys roll in silence.
Nothing happening. Nothing bad happening, either.

Brother have to watch it, here. Situation ain't positive. But stepping to what's wrong will bring ill brothers down on his ass. Just standing there ain't the play, neither. A brother who don't say shit will make ill motherfuckers real suspicious. Low profile is the play. Maintain with the crew. Bullshit with brothers, but don't bring up nothing real. Truth ain't popular when it's dark out.

Break on the five means:
True for real.

When a brother is real it shows. He don't have to broadcast to motherfuckers. Just handles his business. People recognize. There's always a place for a brother who's real like that.

Break at the top means:
Brothers fight in the street.
Blood in the gutter.

WITH IT follows the flow. True Player leads the crew. If WITH IT steps up to run shit, True Player has to break it down. Real bad look. Them brothers go off. Fists thrown, shots fired, both them motherfuckers all messed up and bleeding.

STRESS GETTING STARTED

Some bust ass basketball courts have grass growing right up through the pavement. Shit wasn't easy for that grass. Started out all alone in the dark. Had to push through all that motherfucking dirt. Then it hit the damn concrete. But that grass maintained till it got over into the light. That's STRESS GETTING STARTED.

That's how hard a brother works to get over in the game.

THE FEEL

Stress Getting Started works shit out.
Keeping at it for real.
No jumping the gun.
Reach out for people.

Before shit pops off, it has to come together. That's a hard time. There's lots of stress, talk, and dreams. But nobody really knows how the play will stack up and shake out. Shit's still coming together. Brothers get frustrated here. Some put plays in motion just to have business on them streets. True Player ain't with that. He know that rolling before shit comes together turns into plays that fall apart. But he needs people, and has to put them in motion. Without a crew that's running right, True Player don't have muscle. So he puts brothers together, holds them in line, and pulls through all that STRESS GETTING STARTED. Everybody gets over that way.

THE LOOK

Bad Weather. Lightning. Thunder.
The look of Stress Getting Started.
True Player pulls it all together.

Thunder storms are wild shit. But lightning and thunder work together. First lighting strikes, then thunder rolls. That shit has order, even when it looks bananas.

In the middle of STRESS GETTING STARTED, when shit is all over the place, True Player puts it in order. He takes a bunch of brothers, sorts shit out, and sets them rolling right.

THE BREAKS

Break on the one means:
Half stepping.
Maintain.
Find your people.

If a brother pulls off plays that don't get over, he has to step back. That don't mean he give up. But forcing shit ain't right. So he pulls in some other heads to help. He find his people by being real and chill. No fronting, no stress.

Break on the two means:
Nothing working out.
Brother pull up.
Ain't no crab ass. Wants to help a brother out.
Girl don't put out. She play cool.
Ten years later they hit it.

Player's in a situation where nothing shaking out. Then this brother shows up from nowhere, real helpful. He looks alright. But since Player don't know where that motherfucker come from, Player freezes him out. Business with that brother wouldn't be smart. Since Player's hungry, any help will mean a large piece of action in return. Down the line, when Player has shit together, it's different. If this brother shows up then, the two can talk business.

That's like a female who hears people whispering about her man. Saying he hits shit on the side. She's tripping. In the middle of the rumors, this real clean brother shows up. Looks good and has the right job. But this female waits to find the truth about her man. She learns all the talk was bullshit. So she stays with him.

Down the line, the relationship falls apart for whatever reasons. That real clean brother shows up again, and she decides to get with him. That's no problem now. She ain't lost in drama. Sister has her head together, standing strong. People make the right decisions like that.

Break on the three means:
Live uptown but try and get paid downtown.
Got no people there. Brother's lost.
True Player understands what time it is.
Better to lose weight uptown.
Rolling downtown would make him look bust ass.

If a brother has no people downtown, but rolls there trying to start something, motherfucker gets played. Uptown goes flat sometimes. But if that's the brother's area, he have to maintain there. When crab asses hear about brothers getting paid downtown, they start thinking stupid shit. Like just showing up there will pay out. But since they don't have connects downtown, them motherfuckers end up bust ass. True Player maintains in his area through hard times. Better to lose weight uptown then go bust ass downtown.

Break on the four means:
Train break down.
Pull it together.
Stepping out is the play.
Shit shakes out nice.

Bad situation. Time to roll, but Player don't have the muscle. Then this brother shows up with people. Player shouldn't be proud here. He's fucked and needs help. This brother is real, so shit shakes out.

Break on the five means:
Shit gets twisted.
Push it along.
Big action don't play.

Player has the right ideas but nobody real is listening. Mother-fuckers who are listening twist his words. Real frustrating for Player, but forcing shit is the wrong move. Player have to find some real brothers first. That happens only by rolling right for a particular length of time. When they know Player's for real, brothers will throw in. Then shit will move forward. But that don't happen overnight. So Player just push it along. Little bit here, little bit there. Big plays ain't possible now.

Break at the top means:
Totally bust ass.
Crying in the street all cut up.

STRESS GETTING STARTED shakes some brothers right out the game. They roll wrong, miss the play, and hit streets hard. Just quit right there. See them brothers years later fucked up on drugs or drinking wine. No shoes, falling down stairs, all bleeding and cut up. Real sad shit.

WREXAGRAM 4
SHORTY

SHORTY all over the neighborhood running wild, doing whatever. Young ones don't know better. Little SHORTY got no game.

THE FEEL

Shorty pulls it together.
No time for that.
But Shorty needs help.
First time, break it down, set things straight.
Shorty play the same nonsense,
Shit's over.
Maintain.

Being dumb ain't a crime for little ones. SHORTY will get it together if grown folks show the way. First SHORTY have to realize he don't have game. Find somebody real to break it down for him. Show that brother respect.

But Player don't chase after SHORTY trying to set him straight. Only when SHORTY ready to be respectful and pull his own weight can Player break it down.

When he does break it down, Player makes shit real simple.
SHORTY don't understand no motherfucking gray area. Shit is
right, or shit is wrong. That's all. Problems happen if SHORTY
don't respect or ain't focused. Sometimes SHORTY just straight
up don't believe Player. That happen, it's done. Player got no time
for that. Freeze SHORTY right the fuck out.

But if SHORTY listens, Player have to help that little one put his game
together. That takes a minute. Player has to be patient with SHORTY.

THE LOOK

Stream upstate.
The look of Shorty.
Player breaks it down for him without missing a beat.

Streams upstate in the country just flow. Water moves natural. Fills
up shallow spots then moves through deep parts. SHORTY learns
the same way. Knowledge flows from Player and just fills him up.
Happens natural.

THE BREAKS

Break on the one means:
Don't take no disrespect.
Set Shorty straight.
Chill a minute.

Little SHORTY don't take life serious. Player shows him streets are
no joke. But he don't come down hard all the time. Player never slap
SHORTY for real. He's just a little one. Player remembers that.

Break on the two means:
Good with the hood, even them out brothers.
Handling his women.
Shorty coming up to run shit.

This SHORTY too young for running things, but he's good with the whole block. Have respect for everybody. Big Dogs and ordinary brothers. SHORTY even down with them out motherfuckers pushing grocery carts filled with stuffed animals and shit. Has game with the females, plus respect for his Moms. That's a SHORTY be running shit one day.

Break on the three means:
Back off them gold digging bitches.
Nothing positive happening.

A SHORTY just coming up sometimes fall in with a Player. Starts sweating him. Dressing like him, talking like him, all that. Makes SHORTY like some female who throw herself at a rich brother. Bad look. Shorty shouldn't just throw in with players. Like a female shouldn't throw her ass at brothers. Both have to maintain until the more powerful motherfucker say what up. That's just proper.

Break on the four means:
Dreaming stupid shit and thinking he's all that with no game.
Bust ass.

Every SHORTY thinks they will play in the NBA. Or make millions rapping. But shit like that rarely happen. A young motherfucker who fronts on them streets saying he's famous don't make it real. With a SHORTY like that, it's best to freeze him out. Let him learn the hard way.

Break on the five means:
Brother don't know. Don't act like he do.
All Good.

Little SHORTY ain't supposed to have his game tight. Player knows that. So SHORTY just have to be real. Tell Player: "Yo, I ain't know what's up. But I want to roll with you. I have respect for your business." That's a real good look. SHORTY like that will find a brother to show him the way.

Break at the top means:
Don't shoot somebody just needs a slap.
Set them straight.
That's all.

Sometimes SHORTY act up. If Player tell him to cool out, but SHORTY still going bananas, Player has to break it down. But setting SHORTY straight is different. Player don't break it down hard with little ones. Same goes for Player's operation. The reason Player breaks shit down is to return shit to order. It ain't about slapping the taste out of a motherfuckers' mouth in front of the bodega. People see that shit and start laughing. That ain't right. There are situations where somebody have to be hit. But Player always break it down with respect.

CHILL

Brothers play the game to get paid. Everybody trying to get over. But nobody knows when that shit will happen. Ain't no clock tell a motherfucker when he's about to pop off. Streets decide what's good and when. True Player is down with that. He stays CHILL. His game will hit when it's time. Until that happens, Player maintains.

Crab asses don't know how to CHILL. Them motherfuckers put a joint on the street and stress the situation. Up in every brother's face yelling: "When my shit get over? When my shit get over?" Since they pushy like that, crab asses never hit. They never CHILL and let shit develop.

THE FEEL

Chill. Brother for real gets paid.
Stay with it to get over.
Good look to play Long Game.

CHILL don't mean laying back and fucking off. It means maintaining even when there's no love in the game for a brother. The CHILL Player never hopes his shit will get over. He knows it will.

19

He just don't know when. Holding steady like that, whatever happens, helps him play long game. That mindset lets a brother maintain complex angles at many different levels.

The player who stays CHILL when shit ain't happening for him is a True Player. Don't matter to him what streets saying about his business. True Player stays true to himself, his crew, and the game. He looks at shit straight up and knows what's going down. True Player never wish for shit to be different. He don't act like shit is something it ain't. He's real with how shit is, and finds his way through.

Only a brother who deals with things as they really are will handle business right. Players like that can roll on real moves for the long game. Pull through ill scenarios, no problem.

THE LOOK

Train pulling in the station.
The look of Chill.
True Player has a brew,
Laughing and talking shit with his people.

When a brother's waiting for the subway, he hears rumbling down the tracks. That means the train is pulling closer. Brother just have to wait. Nothing he do will make that motherfucking train show up sooner. Luck's the same. It shows up when it wants to. Some brothers catch a break when they young. Their train comes in early. Other brothers don't get over till they're older. Their train pulls up late. Just how it is.

Sometimes motherfuckers in the subway stress. They wait on the platform. Train don't come, they run upstairs to find a bus. Bus rolls right past them. So they run back down to the subway. But they missed the train chasing the bus. Now they fucked. Wouldn't have a problem if they were just CHILL.

Many motherfuckers in the game are just like that. Stress about when they gonna get over. Have problems waiting for their train to pull up. Play one angle for a minute, but shit don't happen fast enough. So they play another. Both fall through. Motherfuckers like that never make it nowhere.

True Player maintains his angles. Plays his game. But he don't stress about his motherfucking train coming in. That lets him relax and CHILL. Share a brew with his people. Talk some bullshit. His train pulls in when it does.

THE BREAKS

Break on the one means:
Chill in the park.
Do what have to be done.

Streets are talking. Rumors about drama. People say some ill shit heading Player's way. But since it ain't shown up yet, Player just CHILL. He don't stress himself or his crew. Just CHILL in the park. He ain't hiding. Streets feel that and respect Player. Motherfuckers won't be saying he's a brother who lost his head. People will say Player stay CHILL.

Break on the two means:
Chill in the hood.
Bitches be bitching.
Wraps OK.

The drama heats up and moves closer to Player. Ain't safe for him to CHILL in the park no more. Player have to maintain in his area. Stay deep in his people. But tension rising and the crew is stressing. Motherfuckers are talking mad shit. Brothers trying to blame other brothers for the situation. Rumors flying, bitches bitching, people yelling shit from down the block. With that much nonsense, True Player don't try to set the record straight. He don't break it down for crab asses, or yell back at some stupid sister cross the street. Player just CHILL. Down the line, shit shakes out right because he didn't act up.

Break on the three means:
Chill on the bus.
Ill brothers roll up on his ass.

When drama gets thick, some people lose their head. When they hear shit is heading their way, these brothers don't think shit through. Just pull some half ass play to bounce. Like a brother who jump on the first bus that passes. But maybe that shit is running local. Now he's stopped at the light. Them ill brothers he was running from might roll up. If they see that motherfuckers sitting in the window, brother's in a bad spot. Only play he have is praying for the light to change. Plus hoping real hard them ill brothers ain't the type of wild motherfuckers who shoot up no bus.

Break on the four means:
Waiting in blood.
Get out the alley.

Dangerous situation here. Blood gonna spill. Brother standing with his back to the wall, no move to make. A brother trapped like that just have to let shit play out. Only thing that will help him is staying CHILL. That way he don't stress the situation.

Break on the five means:
Chill with dinner.
Maintain. Paid.

Ill times still have patches when shit rolls right. If a brother is strong inside, he takes advantage of good times. He CHILL a minute and gets ready for whatever the fuck is heading his way next. But he can't let an easy stretch like that throw his game. No party and bullshit. Have to maintain and roll forward. That's the way to get over.

True Player running a crew realizes that nobody pulls off everything at once. He lets the brothers in his organization bullshit some. Laugh it up. When True Player lets brothers kick it sometimes, they down for more work. Maintain shit till it's finished right.

CHILL is about staying positive while shit ain't moving. That doesn't mean blocked out or shut down. Those are different situations. When a brother is CHILL, he's just waiting for pieces to fall in place. He stays crisp and in a good mood. He knows shit will lean his way when the timing is right.

Break at the top means:
Fall into shit.
Three brothers show up.
Ain't know these motherfuckers.
Show respect, shit shakes out.

Danger can't be dodged no more. True Player falls right into some ill shit. Seems like all he did to maintain and roll right was bullshit. Right then, some brothers step into his situation. True Player don't know whether these motherfuckers trying to help him or murder him. When shit's real ill, most people feel like telling brothers to just fuck off. But in ill situations, True Player stays mentally crisp. He gets over himself and reaches out to these brothers with respect. They help him crush that ill shit. No more problems. Sometimes good things in life show up in ways that look real fucked up to us.

DRAMA

When True Player meets some Ill Brother who rolls deep, DRA-MA happens. If Ill Brother has a head for the game and real sharp moves, that DRAMA will be serious.

THE FEEL

Drama.
For real but no love.
Hold up.
Maintaining leads nowhere.
Good look to find the Big Dog.
No long game now.

DRAMA happens when Player feels right, but another brother thinks he's wrong. If Player ain't 100% together, static from that brother will shake him up. Streets feel that. People start talking shit then. Run shady plays from behind the scenes. Nobody will get up in Player's face, but his shit will fall off.

Player have to maintain a clear head. Try to meet the other brother halfway. Even if Player is right, war will damage shit too much. So

Player should find a Big Dog with real weight in the game. Big Dog will look at shit fair. Break it down for both brothers involved.

While DRAMA is happening, Player don't pop off real business. Static in the crew ain't a good look. Brothers have to be tight to meet them streets.

THE LOOK

East Side and West Side roll different.
The look of Drama.
True Player watch shit close from the jump.

DRAMA happens because people just do shit different. Some brothers roll West Side, other brothers roll East Side. When they meet, it's DRAMA. But if the situation is made real clear from the jump, so every motherfucker involved knows how shit should be, there's a chance to kill the DRAMA. The other way it shakes out right is if both sides have True Players advanced on some spiritual shit.

THE BREAKS

Break on the one means:
Let shit slide.
People talk.
Shakes out fine.

When a beef is just starting, best thing to do is let it slide. Especially if Player dealing with some ill brothers who just don't give a fuck. Bitches will bitch, but that shit dies down. Situation shakes out fine.

Break on the two means:
Don't step to Ill Brother.
Go on home.
Family and people down.

Player falls into a beef with some real ill brother. Motherfucker just born wrong. Ain't a bitch move to back down. If Player steps up, he's trying to be murdered. Dead Player ain't a good look. Fucks up his family and leaves the crew without a leader. Player don't worry about his rep. Streets knows that ill brother is twisted. Player just say "my bad", then backs off respectful.

Break on the three means:
Some things don't change. Know the score.
Drama.
Ends right.
With it for Player don't stress him.

Player don't throw his money toward everybody who ask for it. Even family, yo. He hold on to what he work for. People will talk some shit, but they respect.

If a brother is rolling with a True Player, he shouldn't bring DRA-MA by looking for the spotlight. He just have to get shit done and let Player shine.

Break on the four means:
Don't bring Drama.
Chill.
Good look.

Brother has problems. Trying to rise in game by starting DRAMA. Even if he steps to soft motherfuckers who fold like laundry, it still ain't right. Brother knows that. So he chills on the DRAMA. That's the right play. Down the line something good comes his way.

Break on the five means:
Reach out to Big Dog sets shit straight.
All good.

Big Dog gets respect. He's for real. Always breaks it down right and ends the beef. When Player have problems, he finds this Big Dog to set shit straight. That's a good look.

Break at the top means:
Hits on the chart. OK.
Tomorrow three other brothers hitting.

Brother played hardcore and buried people. Now he's running the game a minute. He won't be happy long. Life will be filled with motherfuckers trying to take him out, shoot him down, and grab his action. Just how it is.

ROLLING

Player's soldiers might not always be together, but they always there. Player reach out, them motherfuckers rolling. With hard brothers like this, Player have to run shit tight. Some Players maintain like the King, looking down from up high. But the real way to run crews is like a general in the army. When streets is hot, Player right there with them. Brothers follow a Player like that anywhere.

THE FEEL

Rolling.
The crew need to maintain.
Player.
Roll tight that way.

Soldiers are a bunch of hard brothers who have to be organized. If they don't maintain order, shit falls off. Player calls the shots. But he ain't hard, breaking it down on brothers all ill. Player just maintains for real. Brothers feel what he's about. Follow Player into whatever. Player lets brothers run their part of the operation without riding them hard. Just believes in them. Lets brothers flow. That's his part of the deal.

ROLLING on motherfuckers is dangerous shit. People drop. Not just soldiers. Motherfuckers who ain't got nothing to do with shit maybe catch a bullet. Player have to think hard on the reality of bringing violence to a situation. Brothers will die or be fucked up for life. End up retarded, shit in a bag crippled, or do time. That's why ROLLING is the last and worst choice on the list.

True Players only go ROLLING on motherfuckers when all else fails, and shit is do or die.

THE LOOK

Brothers all over the area.
The look of the crew.
True Player finds his people by being real,
Making sure they paid.

Brothers all over the neighborhood. Nobody know who's ROLL-ING or not. But when some motherfuckers step up starting shit, brothers turn into soldiers. Lay them motherfuckers down or chase them out. After that, soldiers go back to being brothers in the neighborhood. That's how it should be.

Player who put his people paid gets love from the crew. If he run shit right but maintains low key, that crew is strong. Broke ass crews got no game. Only paid brothers get respect. That's why Player pays his people right.

Player lets them run their piece without stress. Pays them right. He hit both them beats, Player's crew have real love for him. Those brothers will roll deep and do whatever it takes to win war for him.

THE BREAKS

Break on the one means:
Crew got to roll correct.
Bust ass shit folds.

When brothers ROLLING, shit has to be tight. Player have to be doing it for a damn good reason. His people have to feel it, and roll together. Otherwise they're fucked.

Break on the two means:
Player rolls with his crew.
Money. All good.
Big Dog show respect.

When it's on, Player's right there with his people. Shots fired, he's taking hits. That makes Player for real. Big Dogs see that. Respect Player and his crew. Ain't nobody talk shit about a Player out there fighting. His whole crew gets respect from that.

Break on the three means:
Brothers drive the ride.
Bad look.

The ride got one steering wheel. That's for one brother to drive. Motherfuckers all try and steer, shit goes nowhere. That's bullshit. Player leads, yo.

Break on the four means:
Crew pulls back.
All Good.

When the crew is outgunned, outnumbered, and outsmarted, pulling back is the play. But Players don't do that like a bunch of bitches running. Players pull back tactical. Bob Marley broke it down like this: "He that fight and run away, live to fight another day." Nobody proves they're real by getting their whole crew murdered.

Break on the five means:
Crab ass brothers on the corner. Shoot that shit.
No problem.
Player call the shots. Brothers put them down.
Good look.

Player got crab ass brothers from who the fuck knows where in his area. They spreading out, like Player ain't even there. Coming down hard is definitely the play. But that don't mean ROLLING wild busting shots. Player have to organize that shit. Sweep them motherfuckers out scientifically. Player strategize, then his soldiers make it happen. That's being crisp. Word gets around about brothers who handle ROLLING like that.

Break at the top means:
Player sets the crew up.
People get their piece. Family gets paid.
Half ass brothers don't handle business.

Player ROLLED right and ROLLED deep. Won the war and picked up new territory. Now he breaks that shit off for his people. Brothers who was out their ROLLING get bumped up with better action. When shit went down, some half-ass brothers might have fallen in and helped out some. Player pays them motherfuckers money. But he don't give them business angles. Handing half-ass brothers action will only bring problems down the line.

WREXAGRAM 8
HOLD IT TOGETHER

Times Square is in the middle of New York City. Large avenues flow right into it. True Player is like Times Square. Other brothers are the avenues. Everything leads to True Player. Without that True Player who HOLD IT TOGETHER, brothers just fuck around. Without flow from other brothers, Player have nothing to hold together. Both need the other.

THE FEEL

Hold It Together gets paid.
Player ask once more if he really solid.
Good look.
Brothers with it from the jump are down.
Crab ass late ain't get none.

Brothers in a crew have to HOLD IT TOGETHER to get over. Shit starts with True Player in the middle. Real serious job. Business to handle 24/7. Motherfuckers to organize. Shit to deal with. Plays to pop off. Static to navigate. True Player can't just be strong. He have to roll with some advanced spiritual shit plus be smart as a motherfucker. That's why he should ask himself twice about this job. Being the Player who HOLD IT TOGETHER is no joke.

If a brother ain't sure, he shouldn't try and HOLD IT TOGETHER. He'll just fuck shit up. Brothers will go bust ass. Better to just forget it.

Even if that True Player is ready, brothers might not be down at first. In that situation, True Player just maintains. If he has real style and runs his angle crisp, brothers will throw in with him.

Crab ass motherfuckers who show up late don't have no place. HOLD IT TOGETHER is about timing. Real brothers feel shit before it shows. They recognize Player before he's famous. These brothers go through ill shit trying to get over. Form real bonds. Crab asses who show up late, wanting to be down, really aren't welcome. Them motherfuckers just too late. Crew already been through all the shit that made them tight.

If a Player wants to be part of something, but don't feel large enough to HOLD IT TOGETHER, there ain't no shame in that. He should just look around for brothers putting something real in motion. Throw in with them. That's all.

THE LOOK

Pigeons at the fountain.
The look of Hold It Together.
Old School Big Dogs had whole neighborhoods.
Let all the True Players get their piece.

Pigeons in the park drink water from the fountains. If one bird comes alone, people maybe chase that bird away. But if all them birds fly down together, people let them be. Too many birds to bother with. Water holds them birds together. They get a better dip by flying in there like a crew.

That's how True Players' crew should be. Brothers all dipping their beak, getting that water. They drinking good by not drinking alone. Everybody there together. True Player running brothers got to remember that. Have to make sure people feel that holding together with the crew is better than rolling alone.

THE BREAKS

Break on the one means:
Straight up and down for real.
No stress.
Full brew.
Shit flow his way.

The way to be down with motherfuckers is just by being real. Don't lie about nothing. Don't sweat nobody. Don't stress brothers out. That's being cool, like a full brew. A nice cold brew got nothing but positive things to offer. No tricks. Brothers pick up a brew and know what it's about. A brother who roll like that won't have to look for shit. Situations flow his way.

Break on the two means:
Watch Player's back.
Don't sweat a brother.
Maintain, paid.

When Player needs shit done, a brother should be there for him. Brother don't have to flash or flaunt. Just handle business the way it should be done. That's how a brother stays down. If he's all up in

Player's face about how valuable he is, then goes fronting out on them streets, brother gets played out. Nobody likes motherfuckers like that.

Break on the three means:
Down with the wrong crew.

The game is small. A brother can't help running into people. But he have to watch who he throws in with. Rolling with some ill motherfuckers just because they around is a bad look. A brother should be cool with them motherfuckers, but he shouldn't be down with them motherfuckers. That way he can throw in with a positive crew down the line.

Break on the four means:
Show some love.
Maintain. Paid.

Brother been down with Player from day one. Now Player is getting over. Brother should represent on them streets. Tell motherfuckers who he's rolling with. But he still have to HOLD IT TOGETHER and handle his business. Brother can't lose his grip just because Player popped off.

Break on the five means:
Hold It Together.
In the club Player lets females be.
Ladies choice. No sweat.
People don't freak.
All good.

When True Player looking for females to get with, he HOLD IT TOGETHER low key. He's looking crisp at the club, with bottles on the table. But he don't chase after that ass. True Player ain't no clown for females. He don't run mind tricks just to knock boots.

True Player HOLD IT TOGETHER, showing status. If some female interested, she sends signals. He take it from there.

Same with business. If brothers want to throw in with True Player, that's cool. But if motherfuckers ain't feeling him, True Player let them be. He don't sweat nobody. His people are there because they want to be there. That makes his crew feel natural. Brothers don't worry about what to say, or stress how to act. They down with each other.

Even for brothers who ain't a True Player, that's the right way to roll. Don't sweat motherfuckers to be down. Just be for real. The right brothers will show up that way.

Break at the top means:
Lost his head from the jump.
Bad look.

The jump is the beginning. If shit don't start right, it don't finish right. Some motherfuckers miss the chance to throw in on something real. They trip too hard, wondering if shit will shake out. Brothers roll without them. Motherfucker left all alone then, thinking: "Damn, I missed that one."

WAIT A MINUTE

Shit's coming together, but not happening yet. Player have to WAIT A MINUTE.

THE FEEL

WAIT A MINUTE gets paid.
Clouds coming in from the West Side.
Rain soon.

Shit is dry. Streets need rain. Clouds are rolling in from the West, but nobody know when rain will fall. And no motherfucker makes it rain. So brothers just have to WAIT A MINUTE. That rain will fall when it's ready.

Same when pieces are lining up in the game. Maybe the play looks real nice. But shit is still developing. So True Player maintains business. Stays strong in his heart and mind. Rolls chill with brothers and handles whatever. True Player don't try and force that play to get over.

THE LOOK

Wind in the sky.
The look of Wait a Minute.
True Player keeps his look crisp.

When the wind blows, it might move newspapers cross the street. It don't blow over no motherfucking bus. Wind has some power, but not much. Sometimes True Player in a situation like that wind. Maybe he can move things some, make a little noise, but he don't have the power to move shit for real.

When it's like that, Player have to recognize what time it is. Show up, handle business, maintain his connects, and be ready. But he don't try to roll on large plays. He ain't have that power now.

THE BREAKS

Break on the one means:
Step back.
How that a problem?
All good.

Players make shit happen. But sometimes even the best plays get shut down. When that happens, Player have to step back. WAIT A MINUTE. Decide if he want to try that move again. Or regroup, maintain, and watch shit develop. Ain't about forcing plays right here.

Break on the two means:
Fall back with some brothers sizing shit up.
All Good.

Player wants to make a move. Watches some other motherfuckers try. All them get played. Player knows timing ain't right. So he finds some smart brothers pulling back. Throws in with them. That's the right play. Player won't risk his rep on a move that don't shake out.

Break on the three means:
Wheels stolen off the ride.
Brother and his wife bitching.

Brother trying to force his move in the game. Sees some static out there, but don't take it serious. Thinks getting over will be easy. Wrong play. This brother gets stopped cold, like a ride with the wheels stolen. Bad look. Brother gets frustrated. Starts bullshit fights about nothing, like old married people have. He fucked up. Brother should have taken that static more serious. He didn't. Forced his play, got stopped cold, and now he's looking bust ass, talking like a bitch.

Break on the four means:
If he's for real, beat down fade, ain't gotta worry.
All good.

One brother in the crew have the job of keeping True Player in line. That ain't easy. Brother breaks it down, and True Player gets mad. Shit nearly flips ill. But brother talking truth. Just looking out for the whole crew and playing long game. True Player hears that. After he chills, Player shows brother respect for being real.

Break on the five means:
If brothers down and stand by,
Everybody paid.

Real crews only work if motherfuckers are loyal. For the brothers lower down, loyalty means following Player. For Player, loyalty means honesty. He never play those brothers. And when the crew gets paid, Player spread that shit around. Good times shared is good times doubled. That shit builds loyalty, yo.

Break at the top means:
Start to rain. Streets chill.
This happened because a brother maintained.
Pushing is the bitch move.
Night is dark.
True Player force it,
Bullshit scenario.

Business here chills. Like hot summer streets cool out after rain. Action slows, but Player is set up nice. He maintained, just pushing along without forcing big moves. That worked out for him. Now he have to watch it. Player don't want to push for more. Streets are most dangerous when money stops moving and business cools. Desperate motherfuckers play wild style out there. So Player stays good with the fact that his shit is secure. Pushing for more just leads to problems.

WATCH YOUR STEP

When heavy players and ordinary brothers mix up, shit's slippery. For brothers who ain't The Big Dog, WATCH YOUR STEP. Big Dog do what he want. That's natural. A regular brother can get away with stepping on some toes. But only if he have some real pleasant manners. That smiley motherfucker with his heart in the right place always gets by. Nobody break it down when he fucks up. Big Dog just laugh and be like: "It's cool, yo. That motherfucker don't mean nothing by it."

THE FEEL

Watch Your Step.
Stepping on the Big Dog's tail.
He don't bite the brother. Paid.

Shit is real difficult here. Powerful motherfucker and a weak brother have to roll together. Weak brother follows. Powerful motherfucker is stressed from having to roll with some weak shit. But he don't break it down, because the weak brother stays positive, keeps shit light, and don't threaten nobody or nothing.

Sometimes Player have to deal with real wild, ill brothers. Player can manage the situation by maintaining a respectful style of handling shit. Good manners get over even with real fucked up people.

THE LOOK

Heaven above, streets below:
The look of Watch Your Step
True Player know what's good and who's bullshit.
Strengthen his people.

Heaven is naturally high. Streets are naturally low. They ain't have no beef with each other. Streets ain't looking up at Heaven thinking: "Damn, I wish my shit was up there." Heaven don't look down saying: "Shit, I wish I rolled like Streets." Heaven is good with being Heaven. Streets is down with being Streets. Both belong where they are. That's their motherfucking nature, yo.

Brothers born different. Ain't no motherfuckers all created equal. Some brothers smart, some dumb as a pancake. Some popping off business all over, others can't pop a damn balloon. There's real good looking players, and brothers born looking like Chewbacca. Shit ain't equal in this world.

It's real important for organizations that status ain't based on bullshit. A motherfucker high up the chain have to show he's worth it. When brothers are pulled up just because somebody likes them, that's a problem. People lower down start hating.

If value is clear, there ain't no problem. When status is based on how well a player handles business, people respect. Brothers see a motherfucker up the chain and understand why he's there. Nobody pops off drama.

THE BREAKS

Break on the one means:
Roll chill.
Move forward. No problem.

Brother here ain't part of nothing. Got no crew, no obligations. Just rolling on whatever. If this brother stays chill, ain't no problems. He can roll low key, doing what he likes. If he's good with what he has, and don't stress motherfuckers, shit's fine. But that don't mean he's stagnatin'. Brother have to keep shit moving forward.

Stepping into new organizations is like this. New motherfuckers start way down the chain. If a brother is strong inside, low status don't bother him. If he don't start stress about money and power, that brother will move up, slow and steady. Nobody talk shit about him, neither.

But when a new motherfucker hate living low key, that's a problem. He starts running bullshit plays that ain't good for the game. Tries anything to get money for himself.

Once this type of brother finally gets over, the motherfucker turns real arrogant. Flash how rich he rolls. Flaunts the luxury lifestyle. People hate brothers like that. They might smile in his face, but in their heart they really think he's a motherfucker. So even if he does get over, he's still bust ass.

But if Player is damn good at what he does, and maintains low key, it's a different story. When he blows up, shit's positive. Streets are down with brothers like that.

Break on the two means:
Stepping smooth, straight ahead.

Maintaining like a deep brother.
Good look.

A real deep brother is into the mathematics, spirituality, and all that. He's a lonely motherfucker, holding back from the world. He don't want nothing from nobody, and ain't ever stress people. Just rolls with his knowledge. Since this brother ain't looking for nothing, there's no problems. Bad luck and trouble don't bother with him. That's a good look.

Break on the three means:
A one-eyed brother can see,
A crippled brother can walk.
He steps to the pit bull.
Pit bull bites the brother.
Bad look.
That's how a soldier rolls for his people.

A one-eyed brother can see, but he don't see shit clear. A crippled brother can walk, but he ain't running no races. It's a bad look when Player has real problems, but still thinks he's strong. Try to roll, ill brothers will shut him right the fuck down. Being reckless like that is only right when it's life or death for Player's people.

Break on the four means:
He steps to the pit bull.
Rolling smart and careful,
put this brother paid.

Ill shit have to be handled. Player has the power to do it, but still rolls real smart. That's different from the break before, where a real weak motherfucker is rolling hard. That brother is fucked. But this Player is doing the opposite. He have the strength to break shit down, but still rolls real careful. This lets him deal with seriously ill shit, no problem.

Break on the five means:
Come correct.
Maintain. Real with the danger.

Dealing with a real ill Big Dog is no joke. Player have to handle the motherfucker real careful. Even then, shit is still dangerous. Especially if the relationship have to be maintained for a long time. Only being real about the danger will let Player handle it.

Break at the top means:
Player looks at how he maintained. Sort it out.
When shit's done, good times there.

The play has been made. Player put in all the work he can. If he wants to know whether his shit will get over or not, Player have to look back on how he maintained. If he looks back and sees shit was real wherever he rolled, shit will shake out. Ain't any motherfucker truly know himself. He have to check what effect he had on people's lives. Look what he brought to the game. Then he can judge his value. It will be clear.

PEACE

PEACE is motherfuckers working together right with everybody paid nice.

THE FEEL

Peace. Crab asses bounce.
True Players step up.
All Good. Paid.

PEACE is like heaven in the streets. Big Dogs are looking out for their people. All beefs are settled. True Players are running things. Organizations flowing smooth. Crab asses and ill brothers been shook out the game. The right people are being paid real. That's PEACE.

THE LOOK

Sunshine and streets
The look of PEACE.

Big Dog breaks shit down beautifully.
People hooked up.

Like sun on them streets in spring, PEACE is real nice. Shit stays
this way if Big Dog breaks off pieces for his people, settles beefs
right, and lets money flow. Otherwise, PEACE is just a nice run
that craps out. By working out every angle in the operation, and
making sure the organization is flowing tight, Big Dogs and True
Players set up a system that puts people paid for the long game.
Brothers feel that, and put in work to make the operation pop off.
Shit shakes out nice.

THE BREAKS

Break on the one means:
Pull up weeds, roots come with it.
Brothers connected together.
Getting over gets paid.

When business is rolling, brothers bring in more people. Crew
gets bigger. In times of PEACE, operations expand. Brothers who
are down with each other are connected below the surface of shit.
Have invisible bonds like roots under weeds in the dirt. When a
motherfucker pulls up them weeds, a mess of roots come up with
them. So when business pops off in PEACE, every brother rising
up takes some others with him. They all get over together.

Break on the two means:
Dealing with the bust ass chill.
Cross town strong.
Thinking long game, down with people:
That way True Player steps correct.

Wherever people being paid, some bust ass motherfuckers will show up. They hear shit's good and want some. In times of PEACE, streets aren't dark so Player can let down his guard. Everybody have something to offer. Even the most ridiculous motherfuckers can be put into play. Like them pimps who pay a crack head to watch their car when they stop for a cheeseburger. Give a brother something to do.

But that don't mean just peeling off bills for motherfuckers. Brothers have to be working. Player have to maintain discipline during PEACE. Shit has to stay tight and run crisp. That way, if there's drama cross town that needs to be handled, Player has the power to roll.

Even when life is good, and shit's all PEACE, Player have to keep the long game in mind. Steer details in the direction he want to move towards. He also got to watch out for brothers trying to shut other brothers out. Player can't just hang with a handful of his homeboys. Have to be out there, mixing with people. That helps him make sure motherfuckers don't form clicks that break off into rival crews. Also lets him be sure brothers are running their angles right.

Those are four ways a Player maintains his grip in good times. Most people fuck off in PEACE. That's a bad mistake.

Break on the three means:
Up and Down. In and Out.
Brother who maintains no matter what is OK.
Don't stress on shit.
Happy with what he got.

Streets flip on a motherfucker. One day shits selling so fast he's running out of stock. Next minute, he can't give it away. Money flows for a stretch, then it dries up. That's the game. No motherfucker runs it forever. And bad shit always comes back around. Even if Player chase some ill brothers out the area, them shady motherfuckers will slide back in someday. Just how it is.

That reality might make a True Player sad. But if he's smart, remembering this shit helps him stay crisp when his situation is good. A True Player won't slide if he holds onto the fact that fucked up shit will happen, no matter what. He just maintains, handles business, and have his heart strong. That way no matter what shakes out--getting paid or losing weight—he's still a True Player.

Good Luck is like a woman. She loves a man who has his head up, no matter what's going down. She don't have time for motherfuckers who lose heart or feel sorry for themselves.

Break on the four means:
In the neighborhood, no flashing.
Down with the streets,
Straight up for real.

When streets have PEACE, True Players are out there with their people. Having a bar-b-q, playing ball, checking in at the barber shop, saying what up, whatever. That ain't because they trying to prove nothing. It's just because they like to be with their people. They real and have heart, so it's natural.

Break on the five means:
Big Dog's daughter marries down brother.
Real good look.

Big Dog is a rich ass motherfucker with some fine daughters. Them girls got expensive tastes. But Big Dog don't have nothing against a real brother from around the way. So when his daughter falls in love with one of them neighborhood brothers, Big Dog puts his blessing on that shit. High and low throw in with each other. Strengthen them streets. That's a good look.

Break at the top means:
Shit falls apart. Don't roll on it.

Speak to people.
Step up and its bust ass.

Good times ran their course. Bad times are rising. Maybe them Ill Brothers are back and wilding. Maybe Big Dog got hit with charges. Don't matter. That's life. Best move for Player is pulling back with a few down brothers. Let the ill situation play out. If Player tries to step up while crab asses are rising, he just plays himself. Times are changing. They always do. So player lets the good times go and rolls with reality.

WREXAGRAM 12

STAGNATIN'

Peace is nice and chill, with love on them streets. When shit is STAGNATIN', nothing positive happening at all.

THE FEEL

Stagnatin'.
Ill Brothers shut down movement of True Player.
What's real steps off.
Crab asses show up.

Shit is fucked now. There's lots of confusion on them streets, or in the organization. Ill brothers are driving. Them motherfuckers just don't give a fuck. Since they weak inside, they roll hard on people. Real dark time, here. True Players realize it ain't the moment to positively affect shit. Crab asses running things.

True Players and real brothers don't change their ways. Never try and be ill just to get over. When shit is STAGNATIN' like that, they pull back their game. Spend time at home with the family, read some books, play chess, listen to old records and shit. Wait for streets to lean back their way.

THE LOOK

No sun on the streets.
The look of Stagnatin'.
True Player chill so he won't be mixed up with bullshit.
Lose weight.

When crab asses and ill brothers run the game, nobody trust nobody. Nothing positive can happen.

True Player pulls back. He don't throw in with ill brothers. Even if they running crews paid crazy. Rolling with them motherfuckers would put his ass in ill scenarios. His style don't work with that. True Player don't run shady plays or roll hardcore. He don't want to learn that shit neither. When streets ain't right, he rolls low profile. Tones down business. Don't hang out none. Just chills at his place.

THE BREAKS

Break on the one means:
Grass pulled up and dirt come with it. Everything connected.
Family find each other.
Maintain long game and get paid.

This break is just like the first break in the last Wrexagram. But in Peace, True Player is pulling people together to get over. When shit's STAGNATIN', Player pulls his people back from getting played. When streets is bananas and crab asses running shit, nobody listens to what True Player have to say. He don't force motherfuckers to listen. He don't bother trying to make ill brothers and crab asses give a damn. He don't throw himself away. That saves him from looking bust ass. He might not get over, but he maintains respect and holds his people together. That pays off in the long game.

Break on the two means:
They deal with it;
Good Look for the bust ass.
Pulling back helps move Player forward.

Crab asses talk slick shit to a Player. Charm and bullshit. Try to pull him into their world. They want a real brother to step in and sort out their garbage. That would be a good look for them. But True Player don't have shit to do with them motherfuckers. If that means business falls off, he ain't bothered. True Players can handle losing weight in a mean season. They prefer that shit to throwing in with crab asses. By showing streets he don't roll like a bitch just to be rich, Player maintains status. When the game changes and them crab asses fall off, he's looking good.

Break on the three means:
Shame in the game.

Ill Brothers and crab asses who rise in the game by playing brothers put themselves in a bad spot. They get themselves way up high the chain. But they ain't real enough to run shit at that level. Them motherfuckers might act large, but their hearts are full of shame. They realize they ain't shit. When that feeling happens, even if they don't show it, things takes a turn for the better.

Break on the four means:
True Player with the power do things right.
His people paid.

STAGNATIN' situation is turning around. But only True Players should step in and sort shit out. A regular brother who tries to set streets straight will just fuck things up. That's because he's rolling with a limited view. True Players are different. True Players are advanced in the mental. They see shit from a higher level. True Players move in the rhythm of things, with forces from The Heavens. With that weight behind their moves, plays shake out right. Real mysterious motherfucking shit.

Break on the five means:
Stagnatin' is fading.
Good Look for True Player.
What if it turns left? What if it turns left?
Mind them tree roots.

Times are changing. STAGNATIN' situations are falling off. True Player steps up to set streets straight. That's a good look. But when times are changing, lots of shit is in motion, both good and bad. Things only work out if True Player thinks real hard on everything. Every little move, he have to think: "What if it turns left?" By thinking on all the possible ways shit might flip, he don't make wrong moves. Plus he's ready for whatever ill shit pops up out of nowhere.

It's like a tree just been planted. A brother have to mind them roots when they growing. If he does, the tree turns out alright. But if a brother waits until that tree grows large, it's too late. He's stuck with a fucked up tree.

Old Big Dog break it down like this:

Shit gets all fucked up when a brother just relax and think everything OK.
Brother loses everything when all he thinks about is holding it together.
Shit falls out of whack after a brother put it in order.
That's why True Player don't forget ill brothers out there when he's all set up.
He don't forget the bad times when he in the good ones.
He keeps his mind focused on whatever static might happen,

Even when his personal shit is in order.
That way he cover his ass and watch out for his people.

Break at the top means:
Stagnatin' is over.
First nothing moving, then all good.

STAGNATIN' scenarios don't last forever. But bad times don't change back to good times just like that. Takes real serious effort to put STAGNATIN' shit straight. A True Player has to step up and change things. Once he does, real hard work makes it last. If True Player just kicked back and let shit go, Peace would fall off into STAGNATIN'. So he's always on top of shit. That's how a True Player maintains.

GETTING TOGETHER

Real brothers with tight game are GETTING TOGETHER. This
works out if one brother stays more chill than the others. When
serious brothers GETTING TOGETHER, nobody backs down.
That leads to drama. But if one brother don't mind pulling back,
smoothing shit out, and rolling diplomatic for the whole crew,
GETTING TOGETHER works out.

THE FEEL

Getting Together with brothers in the park.
Paid.
Good look to deal with shit cross town.
True Player maintains, ups his status.

GETTING TOGETHER leads to real shit if brothers think past
their own personal interest. Positive things happen when brothers
think long game for the whole crew, and what's good for them
streets.

When it starts natural, like brothers GETTING TOGETHER in
the park, shit is nice. Nobody have no plan. Brothers just hanging

out. They GETTING TOGETHER because they feeling each other. Connections are real. If some situation pops off, these brothers will work together natural. Handle shit no problem.

Brothers GETTING TOGETHER need one True Player who thinks for every motherfucker involved. True Player puts that long game together. Finds ways to put people paid. Plans out positive shit for them streets. Running a bunch of brothers GETTING TOGETHER is no joke. True Player have to be smart, and real strong.

THE LOOK

Stars in the sky.
The look of Getting Together.
True Player sorts people out.
Decides what's up and who's down.

Stars are different from the sky, but they up in it. Stars been organized by brothers and given names. Back in the day that's how motherfuckers got around. Just looked up at the stars like GPS. Setting up the calendar was the same shit. Brothers organized years to match the movement of them stars. That shit was no joke. Took real thoughtful brothers to organize motherfucking stars in the sky. True Player have to organize brothers GETTING TO-GETHER the same way. Real thoughtful.

GETTING TOGETHER ain't about chilling and talking shit. Nobody gets over that way. If brothers GETTING TOGETHER want to go somewhere, True Player have to decide what's up, and how shit is going down. That's organization, yo.

THE BREAKS

Break on the one means:
Getting Together outside the building.
No problem.

GETTING TOGETHER best starts like brothers just kicking it. That shit is natural. Nobody shows up early to plan their shit separate. Nobody shows up late with some motherfucker ain't nobody ever seen. Moves like that lead to problems. Secret plans break shit apart.

Shit is best laid back at first. The meeting place is important. Shouldn't be no VIP shit. GETTING TOGETHER should happen in a chill place motherfuckers are down with. Like out front somebody's building, or the park.

Break on the two means:
Getting Together with brothers behind the scenes.
Bad look.

It's a bad look for a brother to run shady plays when people GETTING TOGETHER. He don't want to be that motherfucker whispering shit in secret. Cutting some brothers out, or playing brothers off each other will blow up in his face down the line. Motherfuckers get shot that way.

Break on the three means:
Stash his nine in the ride.
Roll the streets.
Three years nothing happen.

Right here, GETTING TOGETHER has flipped into some dark shit. Motherfuckers don't trust each other. Brothers planning ambushes, or spying on players. When it's like that, a brother starts tripping. Thinks everybody trying to play him. Starts looking for proof. Picks up the nine. Takes his ride out at three in the morning, trying to catch motherfuckers in secret meetings. The longer he rolls this way, the farther from reality this brother finds himself. Ends up all alone, tripping on shadows. Years pass with nothing positive happening for him. Bad look.

Break on the four means:
Reach for the nine, but can't pull that shit on a brother.
All Good.

Real serious beef. Everybody just want to put it behind them and move on. But static won't fade. Brothers all jumpy. When Player finds himself in stressful shit like this, he might reach for his nine. But if he checks himself, and recognize that violence ain't positive here, shit will get better.

Break on the five means:
People who down be crying.
Later they laugh.
After ill bullshit play out they get together.

Two people can't get together, but in their hearts, feel really down with each other. Might be a brother who love some sister already married. Or maybe two brothers gay for each other. Or brothers from rival crews who want to do business. Whatever. The way shit shaking out, throwing in with each other ain't possible. They face x-amount of problems. Be crying over this shit. But these two people stay true in their hearts. Don't allow no bullshit to kill their feelings. It won't be easy for these motherfuckers, but they will pull it off. When they finally get with each other, all them tears will turn to laughter.

Old Big Dog break it down like this:

Life puts a thoughtful brother on a long and winding road.
Sometimes that road takes a hard left turn into bullshit places.
Other times it's a chill straightaway.
Sometimes he talking real with people, feeling down with brothers.
Other times it ain't safe to say real shit at all.
But when two people are one in their hearts,
They break through concrete walls and jail cell bars.
When two people feeling each other at real deep levels,
The way they talk is pure and beautiful.
Like a rose, yo.

Break at the top means:
Getting Together in the streets.
No problem.

Player ain't feeling much here. He looked around for a real crew, but didn't find one. Ends up throwing in with some brothers from his neighborhood. He shouldn't stress over this. Throwing in with local brothers will lead to things if he don't force shit to roll his way.

PAID FOR REAL

When a motherfucker gets PAID FOR REAL but stays a down brother, he have it all.

THE FEEL

Paid For Real.
Seriously getting over.

Brothers here got clear heads and strong bodies. Roll in style. Pop shit off that streets love. True Player running the crew stays low key. Brothers love him for that. People feel that positivity, so business pops off more. It's a good time. Streets are loving the real shit. Brothers with talent are shining. True Player gets real powerful, but don't flash. That low key style pulls serious business his way. Deep moves for large numbers. The crew is tight and pulls it off. All them motherfuckers get PAID FOR REAL. Families set for life. Retire to the islands type shit.

THE LOOK

Sun in the sky.
The look of Paid For Real.
True Player puts a cap on the ill shit and shows love for real
    people.
That's why Heaven down with him.

Sun shining down is the look of PAID FOR REAL. But rolling at high levels puts True Player in a position to see problems. Sun shines on what's good and what's bad in the world. Now that it's bright out, True Player sees everything. He can't pretend that ill shit don't exist. And he can't just let it be. A True Player PAID FOR REAL takes advantage of the times. Streets are leaning his way. So he steps to wrong shit and rolls on ill brothers. Takes them out the game. Puts his weight behind positive motherfuckers doing what's right. Heaven have love for True Players like that. Heaven don't have love for the ill shit. So Player gets help from high places, and rolls with real deep forces.

THE BREAKS

Break on the one means:
Not down with ill shit.
All Good.
Mind on the problems.
Nobody talking shit.

When a player first get PAID FOR REAL, he ain't have the chance to blow it yet. Once them champagne parties finish, the problems start. When money rolls in, drama follows. Just how it is. Player don't hide from that shit. Stays aware what's happening.

Holds them problems in his mind. He thinks on all the ways shit might turn left. Recognizes how fast a motherfucker can fall off. That helps Player maintain his game. He won't throw money around if he realize that shit flies away. He won't think he's all that if he remembers every other famous brother who slipped. When Player handles PAID FOR REAL like that, nobody talk shit about him.

Break on the two means:
Large vehicle for rolling.
Make the move.
All good.

PAID FOR REAL ain't just about having large finance. It means having the power to move money and muscle where it matters. Pulling this break means True Player got lots of brothers willing to help him. They down for rolling or representing, and handle shit crisp. True Player can run real deep plays with brothers like that. It's like having one of them large utility vehicles, ready to roll, whenever.

Break on the three means:
True Player give it up like Jesus.
Crab ass can't do that.

When a True Player gets PAID FOR REAL, the money means more than numbers in the bank. True Player's power is there to help other motherfuckers. Just like Jesus rolled. Jesus was real powerful. Pulled food out of nowhere and fed brothers. Changed water into wine. With power like that, Jesus could have run the game. But He used that power to look out for normal brothers and hook them up.

That's how True Player rolls. It don't mean he go die on no cross. (No disrespect to The Lord.) It mean that True Player think of other brothers. He rolls for them streets. Plays long game for the whole area. Sets the game straight so what's good has a chance to get over.

That's the difference between True Player and some crab ass. When a crab ass gets paid, he hold his shit tight. That mother-fucker real afraid of losing his money. Just hides somewhere counting it. Brothers who lock down like that usually fall deep into them drugs or that liquor. Start running whores in the door. Since they ain't real enough to handle power in them streets, it just fucks them up. When they die all that money floats away. Damn shame when nothing positive happens with power like that.

Break on the four means:
He roll chill with them Big Dogs.
All Good.

Player just been PAID FOR REAL. Gets the bump in status. On top with them Big Dogs now. That's a slippery slope. Rich people run serious game. So Player stays chill. Rolls with them only as much he have to. Don't pay their lifestyle no mind. If Player starts looking at how them rich motherfuckers maintain, he starts trip-ping. Wants helicopters and shit like that just to fit in. Pushes his operation harder to bank more. Big Dogs pick that up. Player's competition now. That's a problem.

Them rich Big Dogs been round longer. Learned real deep moves. Play two types of game: hard ball and harder ball. Player don't want to step to that. So when a Player gets PAID FOR REAL and put up in their world, he survives best by showing respect, without really throwing in with them motherfuckers.

Break on the five means:
Brother who is down but not simple.
Paid.

Brothers are throwing in with Player. Not because he's talking bullshit, chasing them down, or trying to buy them out. They just believe in Player. Brothers join the crew because they respect his plays. Bonds like that are for real. True Player is down. Talks with brothers. Everybody relates.

That don't mean True Player is some simple motherfucker anybody can roll with. He maintains high level game. Crisp as fuck. True Player relates with brothers, but still lives at higher levels. He maintains respect. That gets him PAID FOR REAL.

Break at the top means:
Player loved by Heaven.
Paid.
Flowing.

Player here PAID FOR REAL. Rich as a motherfucker. Running business, hits on the chart, love on them streets, everything. But with all that power, he maintains low key. Stays down with brothers. Player don't forget The Heavens, neither. Keeps doing what's right. So Heaven looks out for him, and Player's game just flows.

Old Big Dog break it down like this:

Heaven helps the brother who is down.
Brothers help the brother who is real.
Player who's for real and shows respect for what's right
Gets Love from Heaven.
Player put paid and flows.
Nothing hold him back.

LOW KEY

Foolish motherfuckers flash and flaunt. Heaven loves LOW KEY.

THE FEEL

Low Key makes it happen.
True Player maintains.

The game moves in cycles. Same law running The Heavens runs them streets. Sun up in the sky have nowhere to go but down. The sun never hits high noon and says: "Fuck this, yo, I'm rolling higher." Just don't happen. Same thing on the flip side. Sun low in the morning can't do nothing but rise. There's laws to this shit. Sun is mad powerful, but ain't got shit to say about rising and falling. Laws of Heaven run that motherfucker. Moon is on the same damn program. Full then fade. Every star in the sky answer to that shit.

Brothers think they different but they ain't. If a brother is too high up, Heavens going to bring him down. When's he low, his shit will be brought up. But low don't mean bum in the street drinking liquor. Low means maintaining LOW KEY and real, even when rolling at real high levels. Heaven loves that type of brother. People the same. Streets might give it up a minute for loud motherfuckers who flash and flaunt. But inside their hearts, people just waiting for that brother to fall. Streets only have real love for brothers who stay LOW KEY. Just how it is.

Law of Heavens have a lot to say about a motherfucker's life. Every brother have a Destiny. Destiny can't be fucked with. That's complex shit involving large motherfucking patterns of time and space, yo. But a brother also got his Fate. That's what he can work with.

The place and time a brother is born into is Destiny. Can't do shit about that. Motherfucker born in the Bronx is a motherfucker born in the Bronx. But his Fate in The Bronx depends on his choices. How he rolls, what he does with his time, and the motherfuckers he throws in with all add up. That shit decides his Fate.

Destiny is like a video game. Fate is how a brother plays it. The motherfucking Game is the motherfucking Game. Brothers ain't have no choice on that. But how he plays is up to him. Maybe he run buck wild out there. Or lay up in some sniper shit. Brother might roll in a vehicle looking for hidden levels. Whatever. Everybody decides how to play the game. That decides their Fate.

Fate will lean a brother's way if he roll right. When a brother way high up in the game still maintain LOW KEY, he stays real. People feel that and show respect. Law of Heaven works with him. Shit he does shakes out. Ain't no motherfuckers try and rip him down. But if a brother way high up in the game flash and flaunt, talking mad shit, Fate flips on him. Heavens bring him down. That's law. What's too high gets brought low. What's low is bumped up high. Rules of reality, yo.

Pushy motherfuckers grab headlines, but real life and real business is different. Big Dogs rarely break off a serious piece of action for childish motherfuckers who flash. But brothers who maintain LOW KEY get put onto larger things. That's why true bad boys roll in silence.

THE LOOK

Air and Tiger.
The look of Low Key.
True Player don't play too much.
Don't play too little.
Brings it together and maintain.

When we was shorties, Michael Jordan blew our mind. What he did with that ball was motherfucking magic. Watch him play like: "Oh, shit! He did *what?*" But MJ made it all look natural. Just moved like nothing at all. Same with Tiger Woods on that golf course. Ain't nobody watched Tiger saying: "Damn, golf looks hard." Both them players just made shit look real easy.

That's what a True Player does. He's LOW KEY. Working like a motherfucker, but that shit don't show. True Player might have spent 20 years hitting walls putting his game together. Nobody feel that fight now. Brothers just see him moving smooth, putting points on the board, hits on the chart, and biz in the streets like nothing at all. That's LOW KEY.

True Player maintains that LOW KEY touch when putting his operation together. Sets shit up smooth and flowing nice. He don't hire brothers who roll too hard. Don't employ no soft motherfuckers, neither. True Player balance them books right. He don't pay out some brothers large while other motherfuckers live bust ass. That would just bring problems. True Player run business right. No drama, no static. That's LOW KEY.

THE BREAKS

Break on the one means:
True Player Low Key about being Low Key
Roll on motherfuckers cross town.
All Good.

When bullshit outside the area starts affecting business, Player have to roll on that shit. But rolling on motherfuckers cross town is no joke. Stepping off home turf and breaking down brothers in their area is real ill. But Player can roll in ways that makes this shit more manageable.

If he talks shit up, crab asses know he's coming. Gives them motherfuckers time to plan. Ill situations are best handled simple. Just roll. Don't broadcast. If Player don't talk shit up, he break it down out of nowhere. Catch them motherfuckers cold. Plus his own people ain't have time to think twice. Nobody likes rolling crosstown on motherfuckers. That shit's dangerous. People drop. If Player moves fast, brothers don't have time to trip. Saves him time and energy. When stakes are real high, Player have to be so LOW KEY, it's like being LOW KEY about being LOW KEY.

Break on the two means:
Low Key all the way.
Maintain. Paid.

When a brother is so LOW KEY that every little play shakes out, he gets paid nice. Ain't no motherfucker talk shit about a brother like that. Period.

Break on the three means:
True Player for real and Low Key plays long game.
Paid.

True Player will catch some fame when he changes the game. If he lets that fuck with his head, Player starts tripping. Shit will fall off. But if he maintains LOW KEY when he's blowing right the fuck up, streets show love. Real brothers throw in with him for the long game. Player and his people put paid real serious that way.

Break on the four means:
Alright.
Low Key making moves.

Shit has a limit. Even being too LOW KEY is a problem. But in this situation, real LOW KEY is the right play. True Player is working tight with a serious Big Dog. Shit ain't no joke. Player don't want to disrespect a brother that large. At the same time, Big Dog can't be all blahzay about having True Player in his operation. Have to show respect. Value that motherfucker.

Some crab asses in the game don't do shit. Hide out in their area, never lift a finger. Take money without handling business, have a rep for no reason at all. That ain't LOW KEY. Handling shit smooth and running business right is LOW KEY.

Break on the five means:
Ain't gotta flash.
Step hard.
Flow nice.

LOW KEY ain't about being that nice brother who lets shit slide. Some situations a motherfucker have to step to. LOW KEY Player don't flash, flaunt, or talk shit up. He just steps hard and breaks it down crisp. Ain't nothing personal about it. Player don't come down nasty, just hard. That's how LOW KEY Players handle motherfuckers who step out of line.

Break at the top means:
Low Key saying something.
Good look to step to himself
And break it down.

True Player is real with shit. Crab asses ain't. When a beef happens, crab asses pull back, talk shit, and blame other brothers. They front like they rolling LOW KEY with the situation. But really, them crab asses just ain't handling the beef.

A True Player who rolls LOW KEY sets shit straight. When that beef happens, True Player checks himself first. Sometimes a beef ain't about breaking it down on motherfuckers. Sometimes the problem is in Player's corner. Then it's about stepping to his own damn self. That's hard shit to do. Only a True Player LOW KEY and real enough to break it down on himself will have a serious run in the game.

UP FOR IT

When people UP FOR IT, shit happens natural.

THE FEEL

Up For It.
Put brothers together, shit starts happening.
Get the crew rolling.

Streets are UP FOR IT when a True Player shows up, throws shit down, and moves the crowd. Brothers have to feel that shit. To get people UP FOR IT, Player feels what's good on them streets. He finds out what's hitting. Streets move same way them stars do. Seasons come and go, styles rise and fall. Player respects that rhythm. He checks what streets feeling and flows with it. Player who wants to get brothers UP FOR IT always gives the people what they want.

If Player gets people UP FOR IT, them motherfuckers help him get over. Nobody trying to stop shit that moves the crowd. Everybody feeling it, pushing that shit along. Player gets love and pops right the fuck off. His shit blows up.

Ill movements roll the same way. Like government going to war. Flying brothers around the planet to murder motherfuckers they ain't ever met is real serious shit. Government have to get people UP FOR IT. Roll out some heroes. Make some speeches. Run that shit on TV, in papers, talk shows, whatever. Get people UP FOR IT. Don't happen no other way.

THE LOOK

Thunder in the street.
The look of UP FOR IT.
Big Dogs down with old school MCs. Put that shit on record.
Way back the same. Deeper.

When it's crazy hot in summer, rainstorm is a breakthrough. Before that rain start, air feels strange. Streets get quiet. Light look different. Then thunder rip right out the motherfucking sky and rain pour down. Just like when a brother busts his nut. Mad tense, then all relaxed.

Music does shit like that. Brother might have stress on his mind, tripping. He turn on that music, brother feel better. Them beats work on him. Nobody knows how that happens. Music just be some powerful and mysterious motherfucking shit. Beats been getting people UP FOR IT since way back in time.

Back in the day, ill Big Dogs were bank rolling the first hip hop. When shit first popped off in the park, way before them record deals, hard motherfuckers from around the way were paying for studio time. Music was for real back then. Had to be. Them hard motherfuckers would represent with that music. Be like: "Yo, that's my joint." Shit had to be tight. Nobody put out a bust ass track for no murderer.

Roll it back farther. Way back. Stone age shit. Them primitive motherfuckers took music real serious. Reach their Gods with it. Play joints to get some rain thrown their way when shit was dry. Put on a motherfucking show for the Heavens. That was how shit started. Music turned into theater. Theater turn into movies. Movies turn into TV, then that shit become the motherfucking internet. It all started with music.

Music back then wasn't no entertainment bullshit. Brothers were making music for their Gods. That shit was life or death. Fate of the whole village depend on how well motherfuckers break down a beat and shake their ass. Today God is real friendly. Jesus and Buddha, showing brothers the way. Back in the day, shit was fierce. Motherfucking gods had a damn crocodile head or some shit. Lobster claws. Throw lighting at brothers. That made music real tight. Brothers don't miss a beat when some lobster motherfucker throwing lighting. Please.

All that music happen round the priest. His job was reaching up to The Heavens. Rap with The Gods, dance and get love for the village. His shit had to pop. James Brown style. When the music finish, motherfuckers all over that priest. Be like: "Yo, what The Gods say?" Priest break it down. Tell them where to hunt, what seed to plant, who should marry who, where to fight the next war, all that shit. Motherfuckers thought that shit was straight from Heaven. Believed The Gods blessed them with wisdom. But only when they throw down real beats, shake their ass right, and put on a fierce show. Miss one beat, the harvest is fucked. Rivers run dry. Their music was life or death. That Priest was large. When he bring it, whole world spinning in his hand. Village be like: "Yo, that's the motherfucker talk to God."

THE BREAKS

Break on the one means:
Up For It fronting
Nothing positive.

Some brother have a connect with The Big Dog. He's talking that shit up on streets. Bad look. Fronting about connections don't lead to shit. Just knowing somebody don't get motherfuckers UP FOR IT. Brothers have to feel something real.

Break on the two means:
Solid as a rock. Bounce in a minute.
Maintain. Paid.

True Players see real clear. While streets all UP FOR IT, showing love for some played-out bullshit, True Player stays chill. He don't try and get with it. But he don't disrespect motherfuckers feeling it, neither. True Player just stays solid as a rock. Watch which way the breeze blowing.

When streets all UP FOR IT, shit can break either way. Sometimes it's a party. Home team win the pennant and people happy. But with all them motherfuckers out there UP FOR IT, shit can take a hard left turn, real fast. One minute brothers high-fiving each other. Next they throwing trash cans through windows and lighting shit up.

That's why True Player stays solid as a rock, no matter how many motherfuckers out there UP FOR IT. He don't get caught up in shit. Staying chill like that lets him feel left turns before they break. Shit flips ill, True Player ready to bounce. Maintaining like that protects his business. Player sees real clear and stays ready to handle shit. The operation don't lose money. People put paid, whatever happens.

Old Big Dog break it down like this:

To know shit right from the jump is the mark of the True Player.
When he deals with Big Dogs, True Player don't sweat them.
When he dealing with ordinary brothers, he ain't fronting.
True Player feels a move right from the jump.
Recognize shit as ill or real in a minute.
Bounce or roll with it.
True Player sees shit before other people.
He knows what's real, and what's fucked.
That's why people respect him.

Break on the three means:
Up For It looking around is a bad look.
Half stepping brings problems.

The break before shows a True Player who knows what's up, and how to roll. Here we got a motherfucker without a clue. Shits popping off. He don't know if he should be UP FOR IT or not. Motherfucker looking around to see what other brothers doing. That leads to problems. If a brother miss the moment when real shit pops off, he don't have the chance to throw in later. And if some ill shit pops off that he throws in with, motherfucker gets played.

Break on the four means:
Move the crowd.
Player bring it and shine.
Don't trip.
Brothers tight like sister's braids.

Player moves the crowd. Streets have love because he bring it. Changes the game whenever he throw down. Player have mad talent and not one doubt. Just believes in himself, 100%. That confidence makes other motherfuckers want to roll with him. Shit shakes out nicely. Brothers round this Player are mad tight, all together, like braids in some sister's hair. Crew like that gets paid.

Break on the five means:
Pressure on, still don't drop the ball.

A Player who gets people UP FOR IT is being held back. Like what happens in basketball. Sometimes motherfuckers double up on a high scoring brother, shut him down. Run defense to hold him back. That's frustrating shit. But being played like that ain't all bad. Pressure keeps that Player sharp. Makes his game extra crisp. He develops deep skills to get over on those motherfuckers and bring it.

Same shit happens in life. When a Player gets shut out, it's real hard for him to maintain his game. He lose hope and feels frustrated. Gives up and falls off. But if Player maintains, that shit strengthens him. He develops on deeper levels that other brothers don't deal with. That pressure also keeps Player from having too much time on his hands. Blowing his money on strippers and liquor, stupid shit like that.

Break at the top means:
Up For It the wrong way.
If he settle down and change,
No problems.

It's a bad look when a brother lets himself be carried away on some bullshit just because other motherfuckers UP FOR IT. Once he settles down, and realizes shit he was about to roll with ain't positive, it's alright. Pulling back just before throwing in with ill shit is definitely possible. Damn lucky, too.

FLOWING

An older brother is real polite and patient to some young slim thing he wants to get with. That's what makes her down with him. That's what FLOWING is like. Being real, so people are down.

THE FEEL

Flowing gets paid for real.
Maintain. All good.

If a brother wants motherfuckers to throw in with him, first he have to flow with the times. His shit got to fit what's hitting them streets. Player finds a crew by being real and down, then taking care his people. That way, brothers throw in with him for real reasons. Crab asses run their crew by being hard, telling lies, or running shady game. They work one set of brothers off another. That shit usually blows up in a motherfucker's face. At very least, it leads to x-amount of problems to handle. That shit slows down business.

But just treating people right don't make shit happen. Player have to maintain all the time. Handle business right, deal with situations correct. That's real responsibility. It never stops. Player don't ask brothers to throw in with him unless he plans on FLOWING for the long game. Nobody should throw in with a motherfucker who don't maintain for the duration.

THE LOOK

Movie theater closed.
The look of Flowing.
At night True Player
Chills back home to remain crisp.

Movie theaters ain't open all night long. They shut down and people maintain the place. Keep them popcorn machines working, soda fountains flowing. Make sure no motherfucking seats busted up. Whatever.

True Player's the same. FLOWING all day long, running the operation. Nights he ain't out there popping bottles in the club. That shit's for motherfuckers without responsibilities. True Player rolls home at night. Rests up. Stays crisp for shit he have to handle the following day.

Brothers who wear their ass down trying to get over play themselves. If they do finally make it, them motherfuckers are too tired to hold on. Whoever said it's a long way to the top was lying. It's a real long ass haul just halfway down that road. Then shit starts getting steep. Reaching the top takes all a brother got, for a real long time. Motherfuckers have five seconds to enjoy the view. From there it's a fight to hold tight or fall off.

FLOWING for the long game ain't easy. Brother should chill whenever he have the chance.

THE BREAKS

Break on the one means:
Shit be changing.
Maintain. All Good.
Step out. Mix up with people.
Shit gets done.

The game changes fast. Player starts out in one situation. Then shit flips. He might not know how this new area works. So Player can't be hung up on running things. If he don't know how shit works, he have to talk with his people. Hand over the wheel a minute. Even when Player understands shit, and the operation is FLOWING, he checks in with his people. Some brother might have a look that leads to improvements.

That said, Player have to run his operation the way he feel is right. He don't flip up business just because he saw some motherfucker talking shit on TV. And he don't stay so deep in his people that he miss what streets are saying. Player steps out. Mixes up. Hears what other brothers who ain't got shit to do with him are saying and feeling. That's how he stays FLOWING.

Break on the two means:
Stay tight with the shorties,
Miss that serious brother.

When a brother picks his friends and the people he does business with, that shit is mad serious. He puts real or ill brothers around himself. Can't have both at once. Throw in with some childish motherfuckers still running around like shorties, he miss the chance to meet some serious brothers doing real shit.

Break on the three means:
Down with the serious brother, lose the shorty.
Player Flowing to find what he's after.
Maintain. Good look.

Linking up with serious players can make a brother sad. Shit gets real. He ain't have time for people he used to party with. Party motherfuckers might have heart, but their head ain't in the game. That shit wastes time. Brother has to let them go. He might be sad a minute. But them feelings will pass. If he wants to be FLOW-ING high level, brother's doing the right thing. Life is about focus. Brother has to know what he wants, then stay tight with it.

That ain't easy all the time. Some night a brother might pass his old crew puffing la on the corner. One them motherfuckers shouts out and has a brew ready. Homegirl's there and she gives up that ass real good. Nobody trying to say it wouldn't feel nice. But if a brother want be a True Player, he really don't have the time. He should say what up, show respect, and keep it moving.

Break on the four means:
Flowing paid.
Maintain brings problems.
Flow straight up for real.
Who talk shit about that?

Sometimes when a Player gets over, he starts talking down to people. Act like he on a higher level. His people treat him special. But brothers who talk Player's shit up are not to be trusted. Them motherfuckers try and move up the chain by licking Player's ass. Try to get in tight by talking him up. If Player gets used to brothers like that, he starts to need them motherfuckers. That's a problem. Now he's rolling with a bunch of fake ass bitches. So Player have to be real at every level of the game. If Player acts right, he knows what's right. Maintaining his life correct helps him see through bitch motherfuckers. Then Player's FLOWING nice and nobody talking shit.

Break on the five means:
Down with what's good. Paid.

Every brother got to believe in something. If he's down with what's good, and don't swerve from that, streets will lean his way. A brother have to remember that when shit is thick and motherfuckers up in his face.

Break at the top means:
Meet up with brother seriously down.
Connects made.
Big Dog breaks off serious family piece.

Player been paid out for life. Retired from the game. But a brother shows up who ain't bullshit. Wants to roll on a play real positive for them streets. Player don't tell that brother to fuck off. Since this brother is for real, trying to do positive shit, Player puts himself back in the game. Helps him out. Them two bond for life over that.

Back in the day, Big Dogs had a special place for loyal True Players who maintained a legendary run. Big Dog would offer his niece or daughter for True Player to marry. Break off a family piece of the game to run. Real moneymaking angles only blood be in on. That's how Big Dogs showed love for True Players real valuable to the operation. Made them family. Nothing better can happen for a Player.

SHIT BEEN SPOILT

If a brother leaves food out on the counter for a few days, that SHIT BEEN SPOILT.

THE FEEL

Clean up Shit Been Spoilt.
Alright.
Good to roll cross town.
Before the jump, three days.
After the jump, three days.

SHIT BEEN SPOILT because brothers dropped the ball. It's different from Stagnatin'. When SHIT BEEN SPOILT the problem don't have nothing to do with outside circumstance. It ain't happen from crab asses rising, ill brothers rolling, or streets going dark. SHIT BEEN SPOILT because some brothers let their situation slide. That's all. If brothers put in some work, shit will turn around.

True Players don't back away from putting in real work. They don't stress about handling ill shit neither, like rolling on motherfuckers cross town. But setting straight SHIT BEEN SPOILT have to be thought out. *Before the jump, three days. After the jump, three days.* That means thinking before the play start, and watching it real close. The jump is when a play pops off. Before Player can set shit straight, he have to know where shit turned left. Think real hard about that. Look close at how the situation fell off. Understand the problem 100%. When he pops off the play to turn shit around, that focus don't stop. Just because Player started something don't mean it will shake out. He have to watch the situation real close.

A Player shouldn't try this move unless he crisp as a motherfucker. Usually shit slides because brothers kick back and stop maintaining. It takes just the opposite to put shit right. Real hard work, and tight focus. That's the way motherfuckers turn around SHIT BEEN SPOILT.

THE LOOK

Subway in summer blows ill wind.
The look of SHIT BEEN SPOILT.
True Player motivates his people.
Makes their spirit strong.

Subway in the summer blows a real nasty smell up the tunnel. Shit and garbage. That smell hits the platform where motherfuckers waiting. Tells people them tunnels are filthy and need cleaning.

True Player is powerful like that train. He rolls up to the platform crisp. Maybe he pulls into some SHIT BEEN SPOILT, but True Player is clean. Same way that train takes people somewhere, True Player moves brothers. He takes them from that platform where shit smells bad. Rolls them someplace better. And just like that subway train can hold them people, True Player gives brothers a solid place to stand.

THE BREAKS

Six in the beginning means:
Fixing Shit Been Spoilt by Pops.
If there is a son,
Dead pops ain't rest in shame.
Trouble. Shit turn out fine.

Doing shit the same way, without changing nothing, made SHIT BEEN SPOILT here. That ain't so bad. A brother can turn it around. It's like his pops ran some old-school business that never plugged in no fucking computers. Pops trying to retire, but business is falling off. If his son step up and turn shit around, Pops ain't gonna die broke.

Shit here should shake out. But a brother still got to handle it real careful. Turning around SHIT BEEN SPOILT ain't ever easy. Business that's been running a particular way for years don't turn around on a dime. That shit takes a real close look, and real hard work.

Break on the two means:
Setting straight what been messed up by Moms.
Don't be hard.

SHIT BEEN SPOILT here because people are weak. Not because they bad, bums, lazy, or ill. The motherfuckers just ain't Player material. Brother handling SHIT BEEN SPOILT like this shouldn't be hard. He should work it out gentle, like handling women. Player don't want to hurt people here. That just brings problems down the line. Rolling smooth is the play.

Break on the three means:
Setting straight shit been spoilt by Pops.
Feel bad some. No big deal.

Player rolls real hard setting straight SHIT BEEN SPOILT. He steps up and breaks shit down. Motherfuckers ain't liking that. Have some words for him. Throw a few punches or whatever. But being too hard is better than being too soft. Player might feel bad when that drama happens. But shit will cool down. Really it's no big deal.

Break on the four means:
Not handling shit been spoilt by Pops.
Bust ass look.

Brother is too weak to fix SHIT BEEN SPOILT. The problem has roots in the past. Shit's just beginning to fuck him up. If he doesn't step up and handle this, brother will be seriously bust ass.

Break on the five means:
Setting straight shit been spoilt by Pops.
Big Up. Respect.

Player facing a situation where SHIT BEEN SPOILT long before he stepped on the scene. He's low in the operation. Don't have the status to set shit right. Have to reach out and find some real brothers to throw in with him. Turn things around together. But they dealing with problems been there a long time. Setting shit straight with one move won't happen. That said, just doing something is real. Streets respect them brothers.

Break at the top means:
He don't roll for Big Dog or Players.
Off on some deep shit.

Not everybody got to mix it up in the game. Some brothers maintain on a higher level then streets. That don't mean a motherfucker sit back sipping liquor calling people bitches. Living beyond the game only works if a brother rolls on that deep shit.

Teaches karate. Paints. Writes books. Whatever. That way he's doing something positive for people. Like this book here. A True Player don't find time to write *Yo Ching* if he's busy playing angles, handling crab ass motherfuckers and chasing slim things. Please.

WREXAGRAM 19
COMING UP

A Player with real game is COMING UP. Streets talking about this Player.

THE FEEL

Coming Up gets paid in full.
Maintain. All that.
Summer time come, ill shit.

Shit's looking good here. Big Dogs and True Players are working together, rolling positive plays in the game. Getting over ain't a question. It's about to happen. But Player still has some hard work to put his shit over. And good times don't last forever. He have to be ready for when shit flips. If Player stays ready for ill shit, he keeps a handle on his situation. Nothing blows up in his face.

THE LOOK

Building rise up over the streets.

89

The look of Coming Up.
True Player ain't ever tired of showing brothers what's up.
No limit to what he handle for his people.

Empire State Building stands way high up over New York streets. That's like a True Player who lives on a higher level than other brothers, since he has more knowledge and power. Like that building stand all night and day, True Player never gets tired of standing tall to show the way. When motherfuckers are lost in NYC, they look up for that Empire State. It's always there to show which way is uptown, downtown, east or west side.

And just like that building have room for all them motherfuckers who work there, True Player is down with everybody who comes his way. From janitor to CEO, Empire State Building fits everybody. True Player the same way. He takes care his people. High rollers and simple brothers, too. That's why he's real.

THE BREAKS

Break on the one means:
Coming Up together.
Maintain. Paid.

Some down brothers are catching heat on them streets. Positive shit starts getting over. When that happens, all the real brothers feel motivated. What's good is getting over. True Player rolls when times favor his ass. But he don't lose his shit just because some motherfucker up the chain recognize. He stays tight with his game and maintains. That puts him paid.

Break on the two means:
Coming Up together.

All good.
Everything work out.

Big Dog takes a shine to some player making real moves and pulls him up. He's a True Player in the making. Nobody talk shit about him. Player pulled up don't lose his head over how shit will shake out. He's down with the fact that luck comes and goes. He don't jump up and down when shit pops off. He don't jump off no building when it falls off. He just feels the rhythm of things. Flows with reality, maintaining all the way.

Break on the three means:
Laying back.
Ain't happening at all.
Check himself, nobody talk shit.

Brother doing well. Holds a nice piece of the game. Thinks he has it made. Motherfucker gets careless with his shit. Rolling casual with business and the way he handles people. Shit will slide like that. But when this brother remembers the reason he got over was playing tight game, it's alright. He flips back to running things crisp, and nobody talk shit about him.

Break on the four means:
Reaching out, Coming Up.
All good.

This here Big Dog knows how to spot talent in the operation. Maybe notices some motherfucker clearing trashcans. Big Dog don't care. When he sees a brother with something special, he ain't bothered where he comes from. Just reaches out and pulls the brother up. That's real good.

Break on the five means:
Coming Up smart.

Good Look for the block star.
Paid.

Player have some moves on the block. Recognized around the way.
But Player needs people if he really want to blow up. Has to be real
smart with this. Choose the right brothers. After he finds the right
motherfuckers, Player have to lay back. Let them run their angles
without stress. People put paid nice that way.

Break at the top means:
Coming Up with heart.
For real with people.
All good. No problem.

A True Player who left the game may want to step back in. First, he
have to reach out to brothers with heart. Say what up. That's a
damn good look for them motherfuckers. True Player will show
them shit. Make their angle tight. But since True Player been out
the game a minute, he can't be fronting. He needs help from these
brothers to step back in. Has to stay real. If True Player maintains
low key like that, shit shakes out nice for all them.

LOOKING OUT

When a brother is up in some high office building LOOKING OUT, he sees real far. When he's far away from that building, he can find it just by LOOKING OUT from them streets.

True Player looks up to see how Heaven works. Then he looks down to see how streets run. Player like that understands how shit happens. Plays high level game and puts people paid.

THE FEEL

Looking Out.
Crisp. Tip the drink, ain't break it down yet.
Believing they look up to a brother.

Back in the day people were much more into The Heavens. Had real deep and complex ceremonies for their Gods. First, they wash up with ritual bath and whatnot. Then they offer a drink to the Gods. Then they sacrifice animals to the Heavens. Goat or some shit like that. Every step was real important, and had to be done precise. Like surgery.

They was real careful like that because motherfuckers back then was afraid of Heaven. Talking to The Gods was no joke. People showed up crisp and clean. Poured Heaven a drink and showed respect. They never showed up empty handed, neither. Always broke Heaven off a piece. The Heavens didn't need no goat. Offering that animal was about showing proper respect.

All this had to go down tight. People drop the ball, forget it. Spill that drink, it was a wrap. Gods have nothing to do with them that year. Motherfuckers believed that shit back then. They also believed that pulling off that ceremony real crisp, with respect and heart, made something happen. People felt it. Be like: "Yo, Heaven down with us."

That's like old church mothers today. Them women been doing their Jesus for long years. Believe at deep levels. Lady like that put hands on a brother and pray, it's no joke. Brother feels it. Ain't saying he have to believe nothing. But damn if he don't feel something.

Heaven got laws. Sun rise and fall. Planets moving on point. If a brother thinks on them laws till he understand, he rolls deep and moves people. Most motherfuckers don't have time to study this shit. Brother who want to be down with this level of reality have learning to do. Have to be respectful, too. Like them old school motherfuckers who feared The Heavens. A brother have to clean up before he shows up. Get his life together. Follow them rules and laws without missing nothing. Focus like a motherfucker for long years. But if a brother do it right, he comes through with real power. He's in the rhythm of higher game. People feel that when he show up. Don't know why he's so real, but they feel it. Streets lean his way.

THE LOOK

Wind in the park blowing grass.
The look of Looking Out.
Old School True Players were out in them streets.
Down with people, telling them what's up.

When the wind blows through the park, grass have no choice but to bend. That's the look for Old School True Players. Streets be bananas today. People all messed up. So lots of Players move way the fuck upstate when they get over. Back in the day, neighborhoods was different. True Players were out there in them streets checking on people. Not just looking in on business. Looking in on the whole neighborhood. True Player back then threw block parties. Bought some old lady who didn't have family a washing machine. Maybe helped some smart young brother with tuition for medical school. Even said what up to police, find out what shorties was in school and who was dropping out. Then he pull them wild ones aside. Set them straight a minute. True Player made that neighborhood real.

True Players are superior brothers. First off, they know what time it is. True Players see life for what it is. Nobody ever pull shit over on them. Nobody ever call a situation better than them. True Players change people just by passing through. Like grass blown by the wind. People have no choice but to be moved by a brother that large.

THE BREAKS

Break on the one means:
Looking out like a shorty.
For a regular brother, no problem.
For a True Player, bust ass.

This here like LOOKING OUT at shit from a distance, without knowing what's really happening. There's a True Player is in the game, but streets ain't down with him. That don't matter for streets. Whether motherfuckers down with True Player or not, he make shit positive just by showing up. Ordinary brothers got no responsibility to understand True Player. But True Player got responsibility to understand them. It's his job is to recognize what's happening, and feel them streets.

Break on the two means:
Looking Out through the chained door.
Fine for a pretty sister.

Sometimes a brother open the apartment door and leave that chain on. Looks out through the crack. That's a limited view, yo. He ain't stepping outside to really see what's happening. In life, that means a brother is always LOOKING OUT from his own situation. He never try and understand why other brothers act the way they do. Never see where they coming from. That's fine for a pretty sister. She ain't got shit to do in life but show up looking good. But a brother who wants to play the game right can't roll this way. Looking out at the world like he's standing there with the chain on the door don't work. Player have to step out and see shit for real.

Break on the three means:
Looking Out through his life decides.
With it or step.

Shit's changing for a brother. He don't look around for answers no more. He looks inside to find out what to do. He gets over himself. His ego don't cloud his view. He thinks hard on situations and sees shit clear. But brother don't just think and trip. He handles shit.

Sometimes a brother is rolling with people, but have to make a decision. Either he's with this shit, or stepping off. When a brother have to make big decisions like this, he should look back on his whole life. Think on what he's been through. Remember what he did, and how shit shook out. That will help him decide how to roll in the situation he handling now.

Break on the four means:
Knowing what's up.
Good look to flex like Big Dog's man.

True Player here found real power. He's down with The Heavens, and good on them streets. He did his learning. Did some living. Knows how shit works. Brother like this should be put in play. Big Dog should set True Player up and let him roll. But Big Dog have to let Player move his way. It's a bad look to treat a True Player like some bitch.

Break on the five means:
Looking out on his life.
Nobody talk shit about True Player.

True Player always got to check himself. But he don't trip. Just watches the game, feeling them streets. If things are rolling right, his plays get over. Brothers are down with him. Ain't nobody talking shit about a player like that. He feel good. His shit out there hitting.

Break at the top means:
Looking Out on life.
True Player all good.

The break before is about a True Player checking himself. This break here about a True Player beyond checking himself. He left the game. Made his paper, have no need for business. Rolled off on some monk shit. Player just study them Laws of Heaven. Flows with higher level shit. Learned that staying out of trouble is the best thing in life.

BREAK IT DOWN

Player taking care of business with force. When ill brothers messing with his game, or crab asses talking shit, Player BREAK IT DOWN. Like lightning and thunder.

THE FEEL

Break It Down. Alright.
Good look to come down on what ain't right.

When plays ain't coming together due to bullshit from third parties, BREAK IT DOWN. Maybe motherfuckers won't throw in with Player because some crab ass out there telling lies. Or maybe some ill brothers running sideways game, playing him behind the scenes. Unless Player want shit to be permanently fucked, he have to step up and BREAK IT DOWN. Problems like this don't just go away on their own. When crab asses are actively involved in fucking shit up, the only way out is to BREAK IT DOWN.

That said, a brother have to BREAK IT DOWN the right way. Crisp and clear. When Player BREAK IT DOWN, he don't leave nobody wondering why. He's strong, but not hard or wild. Ain't blahzay, neither. When Player BREAK IT DOWN, he makes sure brothers feel that shit. Inside his head, Player is real clear on the situation. That way, he leaves shit clear in the mind of every other motherfucker, too.

Crisp, strong, clear. That's how True Player BREAK IT DOWN.

THE LOOK

Lighting and Thunder.
The Look of BREAK IT DOWN.
That's how Big Dogs back in the day
Made people know what time it was.

A Player don't BREAK IT DOWN on everything. And he don't BREAK IT DOWN the same way in every situation. There are different responses to the variety of bullshit a crab ass will pull. When Player BREAK IT DOWN, he have to be like lightning. Clear and sharp. People respect the brother who is fair. But he have to be hard, too. Thunder makes people scared. People don't fuck with the brother they scared of. So Lighting and Thunder is how True Player BREAK IT DOWN. He's sharp like lighting, and scary like thunder, so brothers know what time it is.

Player don't just BREAK IT DOWN wherever and however he feel. Have to be a method to his shit brothers understand. If Player do it right, every time he BREAK IT DOWN is a chance to remind brothers who's running shit. He walks away with more respect, and less people who want to fuck with him.

Brothers do whatever the fuck they want when shit ain't clear, and nobody ever BREAK IT DOWN for them. So a Player who want to hold respect does two things. First, he make them rules clear as a motherfucker. Second, he BREAK IT DOWN fast and hard when brothers mess with those rules.

THE BREAKS

Break on the one means:
Bitch slap.
No problem.

The first time a brother fuck up, Player don't go right across his face with all he got. Just a bitch slap will do. Probably that brother will get the message, and there won't be Problem #2. It's like a warning.

Break on the two means:
Like messing with children.
All cut up nasty. Joint in the gutter.
No problem.

This here a clear cut situation of something wrong. Don't have to think about it. Like when some twisted brother messes with little ones. That's real wrong. And because what happen is so ill, Player gets emotional. Forgets to stay crisp when he BREAK IT DOWN, because the shit blows his mind. He cuts that fucked up brother all to pieces. Real nasty shit. Rip off his joint and throw it in the gutter. That shows them streets Player lost his head a minute. But in this particular situation, it ain't no big deal. The motherfucker deserved it.

Break on the three means:
Bites on an old beef.
Rotten and spoilt.
Slightly bust ass. People don't talk shit.

Brother sees something wrong and tries to BREAK IT DOWN. But he ain't have no power in the organization. Ill brothers just tell him to fuck off. This is an old beef. Been around long, long time. Just trying to step to it is poison. Like trying to eat some old salami sandwich been left out all summer. This problem so ill, and so old, it makes everybody hate the brother for picking it up. And since this beef run so deep, brother can't do shit about it. So now on top of motherfuckers hating him, he looks bust ass. However, a problem is a problem. Since the brother had heart and stepped up, people ain't talking shit about him.

Break on the four means:
Bites an old crusty beef.
Hard like a nine. Straight like an arrow.
Heads up on how deep shit be.
Maintain.
Good look.

This break here about large problems, with some ill Big Dogs wrapped up inside. Since they heavy motherfuckers who roll deep, it's some dangerous shit. But the right play is to BREAK IT DOWN. That said, Player have to be hard as steel and straight like a motherfucking arrow. If he really understand how deep this situation is—every motherfucking part of it—shit will shake out right. If he maintains, Player will get over on them ill motherfuckers. But nothing easy about it.

Break on the five means:
Homeboy in the cookie jar.
Solid as gold. Cold like business.
Real with it all.
People ain't talk shit.

This ain't no easy decision, but the case is real clear. Player caught one of his homeboys fucking up. Hand in the cookie jar and all that. Player's heart wants to BREAK IT DOWN light, since he's dealing with his homeboy. But he can't play it like that. Player is the man here. Have to be real with what he signed up for. He wanted to run shit, this here the pain that goes with it. Player have to handle this right. BREAK IT DOWN solid as gold, cold like business. That way streets ain't talking shit.

Break at the top means:
Choke hold.
Brother put to sleep.
Bad look.

This ain't like the first break, where somebody just step out of line. This here about a brother born wrong. Nothing right about him. This motherfucker just don't give a fuck. Slap his mom in church. Brother like this will get the choke hold on him one day. Just put to sleep. That's how it is.

STYLE

STYLE is real important. True Player makes shit look good.

THE FEEL

Style gets paid.
Little bit here, little bit there.
Good look to make a move.

STYLE gets paid. But STYLE ain't the main thing. Player have to be real, with solid moves, then put some STYLE on that motherfucker. If all a brother have is STYLE, his shit blows away with the wind. Streets love STYLE. But it changes with the times. So True Player have to feel them streets and see what STYLE motherfuckers rolling with.

THE LOOK

Light in the VIP lounge.
The look of Style.

That's how True Player rolls
When setting shit straight.
But he don't roll deep like this.

VIP Lounge in the club have nice lights. Real low, shine a little bit here and there. Make everybody look good. Them lights ain't for seeing shit clear. Just for making shit look nice. That's the look for STYLE.

STYLE works with little things. Nice touch for a brother's game. But if he try to roll deep, or run his business on STYLE alone, shit will go bust ass.

THE BREAKS

Break on the one means:
Jump out the ride and walk.

A player who is new in the game got to work his way up. Sometimes a shortcut opens. Maybe another brother offer to boost him up a level. But that shit got strings attached, yo. Brothers who offer shit like that ain't to be trusted. Better for Player to walk his own way then ride in some motherfucker's car he ain't know shit about.

Break on the two means:
Eyebrows done. Beard. Nah.

Sometimes brothers grow little mustache they all proud of. Same type of brother might get his eyebrows done. Please. Manicures are understandable. But eyebrows are just too much. Leave that shit to the sisters. Brothers into that have too much time on their hands. Thinking too high of them self. Never do business with one of them brothers.

Break on the three means:
Style with a drink.
Maintain. Paid.

Shit real nice here. Player living in STYLE, drinking fine wine. Lifestyle like that bump up a brother's status. But dipping too deep in that shit will make him soft. That's why he got to maintain. Keep his mind in the game, even when life is real smooth. That's how a player keeps being paid.

Break on the four means:
Style or street?
Real brother out of nowhere.
He ain't crab ass.
Down and on time.

Player here caught between two worlds. Tripping on if he should flash with a high STYLE crew, or roll with brothers from them streets. Just tripping on that shit tells him the answer. Fake motherfuckers wouldn't think twice. But players with heart like what's real.

Then this real brother from them streets shows up. If Player want to roll with this brother, he have to let go that high STYLE crew. Forget all the champagne and fashion bitches. But in his heart, Player feels down with them streets. So he throws in with this brother from around the way. It feels natural. He's in the right place, even if that brother don't flash high STYLE.

Break on the five means:
Style in the country.
Slim bank roll.
Bust ass, but down the line no problem.

A brother peels off from his crew. They all flashing STYLE and chasing fashion bitches. He ain't feeling that. Brother leaves the city and breaks to the country. Finds a Player out there running real low key operations. Player's people put paid. Brother wants to throw in, but don't have shit to offer. He ain't made his money. Got no weight in the game. But country Players like brothers with heart. Since this brother for real, shit shakes out.

Break at the top means:
Simple Style. No problem.

True Players at the top of the game have real light STYLE. They move so natural STYLE don't matter. That's the highest STYLE there is: hardly any STYLE at all.

FALLING APART

Shit's FALLING APART because ill brothers, crab asses, bad luck and trouble all working on a situation. This happens real slow, piece by motherfucking piece. So quiet nobody notice. Situation just FALLING APART, like some old house with a roof that's rotting. That shit falls apart real slow and quiet. Then one day the damn roof fall right the fuck through. Boom. Whole house ruined.

THE FEEL

Falling Apart.
Not happening to make a move.

Crab asses are running streets. Pushing their bullshit and getting over. Real brothers and True Players don't have power now. That ain't because they fucked up. It's just time for crab asses to have their minute. Shit runs in cycles.

True Player never put plays in motion when crab asses running things. When streets is bullshit like that, he just hold his ground. Roll low profile. Pulling back like this don't make True Player a bitch. It makes him a smart motherfucker, down with the rhythm of things. When crab asses running streets, ain't nothing positive happening.

THE LOOK

Office Tower built on the ground:
The look of Falling Apart.
Brothers high up the chain hold on
By looking out for brothers below.

Them large office buildings in midtown have real strong foundations. That shit goes deep. Without strong foundations, tall buildings fall right the fuck over. The bigger something built, the more support it needs.

Large players the same. Motherfuckers high up in the game are maintaining at top levels because brothers below are working their ass off. Those people are his foundation. If Player up high puts them people paid and shows respect, his position stays solid. That foundation is real deep and strong.

THE BREAKS

Break on the one means:
Split leg on the bed.
Brother make a play is fucked.
Bad look.

The organization is fucked. Crab asses on the rise. But crab asses don't do their shit straightforward. Bitch ass motherfuckers like that roll sideways game. Tell lies about solid brothers. Set people in the organization against each other. It's about to be a fucking disaster, yo. Ain't nothing to do but let shit play out. If Player tries to roll while crab asses are thick like that, them motherfuckers will break his shit right the fuck down.

Break on the two means:
Bed frame split at the edge.
Brothers making moves are finished.
Bad look.

Crab asses got more power now. Just about running the whole game. Their bullshit moving very close to a brother. He sees real clear that shit is fucked now. But since it happened slow, he got trapped. He's losing sleep. Don't have no solid brothers for help. It's a real bad look when the game goes crab ass, and a brother up in it alone. If he pop off some righteous shit, trying to set streets straight, he's finished. Brother just have to adjust to what's happening. Roll low profile, do some business with them motherfuckers. Since streets ain't straight, he have to bend a little bit to survive.

Break on the three means:
Breaks off from crab asses.
People talking shit. No problem.

Brother here tied into an ill situation. Has links with an organization moving in the wrong direction. But he also maintains solid connects with a True Player, running a much cleaner crew. This lets him break off from the crab asses. Them bitches going to talk mad shit. Fuck them. Ain't nothing wrong with what he up and did.

Break on the four means:
Whole bed split and broken.
Bad look.

This ain't just about crab asses running streets. Them motherfuckers right up in a brothers face. Messing with his business, home, and family. Shit don't get worse. Real bad look. Brother here is fucked.

Break on the five means:
Bitches follow. Just like them pretty sisters.
Game all come together.

Miraculous shit happening here. Major crab ass rolls right up on True Player. But instead of breaking True Player down, crab ass sees the light. He realizes how deep True Player is. Drops all his crab ass ways and throws in with True Player.

That's like when some murdering motherfucker walks into church and find Jesus. Turns himself over to police. That shit happens rarely, but it does happen.

Crab asses are a bunch of bitches. Bitches follow. Like when a bunch of pretty sisters all rolling together. All them listen to the finest, most hardcore sister. She tell them how to dress, where to party, who to fuck, all that. Crab asses the same. Just need a motherfucker to follow. Throwing in with True Player saves them from their own bullshit. It shakes out nice from there.

Break at the top means:
Large cheeseburger nobody eat.
True Player gets a nice ride.
Crab ass game falls apart.

Bad times play out. Crab asses and their bullshit have a season like everything else. When them motherfuckers fall off, better times are just waiting there. Like a large cheeseburger, looking real tasty, ready to eat.

True Player is back in the game. Streets are straight, so he's running plays. Brothers got love for him. Real happy he's back. All them crab asses went bust-ass. Their bullshit fell right the fuck apart. Law of Heaven made that happen. Negative brothers ruin shit, but got no head for running shit. So after they fuck up what's real, they fuck up their own damn self. Just how it is. That's why the best move for a crab ass is letting a True Player run shit. Even if he hate that motherfucker.

COME BACK AROUND

Ill times play out. Good times COME BACK AROUND.

THE FEEL

COME BACK AROUND. Good look.
Step out, come back. No problem.
Down brothers show up. All good.
Plays are flowing.
Good look to roll.

After a bad time, things COME BACK AROUND. Real shit that had no chance of being respected gets love. Brothers didn't break it down to make this happen. Just natural changes, happening low key. The old shit falls off and the new joint is on. Because brothers are moving with the rhythm of things, no static involved. Motherfuckers feeling each other throw in with each other. But this ain't no back room deal only a few brothers hear about. Shit happens out there on streets. Any real brother with tight game can step into play.

The feel of COME BACK AROUND is natural. Nothing stops springtime from happening. Same here. Nobody trying to stop positive times when they COME BACK AROUND. And nobody got to stress the development, neither. Brothers just let it flow. That's how Heaven and Earth roll.

THE LOOK

Dead winter.
The look of Come Back Around.
Old School Big Dogs closed the roads.
Nobody buying and selling.
Old Big Dog chill at the palace.

In China, Winter Solstice was a big deal back in the day. It happen on the shortest day and longest night of the whole motherfucking year. That's the coldest, darkest minute on the calendar. But them Chinese motherfuckers celebrated. Because it meant shit couldn't get no darker. Days get longer from there. More sun. Good times.

But they didn't celebrate that shit popping off champagne in the streets. Chinese brothers just chilled. Shut shit down. Big Dogs closed the roads. Business have the day off. People was supposed to rest, celebrate shit laid back.

Motherfuckers today don't chill much. Busy all over. Nobody like to relax. Back in the day, brothers felt the rhythm of things real deep. Watched nature more. Learned from the patterns. Saw there's a time to be doing, and a time to be chilling.

Chilling out is real important when shit is just starting. It takes mad amount of energy to put a serious play in motion. So right before the jump off, players got to relax. Charge up their energy. Same thing in other parts of life. Like when a brother's real sick, maybe gets hit by a bus or some shit. He ain't out that night partying. Brother got to let his body return to strength.

Same shit socially. Like when two brothers fall out, but then patch it up. Trust gets put back on track slowly. Takes time to rebuild bonds.

Any situation where shit COME BACK AROUND, True Players take it slow.

THE BREAKS

Break on the one means:
Come Back Around from a little slip.
No sweat.
Shit all good.

Stepping off the path happens. Everybody drop the ball sometime. But a brother got to COME BACK AROUND before shit gets too fucked. True Players stops trouble while it's still just a thought in the mind. Maybe look at his homeboy's girl, thinking: "Yo, she got a fine ass." True Player crush that thought right there. He ain't lying in bed later tripping on what that fat ass might look like all over his joint. If a brother stops ill shit in the mental, it's alright.

Break on the two means:
Check himself. Good shit.

When a brother COME BACK AROUND it always happens because he checked himself. Maybe he was fucking around with shit that wasn't proper. But he dropped it in time and set his shit straight. That type of decision is easier to make if he's rolling with real brothers who maintain positive lifestyles. If a brother move the way True Players move, good shit will happen.

Break on the three means:
Keep fucking with it.
Bad look.
No problem.

Some brothers play with fire. It's dangerous to keep picking up what should be left alone. Might be nasty pussy. Or some drugs. Or twisted business that plays brothers. Whatever. It's a bad look to keep fucking with that shit. Brother might feel real bad afterward, then stop for a stretch of time. But if he return to that shit, he's fucked. That said, everybody slips now and again. If a brother's heart is down with putting the ill shit behind him, and he's trying real hard, he'll be alright.

Break on the four means:
Rolling with ill brothers,
Pulls out.

Brother here rolling with some ill motherfuckers. But he has a link with a True Player who sets him straight. So he pulls out from that ill crew. Ain't no guarantee here about earning more. But choosing the right path has real mental and spiritual payoffs.

Break on the five means:
Straight up Come Back Around.
No problems.

When it's time for coming back around, a brother shouldn't be making excuses. Just check himself for real. If he fucked up, he should just be straight up and say it. No matter how shit shakes out, a brother who does this ain't ever regret the path he chose.

Break at the top means:
Missing time to Come Back Around. Bad look.
Bullshit inside and out.

Set brothers rolling this way,
Taken clean out the game.
Fucked for real.
Ten years go by
No chance getting over.

If a brother miss the right time to COME BACK AROUND, that's a real bad look. Problem here is because the brother got the wrong attitude. He's looking at the world wrong. So whatever bullshit happens is his own damn fault. Some brothers think they always right, no matter what. Problems happen, they always roll on shit. Always looking to fuck with people. Motherfuckers like that always get hit one day. It never shake out pretty. Brothers like that end up in some wheelchair, or thrown under the jail.

NATURAL

When a brother in the rhythm of things, he move NATURAL. Ain't scheming or planning his shit. Just flowing with what's happening. When a brother rolls NATURAL, things happen he ain't ever think of. Unexpected shit that shakes out nice.

THE FEEL

Natural. Real good look.
Maintain. Paid.
Start fronting, bullshit.
Bad look to make a play.

Brothers born innocent. Ain't no baby try to make problems. Later on, world mess them up. World fucks up everybody. But every brother have that innocent part of him. It stays true. Any situation, if he just listen to what's NATURAL inside, and don't stress how shit will work out, The Heavens look out for him.

But following the heart ain't about just doing shit without thinking. Brother got to sort through what's positive and negative inside. Part of a brother feels pretty damn NATURAL watching titties on that internet all day. That ain't the part bringing a brother places. Have to sort that shit out.

Old Big Dog break it down like this:

Brother who ain't NATURAL and real don't add up to much.
The rhythm of things pass that brother by.

THE LOOK

Thunder rolling in the sky.
The look of Natural.
Old Big Dog back in the day
Maintain tight game. Flow with the time.
Built up his people.

In springtime them thundershowers make shit grow. That happen NATURAL. True Players do the same thing with their people. They let brothers roll NATURAL and grow. True Players have a NATURAL touch. Know when to step up to people, and when to let them be. True Players recognize that they part of a larger system. That lets them flow with reality.

THE BREAKS

Break on the one means:
Act Natural. Paid.

NATURAL feelings from the heart are right. A brother can follow them without stressing. His shit works out. Brother put paid.

Break on the two means:
Brother do his shit.
Don't trip.
All good.

Every part of the game have shit that needs to be done. Player don't trip on what's next. He just does what he's supposed to do, right where he's at. Player don't sweat how shit will shake out down the line. Just do what's in front of him, and does it right. Everything falls into place.

Break on the three means:
Bullshit.
Jacket on the bench.
Crab ass gain, brother's loss.

Bullshit happen. Crab ass brothers lift belongings and whatnot. When a brother's in the park playing ball, he might leave his jacket on the bench. If he ain't paying attention, some motherfucker might walk away with it. Then a crab ass got his jacket and that brother's damn cold. Whatever a brother is doing—from ball in the park to business in them streets—he have to keep an eye on the area. Know what's happening and how shit's moving. Otherwise, some bullshit happen to him.

Break on the four means:
Brother who maintain.
Nobody talking shit.

What a brother truly own won't be lost. That don't mean his jacket or a smart phone. A brother might have that shit, but he ain't own it. What a motherfucker owns is inside him. Talent, The Dream, Love, Smarts, all that shit. So even if a brother mess up real bad and lose something he owns, that shit ain't gone. Motherfuckers can't lose what they truly own. Everybody drops the ball sometime. All a brother have to do is maintain his game, and pay no mind to motherfuckers talking shit.

Break on the five means:
Don't see no doctor for
Illness a brother ain't start.
Shit will pass.

Sometime ill shit happens out of nowhere. If a brother didn't start it, he shouldn't trip. What a brother got to do is take care of himself. Find a better place. Let that ill shit go. Things will work out for a brother that way.

Break at the top means:
Doing shit fucks things up.
No play.

When the time ain't right to move forward, Player just chills. Low key, no plans. Some brothers lose their head and push forward, even when shit ain't ready. They always get fucked.

JUST HANDLE BUSINESS

Player can't always push forward. When he's blocked, he JUST HANDLE BUSINESS. Maintains daily operations to build up power. Then he has strength when it's time to pop off. Player JUST HANDLE BUSINESS mentally by holding his head together, even when he don't like where he's at. Sometimes he have to wait for the right opening. By not forcing plays and acting up, he saves money, builds respect with his people, and don't waste time. While he's looking for the right opening, a brother JUST HANDLE BUSINESS by being sure the operation is running crisp, his people all in line, and personal shit is in order. That lets him make the jump fast when the game opens up.

THE FEEL

Just Handle Business puts player paid.
Out on the town being seen is a good look.
Good move to roll cross town.

To JUST HANDLE BUSINESS and hold brothers together, it takes a True Player in charge. He got to have a clear head, and be respected by the Big Dog. When True Player JUST HANDLE BUSINESS on a daily basis, he stays strong. When times are quiet, having a routine helps True Player stay in shape. That keeps him crisp. And since he got respect from The Big Dog, True Player should be out doing business. Saying what up to brothers around the way. True Player like this stays down with The Heavens, and good on them streets. So even if he got to do something real deep, like roll on motherfuckers cross town, shit shakes out right.

THE LOOK

Money in the bank.
The look of Just Handle Business.
True Player reads them old books of wisdom.
Down with history
To make his game tight.

Money in the bank is power people don't see. It ain't some large diamond in a motherfucker's ear or some million dollar ride. Money in the bank is power a brother got that nobody knows about. That's good to have. Old books are like that. Wisdom from the past is rich shit for a brother. History teaches lessons. Player should be down with how True Players back in the day rolled. But reading ain't about hiding in books all day. It's about learning real moves and putting that shit to use in the game.

THE BREAKS

Break on the one means:
Problems right there. Good look to chill.

Player wants to move on large plays. But ain't nothing opening up.

If Player don't JUST HANDLE BUSINESS, and try to force his way forward, he puts himself into problems. Player here got to check himself. JUST HANDLE BUSINESS, and wait for shit to line up.

Break on the two means:
Wheels off the ride.

Player is blocked by deep brothers with real power. No way he's getting over on motherfuckers that ill. So Player just takes the wheels right off his ride. Don't try to move forward one inch. JUST HANDLE BUSINESS and keeps shit crisp, watching and waiting. Player uses the time to make himself strong. Like when brothers get caught in the system and lift weights or get a motherfucking law degree.

Break on the third means.
Brother following brother.
Eyes on the problem,
Maintain. Paid.
Practice rolling and check the clip.
Good look to make the move.

Shit opens up. Time to roll. Player meets a brother moving in the same direction. Throws in and follows. Streets are ill. They roll careful. Player ready for problems. Has that nine. Maintaining tight street game helps a brother when shit gets thick. But when rolling on motherfuckers, Players always have a goal. They don't just wild on whoever looking squinty at them.

Break on the four means:
Do some pushups or a girl.
Damn good look.

Players in the game have lots of tension in their life. If a Player lets that shit build up, he's stressed. Have to let that tension out. Bust out some push-ups. Run some. Hit some pussy. That takes the edge off stress before it blows up into drama. Always a good look to stay balanced.

Break on the five means:
Horns. No Balls.
All good.

This some old school farm shit. When a real wild bull fucking up the yard, brothers cut off that animal's balls. Chill him out. Bull still got them horns on the head. But without balls, them horns ain't no problem.

True Player think like this when handling ill situations. He don't front right up in the face of that shit. He handle it indirect. Goes around the danger, to find the root of the problem. Cuts it off right there.

Break at the top means:
Brother rolling with the rhythm.
Paid.

Doors open. Player was blocked for a long time, but had the mind to JUST HANDLE BUSINESS. Since he stayed in shape, managed the organization, and kept all his personal shit sorted, Player pops off with mad power. Gets over in a heartbeat. Heaven love this brother's style. Big Dog does too. So Player gets set up nice and calls shots in the game.

TAKING CARE

Player is TAKING CARE of himself and his people with the right food for body, mind, and soul.

THE FEEL

Taking Care.
Maintain gets paid.
Think about what a brother eat.
And what a brother put in his head.

Eating right is important. That fast food is murder for a brother. Motherfuckers make them damn cheese burgers out of the worst parts the animal. Soda is poison too. Makes a brother fat and stupid. Brother who wants to be a True Player treat his body right.

If a Player wants to know what a brother is like, he just watches what part of life that brother feeds. Some brothers put lots of money and time into chasing pussy. Other brothers real into them video games and watching TV. Another brother might spend time on his business, reading up on the market. Everybody TAKING CARE different parts of life. Shows what they value.

Life takes care of everybody. Motherfuckers always manage. Some more than others, for reasons nobody ever figure out. The Big Dog should be TAKING CARE of the True Players in his operation. That takes care of every other motherfucker. Since True Players run shit right, other brothers will be fine. Big Dog ain't got to stress the details.

Old Big Dog break it down like this:

To know if someone is a True Player or not,
Look what part of his body he look after most.
A Brother's body has important and less important parts.
He can't fuck up the important parts of his body just to be
TAKING CARE of less important parts.
Brother live for his dick, his heart going to suffer.
Brother live for smoking la, his head going to suffer.
Brother live for food, his body going to suffer.
Brother who lives life for the less important parts of his body is a less
*   important brother.*
Brother who TAKING CARE of the highest part of himself first is The
*   True Player.*

THE LOOK

In the streets, thunder:
The look of Taking Care.
True Player watch what he say.
Chill with eating and drinking.

Springtime bring thundershowers. Makes the grass and flowers grow. Happens because them seeds in the ground stayed chill. When the rain fall, their shit ready to grow. That's the look for TAKING CARE. Chill before the movement. True Player follows that look to take care his self and be ready.

Words start in a brother's head, then go out the mouth. Food starts outside the mouth, then go in the body. Both are better if a brother is chill. If he chill before speaking, the right words come out his mouth. If he's chill before eating, he choose the right food, so he don't get fat and sloppy. Both together make that brother crisp.

THE BREAKS

Break on the one means:
Let his unicorn go.
Look around frowning.
Bad look.

Unicorn is some magical shit. Fly around and do just whatever the fuck it want to do. That's like a brother who live real free. He just on his own trip. Not following the program at all. Since he was born that way, it's how he should roll. If he decide to give up that freedom, and start wishing he fit in more, this brother gets upset. But being jealous about normal motherfuckers and looking at them all squinty don't lead nowhere positive. If a brother is a motherfucking unicorn, he should maintain like a motherfucking unicorn. Just fly off on his own shit. That's real.

Break on the two means:
Looking for handouts,
Losing his game for charity.
Maintaining this way is a bad look.
Bust ass.

A brother should be TAKING CARE of himself. If he's a lazy motherfucker, and don't handle shit, brother starts feeling bad. That's because a man only feels right when he's TAKING CARE

his damn self. If a brother starts taking handouts, that's bullshit.
Living that way will make him a permanently bust ass motherfucker.

Break on the three means:
Taking Care with wrong things.
Maintain. Bullshit.
Don't do this for ten years.
Nothing works out.

A brother wanting to party all the time puts chains on himself.
Running from high to high will fuck his shit up. Drinking liquor,
throwing dice and chasing pussy all the time leads nowhere. A
brother should never play himself like this. If it takes ten years to
get clean, he should do it. Nothing positive happen from rolling
through life like a party motherfucker.

Break on the four means:
Looking from the top
For people Taking Care gets paid.
Like a tiger.
No problem.

Player is high up in the operation, looking to make some positive
moves in the game. He needs some real brothers to help him out.
So Player looking around like a tiger. Ferocious and focused. Try-
ing real hard to find the right brothers. Since Player is trying to do
something positive for them streets, it ain't wrong for him to be
this hungry.

Break on the five means:
Leaving the game.
Maintaining puts people paid.
Don't roll cross town.

Maybe Player has a problem. He supposed to be TAKING CARE

his people, but don't have the power to do it. So he have to find help from a brother who knows what's up. That might not be a brother up high in the operation. Just some motherfucker who knows shit. Going to him, straight and real about needing help, is the right move. That will help Player put his people paid. But Player have to remember that he's depending on this other brother's help. He shouldn't be fronting in them streets, or trying to handle anything deep, like rolling on motherfuckers cross town.

Break at the top means:
The brother Taking Care his people.
Heads up about static gets paid.
Good look to roll cross town.

True Player here TAKING CARE all the people in his area. That's a large job. If Player keeps his head up for all potential static, and handles his responsibilities, it's alright. Player like that can do serious shit like rolling on motherfuckers cross town. Brothers will throw in. They down because Player TAKING CARE his people.

PRESSURE

When a brother's under mad PRESSURE, the situation has to be changed fast or real bullshit will happen.

THE FEEL

Pressure.
The roof is on fire.
Good look to bounce.
Paid.

When the roof is on fire, whole place about to burn down. That's a fucked up and highly dangerous situation. Only real serious moves will set shit straight.

This ain't no *seed in the ground* shit here, yo. This is drama. Motherfucking roof on fire. Brothers have to move fast and take action. But they can't panic like a bunch of bitches. Busting wild shots ain't help neither. Brothers have to get to the heart of shit. Find out what set off the blaze. Thinking in the middle of all that PRESSURE ain't easy. Takes a True Player to stay cool when the motherfucking roof is on fire.

PRESSURE is real serious.

THE LOOK

Town been flooded:
The look of Pressure.
True Player on his own
Not sweating forgetting the world.

PRESSURE situations are like when New Orleans flooded. TV showed brothers in boats, rolling with shotguns, sleeping in a motherfucking stadium. Shit eventually cleared up. It was temporary. But that temporary situation was still very much fucked up. That's PRESSURE. Temporary shit that is ill, and real hardcore.

The way a True Player handle PRESSURE is by standing strong. He'll stand alone if he have to. Under PRESSURE, a brother got to have a song in his heart. Maybe the whole world around him falling apart, but a True Player stays positive inside. That's the only way to survive PRESSURE.

THE BREAKS

Break on the one means:
Carpet on the floor. Measure the door.
No problem.

When a brother wants to get something done in seriously fucked up times, he has to be extra careful. Like when a real thoughtful brother moves some heavy furniture into his home. First he put some rug on the floor so the wood don't get scratched up. Then he measure the doors, make sure that furniture will fit. Then he sweep the steps, make sure shit ain't slippery. Only after all that's done, does he move the damn furniture. Motherfuckers will laugh and say he's tripping. Being too careful. But they're wrong, and this brother is right. Under PRESSURE, a brother should only make a play if he's ridiculously careful before the jump.

Break on the two means:
Bust ass tree sprout a leaf.
Older brother takes a slim thing.
Everything work out.

Old trees sometimes sprout a whole new branch. That's like when an older brother takes some young slim thing as his female. Even though she's real young for this motherfucker, it works out. In the larger picture, this means that under PRESSURE, a rich brother should throw in with people from them streets. Those motherfuckers know how to handle themselves in bullshit. Everybody gets through that way.

Break on the three means:
Roof is on fire. About to burn the house down.
Bad look.

A brother under real PRESSURE is still trying to force his way forward. Just maintaining is hard enough, but he wants more. Nobody thinks that's right. But he don't listen to people, so they turn their back on this motherfucker. That makes PRESSURE worse. His whole operation about to burn down. Real bad look. A brother who forces himself forward under PRESSURE only makes shit fall apart faster.

Break on the four means:
Fire put out. Good look.
Try to get over, bust ass.

By throwing in with some brothers from around the way, a rich brother gets through some PRESSURE. But if he tries to use them street connects for his own interests, instead of helping the whole area, shit will go bust ass. It won't be pretty, neither. Brothers from around the way don't play.

Break on the five means:
Old school try and make hits.
Old lady takes a man.
No problem. Not paid.

Some old school brother who was big back in the day tries to make hits for them streets. But he's been out of the game too long. He's just burning money. Ain't ever getting over again. Just like when an older sister gets married. If her time for making babies is through, she ain't about to be knocked up. Motherfuckers can go through all the right motions, but they still ain't getting shit from certain situations. Business too. Some motherfuckers trying to rise up in the game will push away real brothers. Start sweating Players high up on the chain. Nothing positive ever happen from that. No matter how hard them motherfuckers try.

Break at the top means:
Running into them Towers.
Falling over his head.
Bad look. Nobody talking shit.

PRESSURE here is at the worst. But some brother trying to do his job no matter what. Like them firefighters who ran into the World Trade Towers when that shit was in flames. Nobody survive that. But nobody talk shit about brothers like that, either. Even the hardest, most murdering motherfuckers from around the way show respect for brothers who roll like that. Some shit is just more important than life.

ILL SHIT

ILL SHIT is a fucked situation that a brother have to deal with. The problem ain't his fault. Just ILL SHIT that's happening. ILL SHIT will last a minute. Like a bad job brother have to hold onto in lean times. Or a fucked neighborhood he ain't have the money to pull up out of. But if a brother rolls right, he pulls through that ILL SHIT. No problem.

THE FEEL

Ill Shit over and over.
If he's a player at heart
Whatever he do works out.

ILL SHIT that just goes on and on makes a brother used to dealing with it. Brother in ILL SHIT should be like water in the river. Water in the river just flows through everything. It don't stop and try to hide from deep places. Water don't stress if shit is shallow neither. Water just fill up every place it have to. Don't miss nothing. Don't stop flowing. Water see a cliff, it jump right off like a motherfucking waterfall. Through all that, it don't change none, neither. Water stays water. And it never stops moving forward.

Player handles ILL SHIT the same way. Not scared of nothing, staying true to himself, and moving forward, whatever happens.

If a brother stays real when facing ILL SHIT, his heart grows strong. With a strong heart, he can understand whatever ILL SHIT he's being put through. Then he gets his handle on the scenario. And once a brother has a handle on how shit is rolling, he does the right thing at the right time.

During ILL SHIT, only three things matter. Doing what has to be done, doing it right, and moving forward. Moving forward is the key, otherwise a brother gets caught up in the ILL SHIT for life.

For real deep Players, ILL SHIT can be put to use. Like how them Viet Nam brothers handled bombs dropping in The Viet Nam War. The U.S. flew day and night for years, throwing shit ton of bombs down on Viet Nam. Instead of losing their head in that ILL SHIT, Viet Nam brothers stayed chill. They looked where those bombs were dropping. Watched that shit real close, with binoculars, because some them bombs were duds. Just hit the ground and lay there. When that happened, Viet Nam motherfuckers run out the jungle with a tea kettle and a handsaw. Climbed up on that motherfucking bomb, sat down and started sawing. Splashed water from the tea kettle to cool down heat from the saw. Sometimes that worked. Other times, motherfuckers blew right the fuck up. Brothers who cut through their bomb and survived pulled out the explosives. Used that shit to make their own bombs. Threw that shit at solders from the U.S. Won the war that way.

Living in some jungle while bombs dropping is ILL SHIT. Rolling with binoculars, handsaw, and a motherfucking teakettle to flip that ILL SHIT on brothers is real high level game.

THE LOOK

Water flows to the ocean.
The look of Ill Shit that go on and on.
True Player moves correct.
Handles his business by showing what's good.

Water reach the ocean by flowing. Fills up every place and don't stop moving. True Player is the same way. He's down with the fact that being real is a 24/7 situation. Not just some shit he does here and there. Part of his business is showing people how to live. That only works if True Player is the same all the time, whatever and whenever. Motherfuckers pick shit up through repetition. So he's always on, rolling right.

THE BREAKS

Break on the one means:
Ill Shit on and on and on.
In darkness brother falls into the pit.
Bad look.

If a brother lets himself get used to ILL SHIT, he starts thinking fucked up situations are just natural. He's lost then. That's a real bad look.

Break on the two means:
The dark is dangerous.
Brother just do little things.

Brother in a bad spot and a dark place don't try to bust all the way out at once. Holding together in some ILL SHIT is job enough.

He just maintains and looks around. Works out how shit is rolling, and gets real about what's possible. That's like a train leaving the station. Them motherfuckers pull out slow. Trains don't pick up speed till down the track. A brother in real ILL SHIT rolls like that. The way out is slow. Little bit here, little bit there.

Break on the three means:
Front and back, Ill Shit and more Ill Shit.
In danger like this, chill the fuck out.
If he don't, brother fall deeper in it.
Don't step like that.

Brother's in a spot where any move he make, forward or backward, will really fuck him up. Getting out of this ILL SHIT ain't about to happen. Brother can't let himself be talked into rolling on a play. Anything he does here will just make ILL SHIT worse. Hard as it is, brother have to chill. Wait for the way out to show up.

Break on the four means:
Just show up.
Quick what up.
Nobody talking shit about this.

Motherfuckers in ILL SHIT ain't tripping on formality. Normally a brother don't just throw in with a Player real casual. He handles shit respectful. Show up with some nice liquor, throws dollars down on dinner. That shit ain't nothing Player can't buy himself. It just shows respect. But in ILL SHIT, all that flies out the window. Brothers just say what up, throw in together, and bust ass to get the hell out.

Break on the five means:
River don't overflow.
Just fill up. Forward.
No problem.

ILL SHIT gets worse when a brother tries to do too much. River only flows through a place by staying low and moving forward. If that water tries to rise, it overflows and turns into a damn swamp. Stays stuck there. Brother in ILL SHIT should be the same way. Just find the flow and move forward with it. Head down, keep it moving. That's enough. If he tries to rise up, he gets stuck in that ILL SHIT.

Break at the top means:
Tied up in chains,
Under the jail.
Three years lost.
Bad look.

Brother who gets lost in the ILL SHIT and falls into fucked up habits won't ever get out. Maybe he start into them drugs because ILL SHIT tripping him out. Or he hits that liquor real hard. Might start murdering brothers, trying to get out. He's trapped then. Like a motherfucker in chains thrown under the jail. No way out of the ILL SHIT, forever.

WREXAGRAM 30
SHINE

Fire is real powerful, but never works alone. Shit has to be sparked before fire can light up and SHINE.

THE FEEL

Shine. Maintain.
Paid.
Looking retarded brings money.

Lot of normal motherfuckers will hold on tight to a famous brother when he becomes a star. Hang on to that brother for life. All them bullshit motherfuckers make a famous Player look even brighter. But stars needs something inside that maintains, or else they burn out. Everybody who SHINE have to hold onto something real inside them self and protect it. That way they stay shining. Sun and the moon hold tight to the sky. Trees and grass hold tight to the earth. Fame is a motherfucker. Mess a brother's head up for real. So famous Players who SHINE have to hold on tight to what's right. That way they don't get lost. Helps them make positive shit happen for them streets.

Brothers try and be famous so they can do what the fuck they want in life. But even the biggest star has limits. Motherfuckers can't just do what they want in this world. Rakim said it best back in the day: *knowledge is when a brother know the ledge*. The ledge is the limit of how far a brother can push shit before he fall off. Knowing that ledge is knowledge. Brothers with knowledge don't fall off.

If a brother don't know his own limits, he try and force shit to happen and falls right the fuck off. If he don't know the limits of the world around him, he starts breaking laws and hearts. Once a brother recognize limits, he realize he need some help in this world. That's why The Heavens there. The brother who recognize limits and ask for help gets love from The Heavens. Finds the right path forward.

Most motherfuckers today don't believe in no Heavens. But that power is real, whether a brother believe in that shit or not. Same Power that runs The Heavens runs them streets. That's the rhythm of things. It's how shit happen in life. Reality have rules. Worst thing a brother can do is turn his back on them rules, or disrespect The Heavens. He's just a motherfucker in the way, then. Always forcing shit, running up in motherfuckers faces, getting played, shut down, shook out, whatever. Motherfuckers like that are lost. Never go nowhere.

True Player flows with reality. Follow where shit leads. That ain't easy for real sharp brothers. They always trying to run shit. Think they're smarter than every motherfucker around. But the simplest brothers do it right. Think on them mentally retarded brothers a minute. They just flow. Their only hope to survive this world is by following what people tell them. Just like children. That don't mean a Player should be retarded. But he should recognize where he stand in reality. One Force rolling through this world, making shit happen. It's older than time and larger than space. This Force so deep and motherfucking magnificent, it makes the smartest, sharpest brother in the game look nothing but retarded. Learning to flow with that Force puts Players in the rhythm of things. They follow where it leads and master reality. Down with The Heavens, good on them streets. Shit shakes out nice.

Players who know their limits, lean on The Heavens, and flow with reality SHINE.

THE LOOK

Sun rise twice.
The look of SHINE.
True Player stays bright and shines all over.

Sun rise twice a day. After it goes down here, sun rise up the other side the planet. Sun ain't ever stop shining. True Player just like that. SHINE on and on.

THE BREAKS

Break on the one means:
Rush hour in the morning.
Head together. No Problem.

Most motherfuckers wake up late and rush to work. That's a bad look. Morning best handled chill. Brother waking up have to let his mind reconnect with reality. The start of shit is important. Day ain't no different. Morning is the jump off. Sets the tone for the whole day.

Break on the two means:
Sun at lunchtime. Paid nice.

Lunch happens middle of the day. Sun is at the highest and brightest. True Player is like that. He stand right in the middle of motherfuckers and SHINE.

Break on the three means:
Day done,
Brothers either party or bitch.
Bad look.

Setting sun reminds a brother that time passes. Nothing stays the same. Shit changes, then a brother die. That's life. We trapped in this motherfucker, without shit to say about how we check out or when.

Knowledge like that hit different brothers different ways. Some feel they got to party all they can while they young. Chase that pussy. Smoke that la. Drink them brews. Live-it-up type motherfuckers. Other brothers get sad. Bitch about getting old. Say life pass too fast. Everybody die. Why bother doing shit?

Both these looks are wrong. For the True Player, growing old or dying don't matter. That shit have very little to do with what's on his plate today. True Player do what have to be done without tripping. He handle his business and maintain through whatever piece of time Heaven broke off for him. Rolling that way makes his Fate tight.

Break on the four means:
Mad fast.
Fame, burnt out, fade away.

Thinking at real deep levels is like fire. Fire burns through wood. Thinking too fierce can burn right through life. A brother might see too much. So he shouldn't trip out on the wisdom. Motherfuckers should think to light shit up, not burn it down. Brothers rolling too deep with their knowledge are like brothers who catch fame too fast. Light up the game a minute, but burn right out.

Brothers should live for the long game. They should chill on knowledge. There's a limit to what thinking can do for a brother. Too much burns a brother's brain right the fuck up. He should learn enough to flow with shit and roll nice. Pick up enough to put him and his people paid. That's enough. Same thing with the body. Live too hard, too fast, a brother's body will just cash right the fuck out. So the smart play is rolling in the middle with this shit, physically and on the mental.

Break on the five means:
Tears and crying, all sad and shit.
Paid.

When a brother hits the high point of something, he have to recognize. Maybe it's his time playing ball. Or his days chasing females. Maybe it's his power in business. Whatever a brother do in life will hit that peak, then fade. That's the rhythm of things. Just like the Sun rise up, SHINE bright, then fall. A brother's run in the game is the same way. Some motherfuckers think they will be on top, riding high forever. Those are the ones who fall hardest when they lose their grip.

A True Player down with reality understands that everything fades. He knows that the biggest of Big Dogs grow old and lose their grip. That makes him recognize the peak in his own life. Once he's living it, he might get real sad. Player knows shit will fall off from there. It has to. He might even cry with a bottle of wine about this one night. That's alright. Player's just recognizing. That helps him do two things. One: appreciate what he have. Two: sort shit out for the ride down.

Heavens have love for a brother that real.

Break at the top means:
Players back in the day roll on Ill Big Dog.
Murder top brothers.
Chill on his people.
Nobody talking shit.

A Player who want to SHINE have to break it down on himself. Discipline his life. But breaking it down ain't about punishing. It's about restoring order. That said, real illness have to be cut off at the roots.

Back in the day, when Players rolled on some Ill Big Dog to take him out the game, they would murder that motherfucker. Next they'd shoot down his top players and clip all the hard soldiers. Minor brothers in the organizations were allowed to live.

Player keeps that in mind when he's trying to set himself straight. Real bad habits get killed cold. Drugs, liquor, crime, or messed up shit in the bedroom will fuck a Player up. Zero tolerance on them motherfuckers. But the little things in a brother's life shouldn't be handled so hard. Maybe he watch bullshit TV now and again. Or eat too many ribs and have a few brews too many. Flip through some titty sites on that internet sometime. Whatever. Let little things be. A brother who come down too hard on himself, all the time for everything, just hurts himself.

FEELING IT

This is about men and women FEELING IT for each other. Brother got to take the first step. Lady lets him know if she's FEELING IT. Once he's in, Player have to hold on even when he's FEELING IT real nice. Make sure the female gets over first. That's how a True Player hits it.

THE FEEL

Feeling It. Paid.
Maintain.
Getting with her is a good look.

People FEELING IT when they both down with each other. But Player stays chill when he meets the right female. If he's FEEL-ING IT strong, Player don't pop off telling every motherfucker. He stays chill in his heart, even when he's real happy. Player knows people are fucked up about FEELING IT. Sometimes a brother will tell his homeboy: "Yo, I met this nice female and I'm really FEELING IT." His homeboy might be jealous. Run sideways game to ruin that shit. Or if a brother straight up tell a female he's FEELING IT for her, she might trip. Freeze him right the fuck out. That's why Player stays chill, even when he's really FEELING IT for somebody. That don't mean he's a cold motherfucker. Just a brother who maintains chill when handling real strong feelings.

Same rules for when Player's knocking boots. He learn to control himself up in that female. If he pops off in a minute, that's a bad look. So Player rolls long game within the female. That shit help the relationship. Females love a brother who FEELING IT and still maintain till she gets over real nice.

FEELING IT is different from hitting it. Sometimes brothers pick up females from the club, just for hitting it. Brothers have to seduce that ass. Seduction is like a mind game. FEELING IT for a worthwhile female don't happen like that. It don't involve tricks. But there is an art to playing it.

Brother who wants to get a valuable female FEELING IT for him rolls polite. Shows some manners. He don't flash his money, but lets her know he have his finance down. Real female only FEEL-ING IT for a brother who have his angle in the game tight. If she FEELING IT for this brother, she send some signals. Brother picks them up fast and moves in crisp. Next she gonna shake him up, just to see how that brother react. Females have a real strong distaste for brothers who fold like laundry or lose their head. They don't like motherfucking nice guys, neither. Brothers like that get played in the game. Sisters want to see a strong brother who ain't hard. He have to roll with her drama, without changing up his game. He have to respect her. But she need to see a part of him that don't give a damn. Her shit cross the line, brother's just walk-ing. If he shakes out nice on all that, she start FEELING IT for him. Then they FEELING IT together.

Many brothers don't have time to deal with them details. Be like: "Why real females such a damn project?" Rather hit it and quit it or rent some shit. But real females take real time. That's just how

FEELING IT works. Have a law and a rhythm to it, like everything. And FEELING IT goes beyond just knocking boots.

FEELING IT keeps the whole universe in order. Earth is FEELING IT for the sun, and stays in orbit with it. Oceans FEELING IT for the moon, so the tides rise and fall. Stars FEELING IT where they shine, so space is balanced. Back before time, our whole motherfucking galaxy started because some molecules were FEELING IT for each other. Broke out their orbit, smashed the fuck into each other, and blew up to make stars and planets and shit. FEELING IT is how everything happens.

FEELING IT is how business gets done. That don't mean sucking dick to get over. It means brothers have to be FEELING IT for a situation to pop off. When a True Player steps into the game, people FEELING IT. Player moves real, plays smart, and rolls crisp. That shit affects brothers. When he's running plays, True Player don't just tell motherfuckers "do this, do that." He has real words, deep reasons, hard facts, and heart. He makes sure brothers FEELING IT. That way they throw in 100%.

If a True Player want to know what somebody is like, he looks at what they FEELING IT for. Brother FEELING IT for weapons and rolling hard is a violent motherfucker. Brother FEELING IT for smoking la and playing video games is a lazy motherfucker. Brother FEELING IT for them books is a thoughtful motherfucker. Brother FEELING IT for his children is a family man. Somebody FEELING IT for the nightlife is a party motherfucker. And so on.

By paying attention to what brothers FEELING IT for, True Player learns invaluable shit about who he's dealing with.

THE LOOK

Brew on the street:
The look of Feeling It.
People reach out to True Player
Since he down with them.

Sometimes Player out in them streets just kicking it with motherfuckers, talking shit. Somebody hands Player a brew. Since he was out there FEELING IT with people, Player got that free brew. Another brother bring up some shit happen in business. Player picks up some real helpful information. That wouldn't happen if he was pulling back from brothers, off on his own shit.

FEELING IT happens through connects. True Player stays down with people, out there kicking it. That helps him pick up knowledge from other brothers in the game. Motherfuckers talk about plays they run and how to handle business. A Player out there FEELING IT with brothers will learn some moves. But Player have to listen. Brothers give up trying to talk to a motherfucker who thinks he know everything.

THE BREAKS

Break on the one means:
Feeling It in the toes.

Brother wearing shoes can move his toes all he want. Since he's wearing shoes, nobody sees that shit. That's like a brother who just starts FEELING IT for something. Maybe that's a fine sister, or a different crew he wants to roll with, whatever. He FEELING IT, but ain't done nothing yet. FEELING IT without moving on it don't effect situations one way or the other.

Break on the two means:
Feeling It in the legs.
Bad look.
Slow down, paid.

When a brother walks, his foot leads and the leg follows. If a motherfucker's leg try to lead, brother trip and fall. Movements starting with the wrong part are fucked. Plays in the game have to start with real feelings in a brother's heart. Bad moves happen when brothers ain't FEELING IT, but roll because other motherfuckers tell them to.

This situation, Player just listen to himself. Not some other motherfucker's thoughts. He hold back, and wait till he's really FEELING IT for something. Player don't roll on a play just because he wants to move. Or because other motherfuckers telling him it's time to move. Player have to wait for real reasons, and make sure he's FEELING IT from the heart. Plays like that get over. People put paid.

Break on the three means:
Feeling It in the heart.
Hold tight to follow.
Maintaining leads to bust ass.

Feelings in the heart are real powerful. That don't mean they real good. A brother who follows every feeling in his heart is fucked. Sometimes a brother's heart will tell him to punch a motherfucker taking forever at the bodega. Other times, his heart will tell him some 16 year old slim thing looks real fine. Neither feeling going to lead that brother any place positive. So if a brother really wants to be free, he don't always follow his heart. He sorts through them feelings.

True Players understand that. They also know it ain't possible to force motherfuckers into FEELING IT. That's why Player don't sweat brothers. Reaching out is fine, but he don't throw himself at motherfuckers. He don't stress about people who ain't FEELING IT. True Players never switch up their game just to get other brothers FEELING IT. Motherfuckers down or they ain't. That's all.

And just like a True Player have to sort through the feelings in his own heart, he do the same for his organization. True Player rolls for the Big Dog. Big Dogs are powerful motherfuckers with lots of stress. Got strong feelings, wild ideas, and say all sorts of shit. Some of this will put people paid, the rest of it will fuck shit up. So Player don't just roll on whatever Big Dog say. He hold off on shit shouted when Big Dog was mad. Part of Player's job is thinking shit through for the Big Dog. If Big Dog wants to roll, but Player ain't FEELING IT, he have to step up. Player don't back down. Big Dog won't like that. But when he chills out, Big Dog understands that Player just looking out for the organization. That's a valuable motherfucker to have.

Break on the four means:
Maintain get paid.
Good look.
Brother tripping and stressed,
Head all over,
Force shit to happen.

True Players and real brothers get people FEELING IT. But their hearts have to be steady. Feelings have to be in check. A motherfucker shouldn't follow his heart all over the place if he wants people FEELING IT for the long game.

When a True Player rolls on what he believes, but don't try to force motherfuckers into FEELING IT, it's real powerful. That force works real quiet. Reaches out to motherfuckers who are looking for real shit to roll with. Them brothers have their mind open, trying to find something real. They feel that force, and get pulled into True Players world. Just by FEELING IT.

But Player don't try to make this shit happen. Manipulating brothers with mind tricks and magic ain't right. That shit is powerful, but stresses a brother out in the long game. Mind tricks only work when a brother focus on that shit. The minute he turn his mind to other things, the power fades. Magic the same shit. Works when a motherfucker put his spell on somebody. When he lets up, that spell falls off. That's why all that ill mental shit just ain't practical.

True Player don't have that problem. He roll correct with his movements, and don't stress about who's FEELING IT. Brothers throw in for real reasons. Player don't have to manipulate them. They roll with Player because they FEELING IT. The organization holds together natural. Don't take magic to make brothers roll on plays. That saves Player time. He don't have stress from running mind games. It gives him more power. Helps the whole organization move forward. Good look for every motherfucker involved, yo.

Break on the five means:
Feeling It from the head.
No problem.

When a brother's FEELING IT in his head, shit's clear. It ain't like FEELING IT in his heart or his joint. Rolling from the mental is logical, so there's no problem. But it's OK to be FEELING IT in life. Some brothers play real cool, never FEELING IT for nothing. That's bullshit. A brother who don't feel nothing will never make other brothers feel anything. Nobody real rolls with a motherfucker like that.

Break at the top means:
Feeling It from the mouth.
Please.

Some brothers talk so much shit there should be a bucket under their mouth. Motherfuckers like that are useless. Just make noise. The worst way to try and get brothers FEELING IT is with words. Talk don't mean shit. True Player or any real brother got no time for chatty motherfuckers like that.

MAINTAIN

Inside, a brother is chill. But outside, he's handling business all over the operation. That's how a brother MAINTAIN.

The way man and woman MAINTAIN together is through marriage. While they dating, female is leading. Makes the man jump through hoops to get some. When they married, that shit flips. Female maintains the home. Man leads out in the world, making money, taking care his family.

Many females today have problems with that set up. Say they want to earn and be powerful. Maybe that's true. But in their heart, females ain't respect a man they make more money than. Marriage only works right when the brother is running shit financially. He have the power then. If he don't have that money, he don't have that power. Females hate on brothers who don't have more power then them. Maybe start off thinking it's fine he don't make much. But in time, the woman will resent her man. That's why so many people today get married but don't MAINTAIN.

THE FEEL

Maintain. Success. No blame.
Maintaining gets paid.
Good look to have somewhere to go.

MAINTAIN means movement that ain't worn down by nothing. A Player who MAINTAIN don't stop. Standing still in the game is like going backwards. So A Player who MAINTAIN moves forward in rhythm with The Heavens. He have his shit together and organized. When he finish one thing, he have the next thing ready to go. Player knows where he belongs. He's in his place, doing what he should do. Brother like this ain't all over the map. Motherfuckers know where to find him. He MAINTAIN his schedule.

Stars and planets MAINTAIN. They have their orbit, and stay in it. That's why they powerful. If planets and stars were flying all over the sky, them motherfuckers would burn right the fuck out. They MAINTAIN their orbit, and stay strong.

True Player understands that playing the Long Game takes real power. So he finds his place, and works there. He ain't run all over the world, trying whatever. He MAINTAIN where he should be, doing what's right. That builds power. Gives him the weight to put something real in motion, and hit them streets with positive shit.

THE LOOK

Wind and thunder. The Look of Maintain.
True Player solid.
Don't change his moves around.

Thunder and wind are free. Motherfuckers can't pin that shit down. Nobody know right where wind or thunder will show up, or how they about to move. But at the same time, wind and thunder don't change none. When thunder boom, people know what the fuck it is. Wind been the wind forever. That shit don't change. No motherfucker going to invent some new improved thunder and wind. Please.

True Player is the same way. He stays down with the times. He feels them streets and changes with them. But shit inside Player stays the same. He flips with the styles, but MAINTAIN his essence.

THE BREAKS

Break on the one means:
Maintaining too fast.
Ain't happening.

A brother who MAINTAIN don't pop off overnight. A rep in the game takes time. Player have to find his place, put in work, and stay on it for real. Time pass, some shit shake out for him. Then some more. After a while, streets say that player MAINTAIN. Motherfuckers who want too much, too fast, don't ever make nothing happen. Their shit falls apart.

Break on the two means:
No Problem.

True Player here stuck in some bullshit. He ready to roll some real moves, but ain't have people to pull that shit off. So Player don't flex too hard. He MAINTAIN without forcing a major play. No problems if he do that.

Break on the three means:
Brother who don't MAINTAIN his character
Goes bust ass.
Look like a bitch.

A brother shouldn't flip his game just because some shit he hear on them streets. Maybe one day a brother wake up thinking his business is tight. Then he sees some motherfucker talking on TV, and that shit changes his mind. He go outside and run into some crew around the way. They look crisp. He starts thinking maybe he should throw in with them. But next morning, he talk to his cousin on the phone. Hears shit that change his mind all over again.

A motherfucker like that ain't MAINTAIN order in his game. He roll hard one day, soft another, run this way, next jump that way, and fuck off all over. Bullshit hits brothers like that. They never see it coming. But them motherfuckers bring it on themselves, since they all over the place.

Break on the four means:
No money in the game.

A brother who wants to be paid has to roll where the money is. Motherfuckers who run plays in bust ass places where shit don't happen are fucked. Trying hard ain't enough. Brothers have to try in the right place.

Break on the five means:
Maintaining after them.
Good look for a sister.
Bad look for a brother.

A female should follow her man. Women should look for a True Player, then listen to him. She find happiness that way. But a brother don't change his life to follow the female. His game will fall to pieces. Brothers always handle business first. True Player got to MAINTAIN his place in the game. If doing that means a female falls out his life, ain't no problem. Always another one round the corner.

Break at the top means:
Impatient brother played.

Some brothers rush and push, trying to make shit happen. Their heart and mind ain't ever chill. Brothers like that don't do shit right. If one them motherfuckers do get over for a minute, they never MAINTAIN. Always rushing off to the next piece of business before the first piece is finished. Stay far the fuck away from them types. Motherfuckers like that real bad for a brother's future.

PULL BACK

When ill brothers and crab asses on the rise, real brothers PULL BACK. They stay out of the way, maintain in their area. Players who PULL BACK dodge wars that can't be won.

THE FEEL

Pull Back. Paid.
Maintain minor moves.

The game leans one way for a while, then the other. When ill brothers and crab asses rise, it's just their time. True Players PULL BACK. That don't mean they run away. Running away is what a desperate motherfucker does to save his ass. PULL BACK is what a smart brother does to stay strong.

Player have to be real smart to PULL BACK at the right time. He have to do it when he still has all his power and finance together. By reading that wind right, he sees how streets set to shake out. That lets him PULL BACK tactical and organized. If he waits too long, ill brothers and crab asses will be up in his face. Then he's fighting wars.

PULL BACK don't mean leaving the game. It means being real about what's possible when streets is ill. When a brother PULL BACK, he still holds onto a few business angles. Plays them from a distance. That makes it hard for ill brothers and crab asses to full on take over the game. Those angles also become a brother's path back into play when times change.

Understanding how to PULL BACK ain't simple shit. Real complex movement, yo.

THE LOOK

Midtown Building under the sky: the look of Pull Back.
True Player pull back from crab ass.
Not ill, but chill.

Midtown office buildings real high. Go way up in the sky. But them motherfuckers don't go further than a certain point. The sky go way up forever. Sky reaches places them buildings ain't ever touch.

This is how a True Player deal with some crab ass on the rise. True Player PULL BACK into his own thoughts whenever crab ass step to him. He don't waste energy hating the crab ass. Hating motherfuckers ties a brother to them. Player just PULL BACK mentally, to places a crab ass ain't able to reach. Gives that motherfucker nothing to work with.

THE BREAKS

Break on the one means:
Last brother to PULL BACK.
Bad look. Don't try nothing.

When crews PULL BACK, a brother better make damn sure he's front of the line. Last motherfucker out of Dodge is the motherfucker shot at. Brother in that situation don't try no dramatic moves. Real big plays don't shake out when it's hot like that. He just stays chill. Maybe be lucky. Pull out in time without being real fucked up.

Break on the two means:
Crab ass hold tight. Wrestle with the angel.
Nobody shake him loose.

In this situation, True Player PULL BACK and crab asses run after him. One crab ass in particular really want True Player to stay around. This crab ass knows his shit will fall apart without help from True Player. So he stress True Player real fierce. True Player can't shake this motherfucker. But because this crab ass is looking for the right thing—some help from a Player who know what time it is—and because he want it so bad, shit works out. True Player lets this crab ass into his crew. Crab ass PULL BACK with True Player's people, and learn how to behave.

There's story in the Bible like this. A Brother way back in the day was praying real hard for something he needed. Just wouldn't stop praying. Heaven had no plans of hooking this brother up. But still, he wouldn't stop praying. Finally, Heaven got tired of hearing his shit. Sent some angel to deal with this motherfucker personally.

Angel show up and be like: "Look brother, it ain't happening. Stop praying for this shit."

But this praying motherfucker wasn't hearing it. He grabbed hold that angel and said: "Yo, I need this shit for real. I ain't letting go till you hook me up here."

That angel was like: "Get the fuck off me you crab ass motherfucker."

But that brother held the angel mad tight. So they fight and wrestle for like, seven days or something.

Finally the angel had enough. Said: "Yo, I'm an angel. I got better shit to do than wrestle with some crab ass over a damn prayer. Let's just give this motherfucker what he want."

So they stop wrestling and Heaven hook that brother up with his prayer.

Break on the three means:
Pull Back slowed down.
Bad look. Dangerous.
Hire them to pack shit.
Paid.

When it's time to PULL BACK, a player ain't want to be held up. The longer a brother stay, the less options he have. Where he can PULL BACK to, how much weight he can bring with him, how much it will cost him—all that shit gets fucked. But sometimes it happen, in real fucked up situations, that a crab ass from out of nowhere jump in to PULL BACK with Player's crew. When time is tight, Player ain't have time for fighting. The best move is letting that motherfucker on for the ride. Nobody want a crab ass in the crew. But that shit will be handled later. PULL BACK is the motherfucking priority.

Break on the four means:
Pull Back nice, good look for True Player.
Bust ass for the crab ass.

When a True Player PULL BACK, it's a decision. He ain't running like a bitch. He does it crisp, and handles shit right. Player ain't upset at all when he PULL BACK. The move lets him stay true to his game. If Player stayed when ill shit was rising, he'd have to slant his moves and play shady game. But True Players don't roll that way. So PULL BACK is a good look. But it's a bad look for all them crab asses left behind. Them motherfuckers stuck with themselves and their bullshit world.

Break on the five means:
Pull Back friendly.
Maintain. Paid.

True Player have to recognize the right time to PULL BACK. If he hits that timing, there's no stress. Player even have a chance to be friendly with them motherfucking crab asses he's leaving behind. Being polite like that means there's no drama. That saves Player energy. But even when he's being friendly, Player's heart have to be dead set on the PULL BACK. Crab asses will tell a True Player all type of shit to make him stay. Like they going to change things, or they need Player, or they love him, whatever. But True Player don't fall for it. A crab ass situation is a crab ass situation, period. Player just smile and PULL BACK from them motherfuckers.

Break at the top means:
Pull Back happy.
Shit work out.

The situation is clear for a brother. It's time to PULL BACK. Maybe he tripped on it for a while. Maybe sorting through it all was real hard. But he finally made the decision. When a brother see shit with no doubt left in his mind, he feels happy. His path is clear. It leads to the right place.

REAL POWER

Brother rolling with strength has REAL POWER.

THE FEEL

Real Power. Maintain.

Player's status been building for a long time. He maintained, did shit right, ran plays crisp, listened to The Heavens, watched them streets, and now he have REAL POWER. That's a good look. The only way shit might turn left is if Player forgets what's right. He's rolling large now, and quite frankly, a brother with REAL POWER does whatever the fuck he wants to do. Brothers with this much weight naturally wants to flex that shit. That's a problem if Player don't remember his place. He's large, but The Heavens are larger. Player have to respect that.

A Player with REAL POWER can force plays since he have so much weight. But there's a difference between REAL POWER and force. REAL POWER is when some brother walks in the room and everybody shut the hell up. Force is when some brother walks in the room and makes everybody shut up. REAL POWER is better to have than force.

163

A Player who built up REAL POWER have to stay true with what's right. That way his power don't turn into force. Force is for bitches, really.

THE LOOK

Thunder in the sky:
The look of Real Power.
True Player don't roll on moves
Ain't positive.

Thunder is up in the sky. That's how it stays powerful. Thunder don't run around in them streets. Thunder don't jump in the ocean, and try to roll there. Since Heaven put Thunder in the damn sky, that's where Thunder rolls. It follows the laws of Heaven. Thunder stays mad powerful that way.

REAL POWER depends on being in the right place, and rolling the right way. True Player with REAL POWER don't fuck around with bullshit brothers. He ain't roll with ill brothers and crab asses. He ain't roll with situations that ain't down with The Law of Heaven. True Player respect The Heavens and watch them streets. Holds onto REAL POWER that way.

THE BREAKS

Break on the one means:
Power in the feet.
Bad Look.
For real.

Feet are the lowest part of the body. Sometimes a brother with REAL POWER is stuck with a low level job in the organization. He don't like that. He want to try and force his way up to a larger place. No matter how much REAL POWER Player has, that would be a bad look. Forcing shit would not work out here.

Break on the two means:
Maintaining gets paid.

Doors are starting to open for Player. He was blocked before, but the crab asses are falling off. He pushes forward. That's where Player might fall into a trap. Start thinking he's the shit. Pop champagne and light up the club. That ain't a good look. A Player shouldn't party when he's just starting to get over. He have to stay chill in his heart and mind. If he don't, his shit will fall right the fuck off.

Break on the three means:
Crab Ass flash power.
True Player don't flash.
Rolling a bad look.
Pushing through the subway line.
All tangled up.

Pushing with REAL POWER is a bad look. A brother gets caught up in bullshit situations that way. Like when there's a bunch of motherfuckers trying to get on the subway. If a brother force his way forward, and push his way through that shit, he gets all tangled up with them people.

When a crab ass gets some REAL POWER, he flashes and flexes like crazy. Lets everybody know his status. That catches him up in all sorts of drama. True Player never has that problem. He knows that flashing REAL POWER just gets a brother tangled up in other people's shit. So he roll low key.

Break on the four means:
Maintaining puts a brother paid.
No problem.
Through the subway line, no tangles.
Power like the ride axle.

When brothers trying to hold back a Player with REAL POWER, he handle them low key. Rolls in silence on them motherfuckers. Break them to pieces slowly and quietly. At the same time, he maintains every part of the organization just as low key. Player don't flash REAL POWER to handle business. A brother who rolls low profile gets paid for real. He chips away at whatever shit holding him back, until it just falls off. This style lets him handle motherfuckers without flashing or flexing. There's no drama to deal with. Less stress to manage. That saves time and energy. Just like a brother who makes his way through them subway lines low key. He don't push, but he's moving forward. Then he's on that train, going where he wants to be. A Player like that might not look like he has REAL POWER. But the less a brother flash RE-AL POWER, the more it works when he have to break it down. That shit comes out of nowhere. Leaves motherfuckers shaking.

REAL POWER is like the axle on a ride. Nobody pay attention to the axle. People see wheels spinning, they think wheels doing all the work. That ain't true. REAL POWER is the axle the wheels are spinning on. The whole damn ride is held up by the axle. Wheels just flash more.

Break on the five means:
Let go being hard.
No problem.

Player finds himself in a place where living is easy. Ain't nobody trying to hold him back. Fighting years are over. Player can enjoy life now, and stop being hard. That won't be a problem here.

Break at the top means:
Brother in the crowd.
Can't go back. Can't go forward.
Nothing helping.
Heads up, good look.

A brother who pushes too hard, when the time ain't right, puts himself in problems. Walls close in on him. He can't move forward or back. Whatever he do just fuck him up further. Like a brother forcing his way through rush hour crowds in the subway. If he push too hard, for too long, he just get stuck in them motherfuckers. Maybe pushed on the wrong train. But if a brother recognizes when there ain't no move to make, he's alright. He don't push or force nothing. Just chills, and lets the situation loosen up on its own. When it does, brother can move without no problems.

RISING

Brother's horizons expanding. Like the sun coming up. He's RISING.

THE FEEL

Rising.
Down Player
Gets major piece broke off for real.
Big Dog shout him out. Show him 'round.

One Player meets up with all the other Players in the area and says: "Yo, we should stop all the beefs between us, and throw in together for the Big Dog."

All the players throw in with this plan. They get tight and turn in-to a fierce unit for the Big Dog. Big Dog love this shit. He breaks off a major piece for the Player who put this look together.

But Player don't start fronting on his new status. He stays on the level with them brothers he pulled together. That's why they roll with him. This Player has a head for getting shit done, and how the game works. But he don't use that power to fuck with the Big

Dog. He puts it to work for the Big Dog. He ain't no threat. That way, Big Dog don't start tripping over Player's power. He recognizes that Player has his back. So Big Dog makes this motherfucker his boy. When there's a powerful Big Dog, rolling with a loyal True Player, positive shit starts to happen. People put paid for real. Good things hit them streets. Everybody RISING together.

THE LOOK

Sun rise.
The look of Rising.
True player
Shine himself up.

Sun rise up out of darkness, spread light everywhere. When brothers are born, their hearts are right. They're pure. But the world twist people up. Teaches them lies and ill moves. But a True Player rises up through all that darkness, shines himself up with knowledge, and spreads light.

THE BREAKS

Break on the one means:
Rising, turned back.
Maintain be paid.
If brothers ain't with a player, chill.
No problem.

Brothers pushing Player to make a move. Player ain't 100% sure the move will shake out. So he just maintain, and run the organization day-to-day. Shit will work out best this way. Other brothers might not see that. Start bitching and shit. Maybe get up in Player's face. Player just have to stay positive. Don't let himself be pulled into their bullshit. That way he don't slip.

Break on the two means:
Maintaining, bad mood.
Maintaining gets paid.
Good look from above.

Player here blocked from RISING up in the organization. He's stopped from linking up with a brother higher up the chain. That brother would help Player. Don't matter. Player can't reach that motherfucker. That's some depressing shit. Player will have to maintain, even though he's feeling real bad. That brother up the chain will hear about Player someday. When that happens, he'll reach out, pull Player up, and it's a brand new day. Player be happy then.

Break on the three means:
All throwing in.
Stop tripping.

Player is making moves, backed by some real serious brothers. But Player don't like it. He wants the power to roll on his own. He don't like needing these real serious brothers. But when Player sees how well shit is shaking out, he stops tripping. He realizes the advantages. He don't have to worry about ill crews fucking with him. The brothers who got Player's back will roll deep on anybody who steps to him. That's a good look.

Break on the four means:
Rising like a rat.
Maintaining. Bad look.

Times is good on them streets. Business popping. With all that money floating around, real easy for ill brothers to roll on shady plays. Take their piece. But shady shit always be brought to light, sooner or later. When times are good, there's more light. So that shit will be brought into the open sooner. Then them ill brothers running shady game are fucked.

Break on the five means:
Not tripping.
Win. Lose. Whatever.
Movements paid.
Shit shake out.

Player is RISING up and getting real power. But he stays low key, running shit chill. Player might trip a minute, thinking he should play hard. Since he have so much weight, he could do whatever. Break it down on motherfuckers, run his angles fierce, even roll on brothers to take their action. All that would break him off a larger piece of the game.

But them thoughts pass. Player don't stress on winning or losing. He just holds onto that powerful position he have. Runs shit right, and maintains chill. By not playing hard, he gets love from his people and them streets. Whatever this Player wants to do will shake out nice.

Break at the top means:
Breaking it down for the crew.
Mind that stress. Paid.
No problem.
Maintain, bust ass.

Player have to break it down here. But he only come down hard on his own people. Player just runs his crew, not them streets. He knows that breaking it down is dangerous. Motherfuckers might come right the fuck back at him. Plus he don't know how that shit will shake out for the long game. Brothers might walk away smiling, but hating Player in their heart. Make plans to take him out down the line.

Still, a brother got to break it down when the situation calls for it. He can't back off. If he stays real about the danger involved, Player maintains. He knows that being too hard, for too long, with too many people, will fuck a Player up. It's real trouble if he starts reaching beyond his crew. Breaking shit down for motherfuckers who ain't his people leads to real bust ass situations. Like motherfuckers laughing at Player, after some brother slaps him in front of the bodega. Or maybe somebody shoot him in the ass, just to shut Player up.

Motherfuckers lose their rep in a minute. Once their rep goes, their people follow. Leave a Player standing there with nothing but his dick in his hand, wondering what the hell just happened.

WREXAGRAM 36
DARK OUT

When it's DARK OUT, streets real dangerous. Brothers get shot.

In the Wrexagram before, a righteous Big Dog had True Players running his operation. That's good for them streets. When it's DARK OUT, an ill Big Dog is running shit. This motherfucker plays hard, dark and twisted. That's a bad look for real brothers and True Players.

THE FEEL

Dark Out. Ill.
Good look to maintain.

Player has to hold himself together when it's DARK OUT. He can't throw in with the ill shit that's running streets. He can't let it break his spirit, neither. When it's DARK OUT, Player maintains his own light. Holds onto that spark inside himself.

Being hard don't help when it's DARK OUT. Player should roll chill and be an easy brother. Not stressing situations. Not stepping to ill brothers. That mindset helps a Player survive when it's DARK OUT.

When the game rolls real ill, Player hides his light. It's not the right time to shine. When it's DARK OUT, Player works shit out mentally. But it looks like he ain't doing nothing at all. Player makes it a point to look like every other motherfucker out there. But he's different inside. His heart and mind are free. That's the only way he makes it through.

THE LOOK

Sun set.
The look of Dark Out.
True Player maintain.
Hide his light. Still shining.

Player stays careful as a motherfucker when it's DARK OUT. He's laid back. Never rude or up in nobody's face. That keeps him from being hated on. When it's DARK OUT, lots of brothers roll ill and live bad lifestyles. True Player don't throw in with them. Same time, he don't judge them motherfuckers or drag their shit into the light. He just plays dumb. Looks like some pointless mother-fucker who don't know shit. He lets things slide as much as possible, without being played. That's how True Players and real brothers survive when it's DARK OUT.

THE BREAKS

Break on the one means:
Dark Out trying to get over.
Head hanging.
True Player hungry, homeless.
But he have somewhere to go.
Streets hating on him. Talking shit.

Trying to change the world ain't smart when it's DARK OUT. But a brother here tries to bring the light. Makes a stand on what's wrong. Ill brothers and crab asses ain't having that. Shut this brother down, hard core. He has to pull back fast, with ill brothers gunning. Now he's on the run and homeless. Crab asses tip off them ill motherfuckers wherever he hides. But this brother stays alive. Living his principles will mean living hungry. But at least he believes in something. Streets ain't ever going to understand a brother like that when it's DARK OUT. Motherfuckers everywhere will talk mad shit and hate on him. Just how it is.

Break on the two means:
Ill Big Dog pops Player in the leg.
Player mad strong, help his people.
Paid.

Player takes a bad hit from an Ill Big Dog. It's like catching a bullet in the leg. Hurts like a motherfucker, and Player's limping. But he stays in the fight, and helps his people pull back. Makes sure everybody alright. Player who stays real when he's hit like that will be put paid nice.

Break on the three means:
Dark Out downtown.
Ill Big Dog taken.
Don't push.

It's DARK OUT and True Player is rolling on ill motherfuckers, fighting wars, trying to put light back in the game. Luck leans his way. Without planning it, Player runs right the fuck into Ill Big Dog. Gets the drop on that motherfucker and breaks it down. Clips all Big Dog's soldiers and rubs that ill bastard right out the game.

That's a real break. But Player don't try to set the whole game straight in a day. When it's been DARK OUT for a long time, little plays are the smart way to put shit right. If Player pushes too hard, too fast, ill brothers will start rolling. They'll fuck Player up, even with their Big Dog down.

Break on the four means:
Drinking with Ill Big Dog.
Heart of the matter.
Shit's fucked.

Player is out one night with the ill Big Dog who's running shit. That motherfucker drinks too much, and starts talking. Tells Player his plans for the game. Twisted shit, real fucked up. Since Big Dog is real powerful, he'll pull it off. Now Player have no illusions about how dark streets will be. Nobody stopping an ill Big Dog that large. So Player just bounces. Drops his angles and leaves town before them bodies pile up.

Break on the five means:
Dark Out like old Chinese prince.
Maintain crazy.
Works out.

China had an ill king way back in the day. He was real twisted. Hacking brothers up, raping their daughters, skinning motherfuckers alive for entertainment. But in those days, the King was the King. He did what the fuck he wanted. And family had to roll with family, no matter what. If they were blood with the King, they had to represent. His people try and bounce, heads start rolling. So this King's family and all of China was fucked. DARK OUT all over the land, while this ill motherfucker popped off wild style.

The King had this little cousin who was a prince. The Prince was a down brother who knew shit was fucked. He was watching motherfuckers getting their fingernails pulled out for wearing the wrong pants to dinner. Shit like that. But he was trapped like everybody else. Couldn't step up, couldn't bounce. So The Prince pretended he went crazy. Started pissing his pants, talking to birds, slapping himself in the face, waving his dick out the window, rubbing shit on the wall, all that. That Ill King was a heartless motherfucker, so he ain't try and help. Just put The Prince in chains. Threw him in some fucked up tower where all the retarded people and crazy motherfuckers were locked up.

It was a real bullshit place to be. But it put The Prince out of the way. King forgot about him. Brother was safe. But he still had to live in chains with a bunch of retarded and crazy motherfuckers. And The Prince had to roll with his act for real. Pissing his pants and throwing shit for *years*, yo. But he lived, while nearly every other real brother and True Player in the palace was murdered.

Finally, that ill King died. Minute it happened, Prince stopped pissing himself, stood up, and was like: "Take me out these motherfucking chains, yo. Let's put this kingdom back together."

That story is a lesson for brothers trapped in a situation that turns real dark. They should hide their real self and put an act together. Play that part to the motherfucking hilt and don't trust nobody. Just like that Chinese Prince. He never winked at a motherfucker saying: "Ha ha, I'm just acting crazy to cover my ass." Prince was in them chains alone, playing that act for *years*. That's what it takes when it's real DARK OUT. If a player is mad careful, and don't lose heart, he'll make it through.

Break at the top means:
No light. All dark.
Run shit to the top.
Fall off into nothing.

It's the darkest of the dark time. Ill Big Dog has mad power. He can fuck up any True Player or real brother he wants. Ill shit is

thick in them streets. But when it's that DARK OUT, bad times
have to fall off. That's the law. When all the light is destroyed,
darkness have nothing left to feed off. It's darkest right before it
falls off. Then light comes back around. Remember that.

FAMILY

Strong leadership comes from the head of the FAMILY. Strong families make a strong world.

THE FEEL

Family.
Maintaining like a woman is a good look.

FAMILY is held together with a positive relationship between husband and wife. What holds them two together is loyalty of the wife. Her place is in the home, running FAMILY. The place of the man is outside the home, supporting FAMILY. When that shit is flipped around, FAMILY is fucked up.

FAMILY needs a strong authority figure. That's the parents. Motherfuckers shouldn't pop out children if they looking for friends. Parents have to discipline their little ones. Shorties learn order that way. When the father act like a father, the mother behaves like a mother, when the older brother act like the older brother, and the younger brother maintain his spot, with sisters being sisters, shit works right. There will be problems. That's life.

But there's order in this set up. When FAMILY is in order, them streets are in order.

Order in the FAMILY depends on different things. Between father and son, it depends on love. Between husband and wife, it depends on loyalty. Between older and younger brother, order depends on respect. Then that shit translate to them streets. The way a son loves his father is how a True Player loves and serves the Big Dog he works for. The way two brothers respect each other is the way friends relate. FAMILY teaches people rules, and shows them how to roll in them streets.

THE LOOK

Energy from fire:
The look of Family.
True Player speak right.
Act right.

Fire makes heat. Heat is power. That's the look of FAMILY. If a father wants to handle his children right, he should have power. Like a fire inside.

If a Player wants his words to have power, he needs something real inside his words. Like wood inside a fire. Fire only has heat if there's wood to burn. Words only have power if they relate to what's happening. Motherfuckers who talk shit about whatever comes to mind lose power. Words should be focused on what's happening in the moment.

If a Player wants people listening to what he says, he have to watch how he walks. If a brother don't step correct, whatever he say don't mean shit.

THE BREAKS

Break on the one means:
Chilling with Family.
No problem.

For FAMILY to work right, everybody have to know their place. True Players bring up their shorties with real clear rules. Start from day one. Shorties don't learn that shit later. They get stronger every year. If they ain't learn how to act when they little, it's a wrap. Motherfuckers grow wild. Ain't nothing harder to do, and easier to put off, then disciplining children.

Break on the two means:
She should not do what the fuck she want.
Take care the house. Feed people.
Maintaining like that is a good look.

The wife should listen to the oldest man in the house. That means her father, her husband, or the oldest grown son. Sisters hate that reality. Think they should do whatever the fuck they want. But the ones who roll however the fuck they please are never really happy. They never find themselves a real man, neither. Woman should be in the home, making that shit run right, feeding the family, showing children love and discipline. If she do that, woman is the center of the universe for them people. Has power and love. She makes that house and everybody in it feel good. Sisters find satisfaction that way.

On a larger level, this break tells a brother to handle day to day business. He should maintain, like a woman running the household. It ain't the time for large plays now.

Break on the three means:
Tempers rise in Family,

Coming down too hard.
Problems but a good look.
Woman and children laugh at the father,
Do what they want.
Bullshit.

In the FAMILY, a man have to find the balance between coming down too hard, and letting shit slide. If he breaks it down too hard, FAMILY don't forget that shit. A father who slaps his children around too hard and too much fucks them up. They grow up and hate on him. So the best play is setting tight rules, but leaving room to slide.

That said, in situations where there is doubt, break it down. When handling order in the FAMILY, it's better to be too hard than too soft. Being too hard will bring some problems. But being too soft leads to real problems. Like children who disgrace themselves and their FAMILY.

Break on the four means:
Jewel of the home.
Damn good look.

Woman has the real power in the FAMILY. She the one people's happiness depends on. She manages the money, minds the spending, and handles the home. A woman who does that right is like a priceless motherfucking jewel.

In the game, this break about a brother in the organization who don't have the weight to run shit. But he's mad loyal, and brings real heart and soul to the operation. Brother like that is worth a million dollars. Makes that place feel like FAMILY.

Break on the five means:
King of the Family.
No stress.
Paid.

A father who has his shit together, loving his FAMILY and making real money, is like a King. Brother like this don't do anything to make his wife and children scared of him. They trust him, because he shows them real love. He lives right, so they respect him and listen to what he says. Father like that hardly ever have to lift a finger. He sets his children straight with just one look. Power like that comes from being real in every other area of his life.

Break at the top means:
Father. Respect.
Day ends, paid.

At the end of the day, the father holds the FAMILY in proper order. If he runs his life right, he have that inner fire. His family feels that. Know he's head of the house. He takes responsibility for everybody. Pays them bills. That's his job. Lots of people today hate on FAMILY order like that. But back in the day, FAMILY rolled this way. It showed people how to act. That's why motherfuckers back then weren't shooting up class rooms with machine guns. Brothers today roll bananas since they never learn order in the FAMILY.

UP IN YOUR FACE

When motherfuckers see shit different they go UP IN YOUR FACE.

THE FEEL

Up In Your Face.
Little plays. Paid.

It ain't time to roll on large plays when motherfuckers UP IN YOUR FACE. There's too much drama. When shit's like that, True Player don't force his moves. He ain't rude, neither. That only brings more motherfuckers UP IN YOUR FACE. True Player limits himself to little plays. Makes minor adjustments in the operation to tighten shit up. He can still get over. Streets ain't 100% fucked, like when it's dark out. Sometimes there's just drama UP IN YOUR FACE. After that's sorted out, brothers fall into place and move forward. People put paid.

Motherfuckers UP IN YOUR FACE is a problem, but it don't last forever. When brothers fight, that shit can be useful. It shows problems in the organization. Lets Player sort them out. That lets him cap drama before it blows up in his face down the line. Ain't right to roll on major plays with ill shit like that in the ranks. Fights also help crews become tight. Motherfuckers who work their way through static and come back around have stronger bonds.

Nobody likes to deal with brothers UP IN YOUR FACE. But differences are part of life. Difference defines life. Without difference, every motherfucker would be just like every other motherfucker. This world wouldn't be shit.

THE LOOK

Uptown. Downtown.
The look of UP IN YOUR FACE.
Hanging out.
True Player stays real.

Uptown brothers normally don't roll with downtown brothers. But in certain situations, a Player have to throw in with motherfuckers from outside his area. Whoever he's dealing with, Player stays real. He can handle ignorant bust ass motherfuckers, ill brothers, party people, crab asses, Big Dogs, ordinary brothers, shorties, whatever. True Player works with anybody, and never lose his essence.

THE BREAKS

Break on the one means:
Problems gone.
Don't chase the cat.

Jump in the lap.
Dealing with ill brothers,
Watch it.

When motherfuckers are UP IN YOUR FACE, that static can be managed. Player don't break it down hard. That only make shit worse. It's like dealing with cats. Brother try and pet one, that animal run away. But if a brother just chill out watching TV, that animal jump right in his lap.

That's the way Player rolls when he falls out with a brother from some misunderstanding. He don't chase motherfuckers down. Just leaves it be. The other brother will sort shit out and come back around.

But that ain't the way to roll with ill brothers. Player have to watch his motherfucking step in that situation. He never tries to shake off ill brothers with force. Shit like that starts real problems for a player. Instead, he just plays it cool and doesn't react. Them ill brothers will wild out for a minute. Pull some UP IN YOUR FACE bullshit. If Player maintains low key, them ill brothers get bored. Leave and fuck with somebody else.

Break on the two means:
Run into brother in the club.
No problems.

There been misunderstandings between two brothers. They the right match for business, and should be rolling together. But static fucked it all up. Then these brothers just run into each other. Maybe at the club, on the corner, in the barber shop, whatever. This gives them brothers a chance to sort shit out informally. That's a good look.

Break on the three means:
Ride stopped short.

Rims stolen.
Bust ass hair cut. Punched in the face.
Bad start. Good finish. Paid.

Many times a brother feels like the whole world spinning against him. Watches every play he make go bust ass. Crab asses shut him down, ill brothers block him out, streets talk shit about him. But a real brother don't stop trying. He hold tight to what's right. Motherfuckers should never stop reaching for the life they want. Long game only shakes out for brothers who maintain.

Break on the four means:
Ain't down with them.
One brother for real.
Ill, but no problem.

If a brother finds himself someplace where he ain't down with the way people roll, he gets mad isolated. That's a bad look. But if he meets just one real brother he trust, that's all he needs. He won't be tripping by himself no more. Shit will get better then.

Break on the five means:
Bad look all over.
Down brother reach out.
Player throw in with him,
How's that a problem?

Player here rolling through some real bullshit. Have his guard up 24/7 since crab asses all around. Then a real brother shows up. But Player don't give that motherfucker the time of day. Bullshit been so thick, for so long, he stopped thinking right. But this real brother reaches out and says what up. When a real brother like that shows up, Player have to let his guard down and work with him.

Break at the top means:
Tripping because motherfuckers Up In Your Face.
See brothers as dirty crab asses.
Car full of crack heads.
First pull the nine.
Then lay it down.
He ain't no thug, he down.
Brothers all good. Rain, paid.

Player been under stress too long. He's tripping. Starts feeling his homeboys are nothing but dirty crab asses. Thinks they dangerous, like a car full of crack heads. He pulls the nine, pushing his homeboys away. But time passes and Player realizes he was tripping. He lays down the nine and all that stress disappears. His homeboys show love. Everybody feel good that the drama is over. Shit was fucked a minute.

Be like that feeling in the air before real big thunderstorms. Shit's all tense. Then thunder crack, rain pour down, and all that tension wash away. A Player remembers that. When drama hits real high levels, shit has to break. It flips in a positive direction if a brother don't trip.

WREXAGRAM 39
SOME BULLSHIT

Player here have his back to the wall, with nothing but SOME BULLSHIT in front of him. Life shakes out like that sometimes. But every bad situation has a way out.

THE FEEL

Some Bullshit.
Pull back fine.
Roll out bad.
Good look to talk with the Big Dog.
Maintain. Paid.

Player here facing SOME BULLSHIT that can't be handled direct. When it's like that, the smart play is to pull back. That don't mean running away. It means thinking shit through, putting a play together, and building up strength to make it through SOME BULLSHIT.

Player in this situation have to find some more brothers. He's facing SOME BULLSHIT that needs muscle thrown at it. Finding a Big Dog is the smart move. Player throws in and rolls for that Big

Dog. Lets a heavy motherfucker like that lead the play. Then everybody get through SOME BULLSHIT together. Maybe Player have to roll with styles that don't feel 100% right. But if he want to get through SOME BULLSHIT, he does whatever it takes. He shouldn't trip on this. SOME BULLSHIT is good for a brother. Makes him stronger and smarter. Makes his game crisp.

THE LOOK

Water on the roof:
The look of Some Bullshit.
True Player look at himself.
Change his game.

Apartment building with a leaky roof is the look of SOME BULLSHIT. People living in that building complain. If they have a bad landlord, that motherfucker just bitch about the costs. Tells them people to put out some pots and deal with it. But the right landlord will fix the roof, even if that shit's real expensive. He understands his responsibility, doesn't bitch about reality, and finishes with a property that have more value.

SOME BULLSHIT makes a brother face himself. When bad times roll up, friends fly away. It's just Player and the game. Crab asses bitch about this. They say people are bad, blame problems on other brothers, hate on the game, whatever. True Player checks himself, first. He looks into his heart and mind. Finds whatever problems there he can fix. That's how he uses SOME BULLSHIT to make himself stronger, smarter, and better.

THE BREAKS

Break on the one means:
Rolling leads to SOME BULLSHIT.
Chilling a good look.

When a brother run into SOME BULLSHIT, first thing he have to do is put his head around the situation. Trying to get over SOME BULLSHIT without understanding it makes shit worse. So Player pulls back. That don't mean he gives up or runs away. He just finds a place to think a minute. That lets him understand the scenario, and put the right play together. Then he roll on that motherfucker and gets over SOME BULLSHIT.

Break on the two means:
Big Dog's player running into SOME BULLSHIT and SOME BULLSHIT all over again.
Ain't his fault.

It's usually best to go around SOME BULLSHIT. But when a brothers' job is handling SOME BULLSHIT, he have to roll right up on it. Like firemen who have to run into burning buildings. Or soldiers in war. A True Player understands his job. If he signed up to handle SOME BULLSHIT, he deals with it. The Player who rolls right into SOME BULLSHIT like that is doing the right thing. He don't have to trip about whether he's making the right play. The ill situation he's facing ain't his fault. Just his motherfucking job.

Break on the three means:
Rolling is a problem.
Back it up.

The break before is about a Player with the job of handling SOME BULLSHIT. He have no choice but dealing with what he signed up for. This break is different. When the father of a family or the leader of a crew run into SOME BULLSHIT, he have to think things through. Brother like that have motherfuckers depending on him. He can't just jump into SOME BULLSHIT and get murdered. So pulling back from SOME BULLSHIT is the right play. He's looking out for his people that way.

Break on the four means:
Rolling leads to SOME BULLSHIT.
Chilling puts shit right.

This SOME BULLSHIT that can't be handled alone. Ain't no fast solution, neither. If Player rolls on SOME BULLSHIT like this without people and a plan, he finds out too late that was some dumb motherfucking shit to do. So the play here is chilling a minute. Player finds more brothers and more information. They roll smart, roll deep, and get over SOME BULLSHIT together.

Break on the five means:
In the middle of Some Bullshit,
Down brothers show up.

Here's SOME BULLSHIT real ill. A True Player gets the job of handling it. His rep is on the line. So he don't try to get out of this, no matter how fucked the situation is. True Player just rolls with heart. Other brothers see him going toe to toe with SOME BULLSHIT. They recognize righteous shit and throw in. Now True Player got real serious brothers rolling with him. They crush SOME BULLSHIT, 100%. Damn good look.

Break at the top means:
Rolling leads to problems.
Chilling gets a brother paid.
Good look to see Big Dog.

Player left the game, and all the drama that goes with it. But SOME BULLSHIT happen in his area. The easiest thing for this brother to do is ignore it. But he can't do that. True Player don't just think of himself. He never let people in his area get played by SOME BULLSHIT. Since he was in the game so long, but don't give a fuck about it no more, Player is the right brother to handle things. He have status plus money in the bank. Don't need nothing from them streets. That makes him see shit real clear. So he puts himself in play. Reaches out to the Big Dog like: "Yo, I heard SOME BULLSHIT going down. Let me handle it for you." That's a damn good look right there.

BAILED OUT

Brother here is moving out of some bullshit. He ain't 100%
BAILED OUT from the problem, but shit is turning around.

THE FEEL

Bailed out.
Downtown and West Side a good look.
No shit to deal with,
Back to business.
Still shit to handle,
Fight static fast. Paid.

When bullshit and static are clearing up, a brother should return
to business as usual, fast as possible. When shit changes for the
better, streets are feeling positive. People all down with each oth-
er. Player takes advantage of this time and sets things rolling. But
he don't overdo that shit. It would be a bad look to move on large
plays. After some bullshit, just returning things to normal is
enough. If there's still some static in the air, Player clears it fast.
He cleans house 100%. That way the crew don't slide back into
some bullshit down the line.

THE LOOK

Rain and Thunder:
The look of Bailed Out.
True Player lets it slide.
Forgive.

Thunderstorms clear the air. True Player handles brothers who fuck up the same way. He is real clear, like that crack of thunder. Lets motherfuckers who slipped know what time it is. But he don't trip out on shit forever. He lets it go. Comes down loud and clear, but lets shit fade away like thunder. True Player forgives his people. He understands they ain't on his level. People fuck up. Brothers drop the ball and make wrong moves. Player gets mad, but then forgives that shit. Like rain wash them streets clean.

THE BREAKS

Break on the one means:
No problem.

Not much to say. Bullshit situation over, brother been BAILED OUT. He just chill low key and rest up. That's the right play when a brother been BAILED OUT from some real bullshit.

Break on the two means:
Brother shut down three bitches in the game.
Paid.
Maintain paid more.

The game filled with scheming motherfuckers, fake ass bitches, crab asses, and ill brothers running shady plays. Some these types might find their way into larger operations. Player might not recognize how bullshit they are at first. He thinks a brother down, while really, that motherfucker playing him behind the scenes. Do it so smooth that nobody ever pin nothing on him. Shady motherfuckers like that can roll a whole lifetime without their shit catching up to them.

But when a True Player recognize bitches like that in his operation, he moves to take them out. He don't fight them on their terms, though. Motherfuckers like that work in the shade, whispering lies. True Player do his shit straight up in the light. So he handles problems like this legit. Jumping them motherfuckers in the parking lot would probably feel better, but True Player don't roll like that. He don't have to, neither. True Player have The Heavens leaning his way. Shit shakes out for him.

Break on the three means:
Brother from the streets
Flash and flaunt
Motherfuckers show up to rob.
Maintain bust ass.

A real brother from the streets just got over, paid in full. If he starts rolling VIP, that's a problem. He's just a brother from around the way. He don't know how them rich motherfuckers roll. He try and flash with them, fashion bitches will play him out. Those types run high level game. Brother will lose his grip and fall right the fuck off. End up bust ass.

Old Big Dog break it down like this:

Riding the train and maintaining around the way is how
Real brother from them streets roll.
Up in the club with them fashion motherfuckers is how
Rich brother roll.

When a real brother from the street start flashing
And rolling with them fashion motherfuckers,
Ill bitches put him in their sights.
Rob him blind.
If a brother is rude to players higher up in the game than him,
And hard on brothers lower down in the game than him,
Ill motherfuckers will break it down for his ass.
If a brother don't pay attention to his shit,
Motherfuckers steal it right away.
If a sister flounce around all tits and ass,
She bring the wrong brothers around.
They get all liquored up and have their way with her.

Break on the four means:
Shake off them crab asses.
Real brother show up,
Real down.

In hard times, when a True Player's game cools off, crab asses show up. They put themselves around Player. He gets used to seeing these motherfuckers. If this goes on long enough, Player starts thinking he needs them crab asses. But when it's time to be BAILED OUT, True Player got to shake off them motherfuckers. There ain't no real bond. They was just in the same bullshit at the same time. If True Player don't break off from them crab asses, real brothers won't trust him. They'll keep their distance and say: "Damn, that motherfucker rolls with crab asses."

Break on the five means:
Player save himself, paid.
Prove to crab ass he for real.

Getting BAILED OUT takes a strong mind. Crab asses a player meets in the bullshit don't shake off lightly. If player really wants to break with the crab asses, he have to do that shit mentally, first.

Just stop thinking about them motherfuckers. Crab asses pick up on that shit. Once they see a brother break it off on the mental, they fall off. Find somebody else to fuck with.

Break at the top means:
Player shoots Ill Big Dog.
Drops him. Paid.

There's a real Ill Big Dog, mad powerful, way high up the chain. This motherfucker keeping Player from being BAILED OUT some bullshit. Ill Big Dog so large it don't matter if The Law of Heaven lean on him. He shake that shit right off. Have a million strings in the system, so nobody ever take him out legit, neither. He's just a wicked motherfucker, hard as nails, dug in deep. Brother like this have to be taken out by force. But Player got to do it right.

Old Big Dog break it down like this:

The Ill Big Dog is the target.
True Player has the moves to take him out.
Player don't broadcast his plan. He don't rush.
True Player chill, think on the best move, and wait for the moment.
When it arrives, he takes Ill Big Dog right the fuck out.
Fast, hard, and crisp.
Why should there be problems that way?
If a brother think shit through, then do it right, he put paid.

LOSING WEIGHT

Business slows and a brother's action cools. He starts LOSING WEIGHT. Money flies away, properties fall off. If a brother plays it right, he survive this shit, no problem.

THE FEEL

Losing Weight and being for real
Puts a brother paid,
No problem. Maintain.
Good look to make a move.
Respect for Heaven.

LOSING WEIGHT is part of business. Shit moves in cycles. A Player feels them and changes his game. When he's LOSING WEIGHT he don't maintain like money's moving. Some brothers borrow. Try to keep up appearances. Then they owe motherfuckers. That's bullshit. When a True Player start LOSING WEIGHT, he rolls with it. Makes lean stretches of the game work for him. Trims fat, sheds unnecessary motherfuckers and dials the operation down tight. Finds focus and builds strength.

A brother on top ain't have trouble feeling good about himself. He's rolling in style and motherfuckers all want a piece. When shit turns left, all that falls off. People think he's bullshit. Streets show no love. Now that brother have to find love and respect in his heart. Build positivity from the inside. Heavens always down with a brother like that. If he's holding property or LOSING WEIGHT, the brother who stays respectful in his heart gets Heaven leaning his way.

THE LOOK

Open freezer in the summer.
The look of Losing Weight.
True Player chill when he mad.
Ain't follow his joint.

Brothers with no air conditioning in the summer open the freezer. Stand in front of that shit. Hook up the fan to blow that cold air on them. Ice starts to melt after a while. Freezer LOSING WEIGHT to help a brother cool down. Sometimes LOSING WEIGHT can be a real good thing. Just depends where a brother standing, and which way the wind blowing.

Every brother has a dick and gets mad. True Player controls both. When he's real mad, True Player cools out. Just like standing in front of that freezer. He chills before deciding the play. True Player don't ever roll on shit when he's mad. He lets feelings die down. When he's seeing shit clear, he puts his play together and rolls on it.

Same shit with his joint. A brother have to handle his dick. If his joint runs his life, business falls off. Chasing pussy brings drama, burns time, and costs real motherfucking money. Especially when them babies start popping out. If a brother trying to build something real, he have to handle his joint smart. Find something steady and hit it regular. Brothers running after every fat ass with their dick in their hand are bullshit.

Brothers who handle their joint and manage anger build power. Less drama leaves more time for business. Business brings money. Money builds power. Brothers with power don't have to worry much about managing anger. Streets don't step to large motherfuckers. Powerful brothers don't chase females, neither. Ass chases them. Top shelf shit.

THE BREAKS

Break on the one means:
Bounce when he's done. Next.
Good look.
Player thinks how much to ask from people.

When a brother in the operation wraps his piece of business, he reaches out. See what else needs doing. He don't make no show of it. Just find out who needs help and throws in. But Players high up the chain have to mind how much brothers lower down are working. Make sure they don't burn out. If a Player runs his people like that, motherfuckers will throw in 100% on everything. They don't worry about working too much. Player pulls them off shit at the right time.

Break on the two means:
Maintaining a good look.
Roll a play is bust ass.
Not playing himself,
Brother put people paid.

A brother has to work real hard without playing himself. He stays crisp that way. Some brothers burn out from jumping through hoops for a motherfucker high up the chain. That ain't a good look. Helps that motherfucker up the chain, but plays the brother jumping through hoops. He loses respect. If a brother wants to play long game, he have to work real hard for people, without being their bitch.

Break on the three means:
Three people throw in.
One have to bounce.
Brother maintaining solo finds people.

Three people is a problem. Jealousy happens there. Two of them motherfuckers will get tight, and freeze out the third. Tight bonds only happen between two people. When a brother is rolling solo, feeling lonely, he don't have to trip. Just maintain his game and make them moves. The right person will show up.

Break on the four means:
Brother check himself,
People happy and get with him.
No problem.

Sometimes a motherfucker have so many rough edges, real brothers don't want to deal with him. Players stay away. So the motherfucker is stuck rolling with crab asses. Their bullshit makes his game fall off harder. But if the motherfucker checks himself, change his game and drop the crab asses, streets recognize. Real brothers and Players will reach out. This motherfucker happy then, and positive shit happens.

Break on the five means:
Someone hook him up.
Ten bad horoscopes don't block it.
Paid for real. Very good look.

If it's Fate for a brother to get over, that shit happens. Don't matter what no horoscope says. Don't matter what them streets say. When a brother has Fate on his side, he ain't have to fear nothing. Luck don't matter. The Heavens are giving this brother a good look. Fate beats luck. Nobody stops him.

Break at the top means:
Brother paid without taking.
No problem.
Maintain. Paid.
Good look to make a play.
Brother gets a crew.
Private life over.

Some players bless the world. Like singers who make people happy. Or crisp brothers who build operations that put people paid. Ballers who bring it whenever they step into the game. That's real positive shit that don't take nothing away from other motherfuckers. Players like that get paid for real. Find solid crews. Get love from streets. But they don't roll just for themselves. They help everybody get over. Be out all the time, meeting people, making connects and building the operation. Players like that ain't have much private life. But it don't bother them, because they're doing positive shit.

BUMP UP

Shit works right when players high up the chain break off real pieces for brothers below. When the whole crew gets a BUMP UP in status, everybody should be paid out nice.

THE FEEL

BUMP UP. Good look to make a play.
Good look to Roll Cross Town.

When a True Player high up in the game breaks off real pieces for his people, that's a good look. Brothers have love for a player like that. If he puts them paid nice, and sets them up with real business angles, they down for whatever. Handle real dangerous shit. Roll on motherfuckers cross town, no problem. A Player uses good times to strengthen the crew. Paying people right shows respect. Respect builds loyalty. Good times don't last forever, so a True Player makes the most of that shit.

THE LOOK

Thunder and wind: the look of Bump Up.
True Player sees something good,
He rolls with it.
Find problems, checks himself.

Wind blowing is one thing. Thunder is another. But when Thunder and Wind both hit at the same time, shit is deep. Both BUMP UP the power of the other, make it more hardcore when they working together.

When a brother find a Player with real tight game, he should find out why. Watch that Player operate. Ask some questions if he can. Then put what he learned into play. If a brother finds problems in his own game, he should change his ways. Shit shakes out right then.

THE BREAKS

Break on the one means:
Good look to make large plays.
Put paid. No problem.

When The Heavens lean True Player's way and really pay him out, he uses that power for positive things. He don't stress how shit will shake out for himself personal. Just rolls on plays that put people paid. Uses his power to BUMP UP the whole crew. Nobody talk shit about a brother like that.

Break on the two means:
Someone hook him up for real.
Ten horoscopes don't stop him.

Maintain for real. Paid.
Big Dog shouts him out to The Heavens.
Real good look.

A real BUMP UP in status don't happen till a brother check him-self for real. He have to drop bad habits, bad thoughts, and crab asses. Maintain with what's right. If a brother start loving what's good in the world, the good in the world starts loving him back.

A brother rolling like this will get a BUMP UP in status. Whatever he wants to do will happen. He gets the BUMP UP because he's in tune with what's good. Nothing can stop this brother. Not bad luck, not Fate, not some horoscope shit, nothing. Only problem might be too much happening for him. It's real important this brother don't lose his head when shit breaks his way. He have to stay strong inside. Love the good, even when the bad shows up real sexy and ready to party. If a brother stays real like that, he gets respect from The Heavens and them streets. Brother like this can do positive shit for the world.

Break on the three means:
Brother paid through bullshit.
No problem, real and roll in the middle.
Letter from Big Dog.

When a real BUMP UP is happening, even bullshit that normally fucks a brother up breaks his way. Player is rolling with what's right in the world, so Heaven is down with him. He's so real that whatever he touch shakes out nice. It's like he have a letter from the biggest of the Big Dogs, that says: "This motherfucker my boy. Let him do what he do."

Break on the four means:
Brother walk in the middle.
Down with Player, followed.
Good look on major plays.

Every crew need a brother who stands between Player and the rest of the crew. This brother ain't whispering shit in Player's ear or playing angles. He just wants shit rolling right. When the crew have a BUMP UP in status, this brother makes sure people put paid. Player shouldn't be holding back no pieces for his rainy day. Everybody has to taste some. Brother in the middle handles that. He's a good influence on Player. That's a real important brother when Player trying to pull off a major play, or roll deep. Helps the whole crew flow tight.

Break on the five means:
Real in his heart, don't ask.
Good look.
Brother recognized.

A real brother don't ask people to say thank you. He just do what have to be done. Players recognize a brother like that. Help his moves get over, since that brother influence shit positively.

Break at the top means:
He ain't Bump Up nobody.
Ill Brothers bust a shot.
Heart ain't steady.
Bust ass.

A Player high up the chain takes care his people. If he gets a BUMP UP in status, the crew have to be paid. If he don't do that, brothers going to peel off from that motherfucker. Then he's alone and ill brothers have a chance to bust a shot at him. Maybe take him out of the game. That's how a player who don't handle the BUMP UP right goes bust ass.

True Player chills out before making a move. He puts his head together before saying shit. He makes his connects strong before he asks brothers for something. If he does all that, True Player's in a real solid place. But if a motherfucker is all fast and rough in the way he operate, brothers just don't give a damn about what he's trying to do.

If he's all stressed when he talks, nobody feeling him. If he asks for shit from brothers he ain't take the time to be down with, they don't give a fuck. And if he ain't have no people, ill brothers show up to play him right out the game.

BREAKTHROUGH

BREAKTHROUGH happens after True Player been held back or blocked for a real long time. Crab asses had power, but they falling off now. Once them motherfuckers lose their grip, it's time for real brothers and True Players to BREAKTHROUGH.

THE FEEL

Breakthrough. Brother have to spell that shit out for Big Dog.
Tell it straight.
Drama. Static.
Heads up to his people.
Not a good look to pull nines.
Good look to make a play.

If only one crab ass is holding a place high up in the operation, that's enough to fuck shit up. If a brother have just one real bad habit in his life, that's enough to play him out the game. If a player want to maintain at high levels, he have to be ruthless on his own self first. Check every angle of his life. Find whatever bullshit holding him back and kill it.

Same thing in the operation. But there's a way to do this. It ain't about being real hard on motherfuckers. It's about being strong and understanding. Lot of brothers miss that. It ain't easy to be understanding when dealing with bullshit from crab asses. But a True Player approach bullshit chill.

He ain't all hard. He don't yell. He don't start swinging fists and breaking brothers down. But he ain't ever cut deals with ill shit, neither. Evil have to be recognized for what it is. Don't matter if it's in some successful brother or some famous sister or whatever. Evil shit is evil shit. True Player calls that out, no half stepping. And he don't never cut deals with it. Evil been around too long. Knows every play in the game. True Players don't dance with that shit.

True Players never let evil slide in themselves, neither. If something is fucked up inside himself, he breaks it down. Some brothers think: "Yo, I work real hard. It don't matter if I pull a few dollars from the operation my way." Or: "Yo, I can sniff some this shit on the weekends and I'm fine." Or: "My girl alright but I really want some of that nasty pussy on the side. I'll pay some bitch for that. It's cool." They think since the rest of their game solid, they can fuck around like that. But if a brother don't check that shit, it will blow up down the line and run his game off the tracks.

But fights with evil aren't won by force. Player roll up hard on Evil, that shit have weapons pulled, ready to party. Player do it favors by fighting. Evil like nothing better than a long, hard, nasty fight. The longer a True Player fight with Evil, the more it twists his soul up. Hate fucks with a brother's mind. Turns him ill.

That's why fighting Evil should start before Player ever meet that motherfucker. He just check himself and maintains the right lifestyle. That way, Evil ain't have no door to step into his life. Evil don't have no place to fight him. When Evil ain't fighting, it starts slipping. Like a motherfucker who starts leaving his nine in the glove-box, instead of stashing it by the seat.

A brother should never fight the fucked up parts of his life head on. Long as he fights with them, they feed off the energy and get stronger. Best way for a brother to fight evil in himself is just doing something else. Maybe he want to do some dark shit with a freak, real bad. He don't stress all night, fighting them feelings. Instead, he finds some brothers playing ball and rolls with them. That keeps his ass busy and his mind occupied. No time to trip out on dark shit.

Best way to fight evil is just doing what's good, 100%, all the time. That way, a brother beat Evil without ever having to see it.

THE LOOK

Toilet overflowing:
The look of Breakthrough.
True Player pays his people out.
Don't just maintain on his name.

When that toilet don't flush right, water gets all backed up. If that shit overflows, it's real nasty and fucks a place up. So the first time a brother sees the flush ain't working right, he should fix it. By handling a small problem, he saves himself stress from a larger problem down the line.

If a Player running the crew piles up money for himself, but don't put his people paid, that's a bad look. Everything stored up has to flow out. That's why a True Player pays his people out while he's bringing that paper in. Makes brothers happy and keeps business flowing that way.

In his personal life, True Player never hard in his ways. He's always checking himself. He crunches out small problems in his life before they blow up. He looks around to stay in step with them streets. Changes his game to roll with what's happening out there.

THE BREAKS

Break on the one means:
Strong from the jump.
Brother not up to it goes bust ass.

Starting is the hardest part. Any Player who wants to get over will hit walls. Plus a bunch of motherfuckers trying to break him down. Just how it is. So Player stays real about how large a play he can roll on. Runs them numbers. Strategizes. If he just dives in swinging wild, hoping to hit something, that leads to problems. Ill shit he ain't ready for. The start of something is when shit a brother ain't thought of will fuck him up the hardest.

Break on the two means:
Shout: "Oh, Shit!"
Nines at night.
No fear.

Being ready is everything. Part of being ready is being real careful. If a brother has his head up, reading them streets, he's ready for static before it shows up. A True Player has his guard up against shit that ain't happen yet. He has his ear out for shit that ain't been said yet. That lets him live in the thickest shit, handling static like nothing. If a True Player maintains real tight game like that, motherfuckers don't even bother getting up in his face. When it's time to be real careful in life, wearing armor 24/7 is the way to roll.

Break on the three means:
Powerful with the mouth goes bust ass.
True Player for real.
Walks alone in the rain.
Splashed with mud.
People talk shit.
No problem.

This a real fucked up situation. Streets are rolling on crab asses. But True Player have some bond to a crab ass he can't shake. Maybe some business or a family situation. Whatever. Player knows he have to shake off this crab ass, but the timing ain't right. If he just fronts on this motherfucker because streets are rolling on crab asses, it will fuck his personal shit up. Plus, this particular crab ass have some real weight in the game. If True Player tries to break it down right now, that crab ass would just break it down harder. So True Player got to roll with a fucked up situation, here. He have to maintain connects with the crab ass, without 100% throwing in with him. Down the line, he'll shake that motherfucker off, but for now, he have to play it cool.

Ain't nobody going to understand Player here. Streets will think he's rolling with that crab ass. So True Player will be out in the cold a minute. He'll feel real alone. His connect with the crab ass will make him look bust-ass, and bitches will be talking mad shit. Turn their motherfucking backs on Player.

But a True Player can handle this. He ain't about to fuck up his own plans just because streets rolling on crab asses. He deals with the hate and the bitches. When timing's right for him to throw off the crab ass, he'll do it. Till then, True Player holds tight and maintains.

Break on the four means:
Rash on the ass.
Hurt walking.

Brother let himself be led like shorty,
No problem.
He hear this, don't believe it.

A brother is restless. He wants to push forward, no matter what. He hits walls that fuck him up. But the problems are only happening because he's trying to force his shit forward. Timing ain't right. If he just chill a minute, things will fall into place. But this brother ain't hearing it. Restless motherfuckers who force shit ain't ever listen to people.

Break on the five means:
Dealing with weeds,
Maintain hardcore.
Roll in the middle,
No problem.

Weeds never die. They always grow back. Same thing with real powerful crab asses, high up in the organization. Them motherfuckers root down. Having to deal with them high level crab asses is ill. A player in this situation might give up. Start thinking shit is hopeless. But he can't do that. He have to maintain and handle his business. Otherwise, motherfuckers will play him right out the organization.

Break at the top means:
No joke.
End of the day bust-ass.

Player here fixed shit up. Crushed most of the bullshit from his organization. Just minor crab ass shit still around. And those crab asses don't look hard to beat. Feeling that shit will be easy is the danger, here. If Player starts popping champagne too soon, them last few crab asses slip out the side door. Then they come back at him harder, down the line. Evil don't die easy. Don't matter if it's in

the organization, or in a brother's heart. Everybody have evil in-
side them. True Players check themselves ruthlessly, yo. If a
brother let something ill inside him live, that shit just grow quietly.
Really fuck him up down the line. Ruin his life.

SAYING WHAT UP

This about some evil that Player thought he shut down. But it comes back on the sly, from inside the organization.

That's like treacherous females who play men for their ends. Pick their target, run their game, and own that brother. Females like that don't do shit proper. Have no time for romance. Just walk right up to a brother SAYING WHAT UP. Look out for them type females.

THE FEEL

Saying What Up.
The sister is powerful.
Brother don't marry that type of sister.

Crab ass shit that rises up sly in the organization is like a particular type of female. Some women give up their body easy, to control a brother's mind. She choose her mark, dress nice, walk up smiling, SAYING WHAT UP. Brothers should beware females who give the ass up fast. Pussy is some powerful shit. Make a brother lose his mind a minute. Female like this gets a brother hooked on her ass, then start dealing it like drugs. Little bit here, little there, until she has power over that brother. Then he's doing whatever she want, just to hit it.

Marriage to this type of female makes it worse. Once she got the courts behind her, she divorce him through the motherfucking floor. Make him move out his own house. Pay her money for life. Brothers come through that shit shell shocked. Be like: "What the fuck just happened to everything I worked for?"

But that shit wouldn't have gone down unless the brother let it. Baby girl didn't pull no nine. Just walked by SAYING WHAT UP. Looked real sweet and pretty. Brother thought slim thing was harmless. Playing with it was fun. Never imagined she roll so hardcore. Burn him right the fuck up.

Just like that type of female, certain ill brothers and crab asses do the same. Just act harmless. Nobody see the danger. Then they get large and it's too late. But if motherfuckers like that are shut out from the jump, they don't rise up to be no problem.

There some rules about SAYING WHAT UP in the game. Brother lower down on the chain ain't SAYING WHAT UP to players higher up in the organization. But when a True Player and his Big Dog SAYING WHAT UP to each other, that puts the organization in order. Brothers born to work together have to meet each other halfway. But they both have to be straight up, without shady plays running on the sly. Both them motherfuckers have to work for the whole organization. Not just each other or themselves. If it ain't real like that, shit falls through.

THE LOOK

Wind in the sky:
The look of Saying What Up.
Big Dog break it down for his people.
Shout that shit out all over town.

Big Dog breaking it down for his people is like wind blowing in the sky. That shit is felt all over town. The sky is far from them streets, but blows some wind to make itself felt down there. Big Dog is high up the chain. He ain't out on every angle, standing over every brother's shoulder. But he sets all that shit straight by breaking it down from a high level.

THE BREAKS

Break on the one means:
Put the brakes on it.
Maintain. Paid.
Brother let that shit go, bad look.
Even little baby tiger rips it up.

If a crab ass slides his way into the operation, that motherfucker have to be shut down immediately. Player have to break it down on him, over and over, till that motherfucker gets the message and bounces. If Player lets just one crab ass slide, the whole organization falls off. Crab asses ruin everything. Takes just one of them motherfuckers to fuck shit up. Crab asses drop the ball or play shady games. Get brothers fighting each other, make business fall off, or put other crews rolling on the operation. That's a bad look.

But not every crab ass looks like a problem when they show up at the door. Some them motherfuckers be friendly and charming. Funny ass brothers that make people laugh. So the organization keeps them around, for amusement and shit. People don't think some funny little bullshit brother like that will be a problem. They just laugh, thinking: "Shit, he ain't nothing. Look at him. What harm can that motherfucker do?"

Here's a story about that.

Up in Harlem, back in the day, some brother got hold a little baby tiger. Maybe through some Dominicans he was dealing with, or shit at the zoo. Whatever. This brother spend the whole spring and summer chilling in front the projects. Wearing a motherfucking 8 Ball jacket and feeding that little baby tiger from a bottle.

Player got famous all over. Motherfuckers from White Plains and Delaware talking about this brother uptown with the baby tiger. Girls from everywhere want to feed that little animal. Motherfucker got more pussy that summer than players all over Bronx, Brooklyn, Staten, Manhattan combined.

But that baby tiger grow. End of summer, this brother can't handle that animal on the bench no more. Have to leave it up in his apartment. Then the pussy falls off, since the girls are scared the damn thing. Now this motherfucker stuck with a wild animal in his crib. He ain't want to call the police, since they arrest his ass. So he shut that animal in a room by itself. Open up the door real fast every day and throw some motherfucking hamburger in there. Be like that for a year, yo. Then one day that brother slipped with the door. Tiger reach out with them claws. Rip his face right the fuck off.

Motherfucker slam the door, run outside bloody and screaming. That shit was legendary. Front page the damn newspapers show them zoo people leading a full grown tiger out the motherfucking projects.

Brother lived through that shit, yo. They did some work on his face in the prison hospital, but it wasn't shit. Came out looking like Freddy Krueger. Hit the streets real hard. Player still notorious uptown today. Brothers from back in the day see him creeping around the parks at night. Be like: "Yo, that's the motherfucker from 135 who had the baby tiger."

He's done. Living like a junkie with no money in his pocket and no face on his motherfucking head.

Just because he thought that little baby tiger was cute.

Break on the two means:
Dog on a leash. No problem.
Not a good look for brothers.

This situation about a crab ass who ain't beat down with violence. Just kept under tight control. The crab ass ain't allowed to run free. It don't have the chance to grow. It's kept far away from people. If it started to reach out and connect with brothers, the whole organization would fall off.

Break on the three means:
Rash on the ass,
Walking hurts.
Heads up on the problem,
Brother don't slip.

Brother really wants to throw in with some evil shit SAYING WHAT UP. Maybe it's fast money, hard drugs, or nasty pussy. Either way, the shit is real dangerous. Fortunately it just don't work out. For whatever reasons, the situation falls apart. But that brother still tripping real hard. He wanted to throw in with that evil shit real bad. Can't stop thinking about it. He's all mixed up. Moving forward happens real slow and difficult. Like walking with a rash on his ass. But if he finally pulls his shit together, and realize how dangerous that evil situation was, brother won't make no bad mistake.

Break on the four means:
No crabs in the bucket.
Bad look.

Crab asses are part of life. They everywhere in business. A brother will even need one at some point. Maybe just to sign some papers or introduce him to a motherfucker. So if a brother act all righteous on crab asses, and have nothing to do with them, that's a bad look. Them crab asses will turn their back on him when he needs some shit. But that's his own damn fault.

Break on the five means:
Made in the shade.
Drop right down.

Some shit grows in the shade. Like hip hop MCs from real rough neighborhoods. If they was brought up where life was soft, their flow wouldn't be shit. Took darkness to make them develop. That's the way to run business in certain situations. Like when a Player pull some rough brothers into his crew who don't know shit. Instead of putting them motherfuckers in the spotlight every time they drop the ball, Player just watch from the shadows. Maintain his presence in the operation and let his style influence the situation. Let them brothers develop without shining too hard on them. That way they ain't feel foolish, or hate on him. Just pick up Player's moves, and everything falls in line.

Break at the top means:
He say fuck off.
Bitches bitch. No problem.

Many times, when a Player makes his paper and pulls out the game, he ain't have time for them streets no more. That shit's a headache for him. Brothers try SAYING WHAT UP and he tell them to fuck off. So people talk mad shit about him. Saying Player all proud and high on himself. But since Player made his money and checked out the game, it really don't matter. He don't have to give a damn what some bitches think. If motherfuckers hate on him, he ain't particularly bothered by that shit.

BRING IT TOGETHER

This is like GETTING TOGETHER, but stronger. Instead of a situation just flowing together naturally, True Player pulls brothers in, and BRING IT TOGETHER. Makes that shit happen.

THE FEEL

Bring It Together. Paid.
Father bow the head.
Good look to see Big Dog.
Maintain. Good look.
Help out. Paid.
Good look to make a play.

Nothing BRING IT TOGETHER like family. Blood bonds are strongest. Business BRING IT TOGETHER, but it's more formal. Family just happen naturally. Family BRING IT TOGETHER around the father. The man is the head of the house. He should have some spiritual strength to run that family right. Maybe that means church. Or maybe it's being down with the Laws of Heaven. Might just be living right and showing respect for what's good. That makes Heaven look out for his little ones and his lady. Adds an invisible power to that family, holds them together through hard times.

Business the same way. If a True Player puts his shit correct with The Heavens, all his plays have more weight. Shit leans his way. His people put paid.

To BRING IT TOGETHER, brothers need a leader. A True Player with his heart chill and mind steady. He should live right, so his plays are solid. It's a good look when he shows respect to The Heavens. Throws some money at church or charities. Builds a playground. That makes The Heavens recognize Player. Lean his way when shit gets thick.

THE LOOK

Rising water in the sink:
The look of Bring It Together.
True Player stay sharp
For what's next.

If water rise up in the sink, that shit overflows. It's a mess. Nobody wants that. So Player makes sure the drain is clear, and them pipes are clean.

When a whole lot of brothers throw in for a play, all them heads are thinking different ways. There's drama and fights. And wherever real money stacks up, real criminals show up trying to take it. So when it's time to BRING IT TOGETHER, True Player have to be ready for shit he ain't ever thought of. Most problems are made by shit a brother never imagined, happening when he isn't ready. If a Player is ready all the time for whatever, he rarely have problems.

That's like keeping that sink clean so it don't overflow.

THE BREAKS

Break on the one means:
For real, then tripping.
Static, but sometimes shit come together.
If he shouts out, after a pound they laugh again.
Don't trip. Movement a good look.

Brothers want to throw in with a player they respect. But large groups have lots of bullshit about how to do things. Motherfuckers fight. Shit has no center. But if brothers realize they need a True Player to run things, all they have to do is shout that Player out. He steps in and puts shit right. All them brothers stop tripping. If they follow True Player, everybody put paid nice.

Break on the two means:
Let it flow,
Paid no problem.
Brother for real,
Good look to bring a little.

Sometimes The Heavens BRING IT TOGETHER. Brothers don't have to steer nothing, then. Mysterious forces work shit. Bring players together who belong together. Motherfuckers just flow with it. No problem.

When brothers really down with each other, nobody have to be formal with shit. Motherfuckers just feeling it. Brothers know everybody's all good. Have an understanding, without spelling shit out.

The Heavens have an understanding like that for all brothers. Like a real poor motherfucker who don't have shit to his name. Maybe he really want to do some good. But all he have is one dollar for charity, or helping somebody in the street. Heaven understands that brother don't have much. Heaven loves that brother for giving what he can, since it comes from the heart.

Break on the three means:
Bring It Together feeling down.
No move to make.
Reach out, no problem.
Slightly bust ass.

Sometimes a brother wants to throw in with motherfuckers, but shows up late to the party. The crew is already set. He's on the outside looking in. A brother in that spot have to reach out to one player in the middle of the crew. Have to be straight up and real with this player. Talk about respecting the crew, but having no connects. He's sweating Player slightly, but that ain't wrong. Just makes this outsider motherfucker feel bust ass for a minute.

Break on the four means:
Seriously paid. No problem.

Player here brings brothers together, then organizes them to roll for the Big Dog. He ain't just looking out for his own ass. He BRING IT TOGETHER so all them motherfuckers plus Big Dog are paid nice. That's a damn good look. Since Player ain't just thinking of himself, everybody here get over together.

Break on the five means:
Brothers Bring It Together.
Player has status.
Nice look.
For halfhearted brothers,
Be real, run plays, maintain.
All good from there.

When brothers first throw in with a Player, it's natural. When the crew grows and Player has status, shit gets different. Brothers start throwing in just because Player has a name in the game. But in their heart, them new motherfuckers don't think Player's all that. Only way Player can flip them is by being real. Rolling on solid plays, putting people paid, maintaining crisp game, and not missing a beat. That wins brothers' hearts. It's all good from there.

Break at the top means:
Depressed and sad.
No problem.

Some brother wants to throw in with Player. The brother has heart, but Player thinks he's bust ass. Freezes him out. This brother gets depressed and real sad. That's alright. When Player sees how bad this brother feeling, he'll realize he was wrong. He'll reach out and link up. That's a good look. Everybody need people.

GETTING OVER

A brother from them streets put his game together, made it tight, rolled right, and now he's GETTING OVER for real.

THE FEEL

Getting Over. Paid for real.
See the Big Dog.
Don't trip.
Step downtown.
Paid.

Player is GETTING OVER with no problem. His shit is popping off. But Player ain't GETTING OVER by being a motherfucker. He stays real low key, flowing through whatever's out there. He's feeling the times. His style matches what's hitting on them streets.

Now that he's GETTING OVER, Player have to roll with some real Big Dogs. Player doesn't trip on that. His game is tight and his style is hitting. He shows respect and maintains his angles. Starts to play long game with his finance and business. Heads downtown, learns that Wall Street shit. Put his money in properties, bonds, all them deep investments.

THE LOOK

Tree growing in the park.
The look of Getting Over.
True Player does little things over and over
To blow up large.

Trees in the park start in the ground. Just some seed sending out roots. Them roots wind up through the dirt to find the sun. If they hit rocks blocking them, roots don't stop. Just work around that shit. Roots don't rush and don't stagnate. They just push it along. Nobody sees motherfucking roots on the move. But that's all they're doing, real slow and low key. Same thing with True Player who's GETTING OVER from the streets. He's always moving forward. But he's chill about it. Never rushing, never stagnating, just pushing shit along, bit by bit, till one day he's GETTING OVER. Then everybody see how large he is. Like some motherfucking tree in the park.

THE BREAKS

Break on the one means:
Getting Over that gets a good look.
Paid large.

This player just starting. Don't have shit. Came up around the way with real rough motherfuckers. That hard shit made him strong. If this brother was born rich, he would never have the power to feel them streets. Having nothing is what lets him get everything. Since he has heart, and makes real crisp plays, Big Dogs recognize. When Big Dogs say this brother's down, streets show love. Now he has that power base. Player starts GETTING OVER from there.

Break on the two means:
Brother for real, good look with a little bit.
No problem.

This brother rolls rough. Motherfucker came up hard and it shows. But since he's a real brother who makes shit happen, people feeling him. The fact that he really ain't smooth don't matter none.

Break on the three means:
Getting Over all city.

Normally, GETTING OVER is real hard. Bullshit slows a Player down, motherfuckers block him out, whatever. But in this situation, all that falls off. GETTING OVER is real easy for Player. Doors just open. He don't slip or trip. Just flows with the run. From the outside, it looks real good. But a run like that ain't normal. It don't last forever. Player don't trip on that reality. If he stresses on how long his run will last, he starts to slip. So all he does is roll. Stays 100% focused. No tripping. Moves through every door he can before they start closing. That's all.

Break on the four means:
Real deep real estate.
Good look. No problem.

True Player 100% got over. He has real large success and maintains it crisp. Went from the streets to the stars without missing a beat. So True Player gets a special bump up from the Big Dogs. They let him buy a house in some deep real estate.

There zip codes in the world off limits to normal motherfuckers. Classic addresses in the city, particular beaches on the island, certain towns upstate. Only power put down there. No matter how much money or fame a brother have, he ain't buying in without a nod from the Big Dogs. That's because Big Dogs real particular about neighbors. They decide who lives next to them. So when True Player gets the nod to put down in this area, it's a real motherfucking honor. Respect beyond money and fame.

Break on the five means:
Maintain. Paid.
Getting Over, step by step.

When a brother is just GETTING OVER, he have to watch the fame. That shit fucks up lots of Players. When it's all popping off like crazy, he has to be the most steady. Can't party like a motherfucker. Can't miss any beats in his game. Business moves real fast in this situation. Motherfuckers show up from nowhere with plans out the ass, pushing for their piece. Player have to handle it clear headed. The only way to maintain at the top is by minding details. Step by step, no matter how high them steps lead, or how many motherfuckers pushing. True Players don't rush shit.

Break at the top means:
Getting Over in the dark.
Good look to maintain for real.

Moving forward means different things at different times. Sometimes the smart play is chilling a minute to build strength. Or pulling back to shake off crab asses. True Players will do whatever. Maybe lean right or left, lose weight a minute if they have to, then maintain forward when timing is better. But brothers who force it forward all the time, no matter what, get played. Since they moving fast, they roll with whatever business show up. Start making plays because they feel like it. Not because the plays are smart.

Like when famous people launch some bullshit perfume line. Or open up a restaurant without ever having cooked a motherfucking steak. Stupid shit like that makes a brother lose money and look bust ass. True Players think through every angle, step by step, at every level of the game.

PLAYED

Streets are thick with crab asses. Them motherfuckers lock down the game. True Players and real brothers got no moves. People who step up get PLAYED.

THE FEEL

Played. Maintain.
Big Dog puts people paid.
No problem.
Brother try to talk,
Nobody believe that shit.

Being PLAYED is the opposite of being paid. Nothing positive is happening for a brother. He's being shut down left and right. Stopped cold, even straight-up robbed. When a True Player gets PLAYED, he stays positive, even in the middle of ill shit. That positivity makes him stronger than whatever Fate throw at him. A brother who folds when he gets PLAYED never makes it. The game is hard. Everybody gets PLAYED sometime. Until a brother gets fucked, he's just visiting.

If a brother who's PLAYED gets all bent up, but straightens shit out, it builds his power. He comes through it with more strength than he had going in. Crab asses don't do that. Them motherfuckers get PLAYED and fold right the fuck up. Bitch and moan, drop out the game.

True Player turns a bad run into good things. Nobody talk shit about him when he's through the other side. But while he's being PLAYED, his status is bullshit. Player's words don't hold weight on them streets. Brothers see what he's going through. Be like: "That motherfucker being PLAYED right now. What the fuck he know? I ain't listen to him."

That's why True Players getting PLAYED rarely talk. The best look through real ill shit is staying strong inside, without saying much.

THE LOOK

No water in the pool:
The Look of Played.
True Player has heart.
Decides his Fate.

Shorties in the summer love to swim. Run all the way cross town to that pool at the community center. Jump right in. But a few days every summer, park service drain that motherfucker to clean it. Shorties run 15 blocks in the sun, then stand there staring at an empty pool. That's the look of being PLAYED.

Motherfuckers get PLAYED all the time. Fate, ill timing, and bad luck will fuck a brother up nicely. Sometimes there ain't nothing to do but feel the hit. Like staring at that empty pool on the hottest

day in the summer. What happens in the outside world ain't some-
thing a brother can control. But a True Player has heart. He stays
stronger inside than whatever happens outside. That lets him han-
dle anything Fate throw his way.

THE BREAKS

Break on the one means:
Drinking on the corner.
Down the alley.
Three years gone.

When a brother gets PLAYED, he have to stay strong inside. Hold
his heart and mind together. When a crab ass gets PLAYED, he folds.
Instead of moving forward, he picks up liquor or them drugs. Starts
drinking or shooting in the alley with a bunch of motherfuckers
bitching about life. That only makes shit worse. People lose years that
way. So when a True Player gets PLAYED, he's fierce about shaking it
off mentally. He don't let that shit break him down.

Break on the two means:
Played with food on the table.
Brother with the crisp look coming.
Good look to say What Up to The Heavens.
Making the jump a bad move.
No problem.

Brother's PLAYED in his own mind. Life ain't bad. Food on the table
and business rolling. But brother's bored. Makes him feel PLAYED.
He's losing heart, but don't know how to change the scenario.

Then some shit breaks his way. A crisp player, tight with the Big
Dog, is looking for real brothers to handle a particular piece of

business. This bored brother is feeling it. But that job ain't falling into his lap. Lot of motherfuckers out there want in.

The best way for this brother to roll is turning to The Heavens, first. Show respect and get help from the other side. Jumping right in and fighting for the job would be bullshit. This brother been PLAYED in his mind too long. He have to set his spirit straight, first. Brother have to be patient. Say what up to The Heavens, see where that power leads him. Shit shakes out right that way.

Break on the three means:
Brother lets himself be Played by hard brothers.
Falls back on bullshit.
Goes home his woman gone.
Bad look.

This brother don't hold his head together when he's PLAYED. Instead of taking the hit, he steps up to roll on the ill motherfuckers who PLAYED him. But he don't have the muscle to handle them, so he only gets PLAYED harder. Scrambles for shit to fall back on. Maybe crab ass motherfuckers, business that ain't proper, some bullshit crew he ain't ever met, whatever. Finally this motherfucker realize he don't have a chance. He says "Fuck this, yo," and goes home. But since he been so foolish out there on them streets, his woman up and left him.

Old Big Dog break it down like this:

If a brother lets himself get PLAYED by situations
Real Players don't bother with,
Streets be talking shit about him.
If he falls back on motherfuckers he ain't supposed to lean on,
Ill brothers roll on his ass.
First he plays himself, then he puts his ass in danger.
What type of female live with that?

Break on the four means:
Half stepping. Living nice without feeling streets.
Bust ass, but it shakes out.

Streets is real dry. Nobody getting paid. A rich brother wants to roll on business. Put brothers paid and do something positive for people. But instead of jumping off strong, he half steps. Talks too much, trips himself out, holds back on laying money down. The other rich brothers hear about this shit. They ain't want new business in them streets. Have that shit locked up for themselves. So they reach out to this rich brother and pull him into some upscale lifestyle shit. Take him to parties, nice restaurants, throw fine females his way, whatever. Tell him to live the good life, and forget brothers on them streets. Why bother with business since he's already rich?

Now this brother is in a real bad place. He's trapped with some powerful motherfuckers who could shake him right out the game. The smart play is acting like he's down with them. Just do what they say a minute. That makes him look like a bitch to brothers on them streets. But this shit will pass. Rich brother have a good heart, and he's strong inside. He'll turn it around. Peel off gradual from them other rich motherfuckers. Pull his business together for them streets. Put some brothers paid. Help out in tough times. That shit shakes out.

Break on the five means:
Bullshit neighbors upstairs and down.
Played by the crisp brothers.
Shit turn around slow.
Good look to say what up to The Heavens.

A brother with positive plans is being PLAYED by ill motherfuckers high up the chain, and crab asses below. Bullshit all around stops him cold. Normally, brother like this would get help from down Players rolling with the Big Dog. But in this particular situation, even them motherfuckers ain't got shit to say. Things will turn around slowly. Till they do, this brother got nothing to do but chill and pray.

Break at the top means:
Played by weak shit.
Tripping: *making a play will fuck shit up.*
If a brother feel bad about this and move, paid.

Bad times are just starting to fade. But a brother still being PLAYED by minor shit that shouldn't hold him back. Problem is happening because he's still tripping on the bad times. Thinks whatever he does will fuck him up. Finally, he understands the bad times are really fading. Sees that just some minor shit is holding him back. This brother pulls his shit together, puts a play in motion, and moves forward.

WATER FOUNTAIN

WATER FOUNTAIN in the park is a damn good look on a hot day. Press that button, water is right there. Everybody love the WATER FOUNTAIN.

THE FEEL

Water Fountain. Streets may change,
But water don't.
Water stays the same.
People use Water Fountain all over the park.
If one goes bust ass, bad look.

Back in the day motherfuckers had wells. Drop their bucket down, pull up some water. Life changes, and people do shit different. Motherfuckers today use the WATER FOUNTAIN. But that don't change water. Water still the same. It wasn't less watery yesterday. Won't be more watery tomorrow. Millions of years, that shit ain't ever change. Water don't change, because water is life.

Life don't change none, neither. Technology flips shit up, styles come and go, but life still the same. Motherfuckers are born, grow up, chase pussy, find work, get old, then die. Same as it ever was. Some motherfuckers are rich, some are bust ass. Some brothers have a head for business, some be dumb as a pancake. But everybody have a heart and mind. Everybody have the same shit to do: be born, get paid, die.

If brothers live deep, like water far down in the earth, they have a real life. Problems happen when motherfuckers live shallow, and don't lower the bucket into what's real and deep in the world. Or they don't maintain themselves. Ain't nothing worse than a bust ass WATER FOUNTAIN at the park. If shit's rusty or fucked up, nobody can drink from it. But if that WATER FOUNTAIN is maintained, there's water for everybody. Same thing with a brother's life. He have to maintain himself and stay useful. If he lets himself go, people won't have no use for him.

THE LOOK

Water spraying up: the look of Water Fountain.
True Player helps people do their job,
Gets them helping each other.

WATER FOUNTAIN has different parts that work together. Press that button, water's there. A crew is the same way. True Player helps brothers work together. He organize them right, makes sure they tight. When different parts of the organization are working right, shit just flows. Press a button, it's on.

THE BREAKS

Break on the one means:

Dirty broken Water Fountain.
Nobody drink that shit.

If a brother runs around with dirty motherfuckers, doing dirty things, he become a dirty motherfucker. Mess with them drugs, drink too much, fucking ill whores, whatever. That shit fucks him up. Real brothers stop rolling with him. Then they stop bothering with him. He's like some bust-ass WATER FOUNTAIN at the park. Nobody even press the button. Just look at it like: "Yo, that shit is broken."

Break on the two means:
Pigeons in the Water Fountain.
Broken and leaks.

Sometimes the water is fine, but the WATER FOUNTAIN is bust ass. All blocked up. Pigeons fly down for a bath. Nobody drink from a WATER FOUNTAIN where them dirty motherfucking birds be chilling.

That's like a brother who have talent, but don't do nothing with it. The lazy motherfucker could make some real plays in the game. But he don't do shit. Just fucks around hanging with crab asses on the corner. Nobody real bothers with that motherfucker.

Break on the three means:
Nice Water Fountain, but nobody drinks.
Sad.
Brothers can drink from it.
If the Big Dog were real,
Everybody paid.

A real crisp player is on the scene. He's like a perfect WATER FOUNTAIN in the park. Clean and cool. But nobody bothers with this player. He has real good shit to offer the game, but nobody puts him in play. This makes every brother who knows him real sad.

Everybody wants the Big Dog to hear about their boy. Then they would be his crew. Get over together. Put paid.

Break on the four means:
Water Fountain being built. No problem.

When a new WATER FOUNTAIN being put in the park, motherfuckers can't drink from it yet. Have to wait till the work is finished. Same thing when a brother put his life in order. There are times a brother drops out the game to focus on himself. While that's happening, this player ain't useful to nobody. But it's a good look. After putting his shit together, player will be real crisp. Jump back in the game better than before.

Break on the five means:
This Water Fountain the best.

When we was shorties playing ball in the park, we had a favorite WATER FOUNTAIN. It was shiny, had real cold water, and flowed strong. Even with WATER FOUNTAIN all over the park, we still lined up for this one. Best drink in the park.

That's like a True Player who makes his life real crisp. He's real, down, smart, strong, and rolls on some spiritually elevated shit. Runs tight plays that put people paid. But streets have to reach out to this player, listen to what he have to say. Otherwise, True Player can't help them out.

Just like the best WATER FOUNTAIN in the park. Shorties don't know about it till somebody points it out. Then every motherfucker lines up to drink at it. So when a brother finds a real True Player, he should let people know.

Break at the top means:
Brother drinks from the Water Fountain.

No problem.
Shit works.
Damn good look.

WATER FOUNTAIN is there for everybody. No locks on that shit. Nobody have to join no WATER FOUNTAIN club. Motherfuckers just walk up and drink the water. WATER FOUNTAIN works all day. Don't matter if five or five hundred brothers have a drink. That water just flows. Same thing for the True Player. He ain't ever run dry. No matter what the situation, True Player has something to offer. He ain't ever turn brothers away. The more this brother is put in play, the stronger he gets. The operation grows, shit rolls better, more people put paid. That's a damn good look.

THROW SHIT OFF

This is about large changes happening fast. Like a revolution. Brothers THROW SHIT OFF when it ain't working.

THE FEEL

Throw Shit Off.
Recognized.
Real good look.
Maintain and make that play.
All good.

Real serious to THROW SHIT OFF. It should only happen in dangerous situations, with no other way out. Not just any motherfucker can THROW SHIT OFF. A True Player who everybody trusts and believe in have to lead. Timing has to be right on. If Player rolls too early, people aren't ready to THROW SHIT OFF yet. If he rolls too late, the bullshit is too thick and people are trapped.

Player have to THROW SHIT OFF right. He can't roll hard. He don't roll wild style. THROW SHIT OFF ain't about pouring gasoline on

244

motherfuckers and lighting them on fire. True Player have to maintain positivity and handle his people. And Player have to be thinking of everybody, not just himself. Some motherfuckers THROW SHIT OFF just to set themselves up in the new situation. That's bullshit. True Player leads motherfucker to THROW SHIT OFF because it's the right thing to do. Not because he wants to run shit.

If Player hits all them beats, brothers THROW SHIT OFF right.

THE LOOK

Sunshine and Snow: the look of Throw Shit Off.
True Player know the calendar.
Checks the season.
Roll with the weather.

Sun and snow work against each other. In spring, sun melts the snow. But in winter, snow falls blocking sun. Sun runs shit in spring. Snow runs shit in winter. Like two Big Dogs at war.

Players have to stay in touch with the calendar. Know what season it is. Check them streets and see who's running shit. Stay real with what's happening. Different seasons, different plays.

THE BREAKS

Break on the one means:
Yellow light.

Brothers THROW SHIT OFF only when nothing else is working. Last resort. Since it's such a serious move, the Player leading has to be real careful, right from the jump. Can't be nothing wild in the way he's rolling. This break here is telling a brother to slow down. It's like seeing a yellow light in the intersection. Be careful. THROW SHIT OFF too soon, or too fast, and ill motherfuckers show up from nowhere. Break it down, real hardcore.

Break on the two means:
When timing is right, brothers lead a revolution.
Roll on them motherfuckers. No problem.

When a Player tries to fix a situation, but nothings working, it's time to THROW SHIT OFF. But a play this large has to be thought through real deep. It has to be lead by a player who has the weight to pull it off. Streets have to believe in this player. A brother others will follow. Once that's set, motherfuckers involved have to prepare for a world of shit. Movements like this come with mad static. Brothers have to stay focused on what they want to happen after they THROW SHIT OFF. People who THROW SHIT OFF with no plan for what's next are fucked.

Break on the three means:
Jump off. Bad look.
Maintain. Left turn.
When talk goes three rounds
Player throw in.
Motherfuckers believe.

When it's time to THROW SHIT OFF, brothers slip up two different ways. The first mistake is moving too fast, and breaking it down too hard. Shit like that leads to war. The other mistake is moving too slow, and being too soft. That lets ill brothers slip out the back door, and fuck shit up down the line.

There's something else real important. Every time a motherfucker says: "Yo, shit have to change here", it don't really mean shit have to change. But if lots of brothers are saying this, all over the operation, a player listens up. He thinks on it. If their shit makes sense, he throws in with them motherfuckers. Positive brothers believing the same thing, moving together, will lead to better shit.

Break on the four means:
No more tripping. Brothers believe.
Change is a good look.
Paid.

The Player who leads brothers to THROW SHIT OFF has to hold weight in the operation. Be high up the chain. The play should be made for real reasons. Not personal shit. Real nasty motherfuckers might be running the organization. It don't matter if brothers like them or not. If shit is rolling legit, with people put paid, there ain't no reason to THROW SHIT OFF. But if shit's ill, and getting dangerous for brothers, that's the right reason to THROW SHIT OFF.

If Player tries to THROW SHIT OFF for personal reasons, it don't shake out right. He might get some brothers up for it a minute. But that don't hold for the long game. On a move this deep, brothers only roll for real reasons.

Break on the five means:
True Player Throw Shit Off like a tiger.
Even before he ask Yo Ching,
Brothers believe.

Tigers have stripes. People see that shit clear. Motherfuckers see a tiger and know what it is, real fast. It's like that when a True Player THROW SHIT OFF. The reasons and rules are made real clear. Just like seeing that tiger, people understand in a minute. No questions at all. When reasons are clear, and rules understood, Player don't have to check with *Yo Ching*. What he's doing will shake out.

Brothers will roll with him. Together they THROW SHIT OFF right.

Break at the top means:
True Player change the body.
Crab ass change his face.
The jump is a bad look.
Maintain. Paid.

People THROW SHIT OFF to solve large problems. Once them large problems are sorted out, details remain. Brothers can't just change the face of something. Have to deal with the whole body. That's some complex shit to do. After brothers THROW SHIT OFF, crab asses will remain. Maybe they get with the new program, but they still crab asses. Change their face, smile more, but it don't go deep. Player have to be satisfied with that. If he goes too far, and tries too much, he would stir up too many crab asses. They might organize and bounce him out the operation. The reason a player THROW SHIT OFF is to put the operation correct, and make it stable. He have to be happy with that. He shouldn't try for everything at once.

THE POT

THE POT is on the stove. People make meals and feed themselves with THE POT. It's about nourishment.

THE FEEL

The Pot. Very good look.
Paid.

WATER FOUNTAIN is about water. Every motherfucker need water. People need food, too. But food is different from water. Water is natural. Just flow right up out the ground. Food have to be prepared. Animals eat their shit raw. People more advanced. Put food in THE POT, follow recipes, serve that shit up in homes. THE POT is about motherfucking civilization.

When civilizations first started, brothers built shit for The Heavens. Huge ass temples and pyramids to show respect. They believed by showing love and respect, The Heavens would hook them up. Bless the tribe with real smart brothers to tell people what's right and wrong. Prophets.

Prophets broke it down for motherfuckers. Taught them laws. Showed them how to act. Told them what to eat. Prophets got brothers out of caves and put them into civilizations. Everything them motherfuckers taught people, from reading, to writing, to science, to recipes for THE POT, was sent from The Heavens. That's what brothers back then believed. Thought heaven was hooking them up with the right ideas and information, since they showed respect.

We ain't having that today. Prophets don't exist. Streets don't like anybody who say: "Yo, this is right. And that is wrong." Tell motherfuckers like that to eat a dick. Brothers all sophisticated and into science today. When new shit like computers happen, they ain't think it's a gift from The Heavens. Just some smart motherfucker inventing shit. But nobody think on where that idea come from. Back in the day, brothers thought good ideas came from The Heaven. Like a gift.

That's why brothers back then ain't ever forget The Heavens. Especially when they have food in THE POT. Back in the day, brothers would cook a whole dish for The Heavens. Put that shit on the table and be like: "Yo God, that's for You. Please look out for my family, and watch over my motherfucking ass. Thank You." Heavens had love for brothers like that.

THE LOOK

Heat on the stove:
The look of The Pot.
True Player makes his game tight by having his shit together.

People put THE POT on the stove to heat up food. Power beneath THE POT heats it up. Life has power that heats up a brother's life, too. If a brother puts his life in order, that power starts to heat up his moves. He starts rolling with forces other motherfuckers don't have access too. That power changes his game and makes him a True Player. Brothers who don't live right never feel that power. Them motherfuckers stay cold.

THE BREAKS

Break on the one means:
Pot turned over.
Clean shit out.
Single sister have a son.
No problem.

Brother can't cook something new until he cleans out the old. Turn THE POT over, pour old food out.

When shit's running right, everybody with heart can make it. Don't matter how low down the chain a brother is. If he clean his shit up, get rid of whatever nonsense was fucking him up, there will be a place for him.

That's like a single sister who made some bad choices in her past. She forced to bring up her little boy all alone. Maybe she picked the wrong father, plus made some mistakes herself. But if she raise him up right, that boy bring her respect in the community. She's recognized for that.

Break on the two means:
Food in The Pot.
Jealous brothers can't touch.
Paid.

When a Player finally catches his break, he ain't holding back. Doors don't open much. When they do, he just pop off like a motherfucker. Players who shine like that make other brothers jealous. Way to handle it is staying tight with business. Player don't just hang out. Motherfuckers who hang out talk shit. Player misses all that. Just maintains his angle, 24/7. Jealous motherfuckers don't have the chance to reach him that way.

Break on the three means:
Handle on The Pot bust ass.
Brother blocked out the game.
Good food nobody eating.
Rain come no more tears.
All good. Paid.

If the handle on THE POT is broken, brothers can't serve the meal. Might be real tasty, but if a motherfucker can't serve it, nobody eats it.

That's like a player who ain't been recognized. He have real talent for the game. But it don't mean shit since nobody put him in play. Player in that situation have a hard road. He has to make his spirit real strong. Stay mentally above the bullshit he's living through. Sooner or later, some Big Dog will recognize him. Put Player in the game. Shit will be alright then. Like when rain finally falls, after streets been dry forever.

Break on the four means:
The Pot cracked.
Spill food on the Big Dog.
Mess up his shirt.
Bad look.

Brother here have a big job, high up the chain. But he don't know what the fuck he's doing. Plus this motherfucker lazy. Don't bother to learn nothing. Just run around partying with crab asses. Naturally, this bullshit brother drops the ball. Everybody in the organization think he's bust ass after that.

Old Big Dog break it down like this:

Weak brother high up the chain.
Stupid brother with big plans.
Brother with no weight trying to roll heavy plays.
All this leads to bullshit.

Break on the five means:
The Pot have gold handles.
Maintain, good look.

A powerful player high up the chain stays real. Since he's down, all the best brothers want to work for him. Money stacks up in his part of the operation. It's real good. All Player have to do is stay low key, no matter how large he gets. Player check himself like that, it's a good look for him and his people.

Break at the top means:
The Pot has soft handles, still strong.
Real good look.
Everything get over.

Here's how a brother should live to lean shit his way. Roll strong but have a light touch. Move real deep but stay chill. Have high power but live low key. Heavens love a brother like this. Streets have love for him too. Rolling that way lets a brother get mad weight in the game. If he don't throw it around, whatever he wants to pull off will get over.

BOOM

BOOM is powerful, shocking shit. Like thunder or shots fired. Scare the hell out of every motherfucker around. But some shit that happen without a sound still BOOM. Like when real fucked up information brought to light. That hits brothers like: BOOM.

THE FEEL

Boom gets paid.
Boom! Oh, shit!
Laughing.
Boom scares motherfuckers all over town.
True Player don't miss a beat.

BOOM fuck up everybody. Nobody sees it coming. Like when earthquakes hit, or floods put a city underwater. Heavens throw a BOOM down whenever. True Player have mad respect for that power. He ain't trying to front on no BOOM. Just be real happy when it passes. Player laugh with his people after it passes, like: "Oh, shit!"

When a True Player deals with danger for a long time, he learns to handle fear. He feels fear but faces it down. Then nothing scare

him no more. Player like that is chill about his life. He don't want to die, but he ain't afraid to check out. So BOOM don't bother him none. Other motherfuckers run and hide when BOOM hit. Scared as hell. True Player pour tea in the middle of a damn earth quake. Not spilling a drop. That's the look for True Player. Shit motherfuckers run from bounce right off him.

THE LOOK

Thunder don't stop.
The look of Boom.
Respect for the Lord.
True Player pulls his shit together
And check himself.

Thunder that don't stop be like: BOOM! BOOM! BOOM! Send brothers running scared. That's powerful shit. True Player respects that power. When frightening shit is happening, he puts his life in order. True Players are ready to check out crisp. If a BOOM have their number on it, that ain't their business. True Player is down with whatever shakes out. Heavens do what they do. Respect like this leads to good things.

THE BREAKS

Break on the one means:
Boom happen. Oh, shit!
Then brothers laughing.
Paid.

This BOOM so large Player thinks he's done. But it passes. Player don't believe he survived. Now he have some new appreciation for his life. Shit only gets better for a Player like that. Put paid nice.

Break on the two means:
Boom is danger.
Hundred thousand times lose money.
Have to roll way uptown.
Player don't chase shit.
Later get it back.

BOOM hits Player real hard. Major losses. But he can't fight to get it back now. Player lost too much weight from the BOOM. Have to pull back someplace where he won't be fucked with. Leave town, roll upstate. Some shit will be left behind when he makes the break. Player have to be good with that. When the BOOM passes, life will turn back to normal. Shit will come back to him.

Break on the three means:
Boom set brother tripping.
If that shit make him move right,
No problem.

Three types of shit go BOOM on a motherfucker. First BOOM from Heaven. That's ill natural shit, like earthquakes. Next is BOOM of Fate, where some ill shit happen out of nowhere. Like some drunk drive up the sidewalk and run a brother down. Last BOOM hits the heart. Like a brother go home early one day and find some motherfucker tapping his girl. All these BOOMs will shake a brother up. But this break here about the BOOM of Fate. That's the one breaks brothers down hardest. When ill shit hits from out of nowhere, that shocks people. Some brothers panic, or freeze up, or just fall to pieces. But when Fate go BOOM like that, a brother have to hold his head together. If he think shit through, no matter what's happening, he finds the right path forward.

Break on the four means:
Boom be stuck.

Putting a crisp game together depends on the environment. If there ain't ill shit a brother got to work through, he don't develop his strengths. But if shit is too hard, for too long, brother stops trying at some point. He gets stuck. That's a bad look.

Break on the five means:
Boom all over. No stopping.
Ill.
No shit lost.
But shit to do.

Sometimes shit hit a motherfucker from all sides. BOOM! BOOM! BOOM! He ain't even have time to breathe. But a brother who don't lose his head will be fine. He rolls with it, instead of being thrown by it.

Break at the top means:
Boom fuck everything. Brothers scared.
Looking around. Running around.
Rolling plays is a bad look.
Hit the motherfucker next door, no problem.
Bitches be bitching.

When BOOM hit, people panic. Brothers don't see shit straight. It's bananas on them streets. But True Player stays chill. He don't roll until shit becomes clear. Ain't easy to maintain while brothers all around losing their head. But True Player don't roll with no running and screaming motherfuckers. He pulls back. Brothers won't like that. Hate on Player because he break away. Player lets them hate. He pulls out and saves his ass.

WREXAGRAM 52

STAYING CHILL

True Player STAYING CHILL in his heart and mind. It's hard to chill the heart. Near impossible to chill the mind, yo.

THE FEEL

Staying Chill.
Chill so much he stare at the wall.
Out in the yard don't see his people.
No problem.

Player STAYING CHILL when it's time to chill. Move when it's time to move. Brother like that rolling with the rhythm of things.

When a Player STAYING CHILL on deep levels, his mind and heart turn real calm. He sees shit clear. That helps him move right. True Players meditate. Ain't have to be no monk for that shit. Just sit there breathing, stare at the motherfucking wall. Do it right, the whole world chill out. Drama just disappear a minute. Players STAYING CHILL at a deep level like that tune into rhythm of things. Make the right moves, at the right time. Ain't ever roll on bust ass plays.

THE LOOK

Buildings close together:
The look of Staying Chill.
True Player
Don't trip out on what ain't in his area.

Ain't no motherfucker ever stop thinking. But a True Player focus his thought. Thinks right here right now. Crab ass have his head all over the place. Tripping on shit downtown, while handling business uptown. Stresses on shit from last week, while dropping the ball today. True Player have his head where he's at. That's all.

THE BREAKS

Break on the one means:
Chilling his feet.
No problem.
Maintain a good look.

STAYING CHILL in the feet is about stopping before shit starts. A player sees things clear at the beginning. When the crew is small, brothers are tight. Motherfuckers know who's who, and what's up. But the more that crew gets over, the deeper into the game they go. Shit gets twisted. So Player stop a minute before he starts something. Holds onto that pure feeling while it's there. That helps him later, when the bullshit piles up.

Break on the two means:
Legs Staying Chill.
Can't help the brother he throw in with.
Damn shame.

Player throws in with a real brother. But then that motherfucker start rolling ill. Player knows shit won't shake out right, but that brother is mad powerful. Plus, his operation moving real fast. That's like running full speed and trying to stop one motherfucking leg. Ain't about to happen. This bullshit makes Player sad. No matter how bad he wants to help, he can't do nothing. The brother rolling ill will have to learn on his own. And lessons like that only learned the hard way. Damn shame.

Break on the three means:
Staying Chill with his joint.
All backed up.
Bad look. Pressure.

When a fire is smothered, flames die. But smoke is everywhere. That shit choke a brother to death. This break here about wanting something real bad. Like pussy a brother dying to hit. But the situation ain't right. Maybe it's another brother's woman, or she ain't having him, whatever. Brother shouldn't pretend that pussy don't have him hot and bothered. Them feelings too strong. If he try and smother the fire, he'll choke on the motherfucking smoke. Brother should just hit some other pussy, or play sports. Put that fire someplace to burn.

Break on the four means:
His heart Staying Chill.
No problem.

Brother here STAYING CHILL in his heart, so he sees real clear. But his head still tripping. Brother feel stress and doubt like a motherfucker. It's still a good look. Most brothers never even handle STAYING CHILL in their heart. Having the heart chill is the first step towards chilling the mind. So this brother will be alright.

Break on the five means:
His mouth Staying Chill.
Ain't talking shit.
Not a bad look.

In ill situations, some brothers talk too much. Telling jokes and rapping bullshit since they nervous. That fucks shit up more. When it's thick, True Player don't say much. His mouth STAYING CHILL.

Break at the top means:
Staying Chill on everything.
Paid.

Player here STAYING CHILL about everything. He knows how ill the game is. Don't bother him. He just do the right thing, whatever the situation. Then he handles what's next. Player don't trip on how shit shakes out. Don't stress about who's getting over. He ain't listen to shit streets saying. Just stays above all that, handling business. Brothers like that always get paid.

PUSH IT ALONG

Large trees in the park grow mad slow. Because that shit takes time, they have real strong roots. That's what's happening here: something large that builds slow.

To PUSH IT ALONG in the game, a brother have to be mentally chill. That way he don't stress situations or roll on stupid shit. His plays are smart and small. Little bit here, little bit there, he PUSH IT ALONG. Player like this grows slow, but he grows real strong. One day, he's so large that motherfuckers don't even think of stepping to him.

Like one them large trees in the park. Brothers never think of pulling that shit down. Thought never cross their mind. Them trees too large, yo.

THE FEEL

Push It Along.
Getting with fine female.
Paid.
Perseverance furthers.

Dealing with a fine female takes time. Player have to move slow. Real sisters make a brother invest dollars and time. She shake off the suckers that way.

Same feel for business. True Player handles investments slow. He don't throw down real dollars till shit been felt out for real. Motherfuckers who rush their business always get played. True Player lets situations develop. He PUSH IT ALONG, but don't force nothing. Large plays have their own timetable. True Players respect that.

Same shit for a brother who wants weight in the game. Player who wants to run shit have to be 100% together. If he wants brothers throwing in with him, rolling on his plays, he have to build respect. That takes time. Serious players don't just throw in with a brother. They watch the way he rolls, how he handle business, and ask around. If they respect what they see and like what they hear, maybe they throw in. That ain't happen overnight.

Always be some flashy motherfuckers. Talk game and put on a show. Brothers like that will always trick a few people. But their status don't hold, since their shit ain't real. What's good takes time. It takes time for a brother to set his heart right, get his head straight, and pull his game together.

To maintain his angle, Player stays chill. He PUSH IT ALONG, flowing with the times, switching shit up when streets change. Some brothers push hard. All they have is force. They hit walls and break them down. But one day, they hit a wall that's too hard to break. All they know is hitting shit hard. So they hit harder. That wall won't move. Those brothers don't stop. Just bust themselves to pieces.

A True Player who PUSH IT ALONG is like tree roots. Roots are always working, growing, and taking more ground. But they do it real slow. Nothing stop them motherfuckers. Roots hit a wall, they work around that shit. Roots hit a rock, they push that shit away, real slow. Little bit here, little bit there.

PUSH IT ALONG is a tough angle to maintain. Brothers feel like nothing's happening. So they fall off. It's hard to stay with shit day after day, bit by bit, and just PUSH IT ALONG.

THE LOOK

Large tree in the park:
The look of Push It Along.
True Player roll correct.
Set the standard.

Large tree in the park is something brothers see from far away. Like a landmark. But that tree ain't come up over night. Them roots PUSH IT ALONG and grow mad slow.

Becoming a True Player happens slow. Years of Player maintaining correct at every level he's rolling on. Years of Player checking himself. Then word gets around. Brothers recognize crisp game. Want to throw in with Player. Status like that takes time to build.

THE BREAKS

Break on the one means:
Bird find the fountain.
Young brother in a bad way.
People talk shit. No problem.

Little bird flies into the park alone. Real tired from all the flying to find the damn park. Lands at the first fountain it finds. This bird ain't from the area. Don't know if that fountain is bust ass or real. Bird just need some place to land and drink a minute.

That's like a brother first stepping into the game. He ain't have no people. Nobody give a fuck about him. This brother don't know nothing. Have no idea what angles to play or how. He's moving slow, looking around, trying to find what's real.

That's a dangerous spot to be. Because he don't know nothing, other brothers talk shit. Be like: "Who the fuck that dumb ass motherfucker?" But that makes this new brother extra careful. He check himself before he does anything. So them motherfuckers talking shit really help him, in the long game.

Break on the two means:
Bird find the right fountain.
Drinking chill with other birds. Singing.
Paid.

Every park have one fountain birds down with most. Built in some shade, far away, where people don't bother. If a bird new to the area finds that fountain, it's a good look. He's in the right place, with the right birds now.

That's like some brother who finds his first real place in the game. Put paid nice in a situation rolling right. First job like that really make a brother happy. Now he believes in himself more.

Birds in the park sing when they happy. Splash in the fountain, singing with all them other birds. That's the look for a brother who found his first place in the game. He should buy drinks for his friends. Get his girl some presents and shit. A brother should share his luck when it happens. Makes him feel good.

Break on the three means:
Bird fly to the high building.
Brother go out and ain't come back.
Family dropped.
Problems.
Good look to break it down on crab ass.

Very high buildings ain't no place for a bird to chill. Too much wind and shit. Little bird that try to build his nest there is tripping. If he fly up and start building, his shit will blow away.

That's like a brother new to the area. He really don't know the situation. So he just let it develop. If that brother fly off making moves, he upsets people. Ill motherfuckers he ain't even know about. Motherfuckers who don't play. Drop that brother and his whole family, just to set an example.

It don't have to be that way. If a brother new to the area just maintains a minute, he learns shit. Like who not to fuck with. If he don't bust off on plays, he don't start no beefs. All he have do is maintain his angle. Fight off crab asses who roll on him. Brother like that will be alright. Shit will open up for him that way.

Break on the four means:
Bird in bullshit tree.
Find that branch.
No problem.

Trees in the middle of the city ain't the right place for birds to build their nest. Those trees are bust ass. All them cars around blow smoke. Bird wants a motherfucking tree in the park. But sometimes a bird is real tired from flying. Just have to lay up a minute. So he land in one of them bust ass trees, right there in the city. It ain't the best spot. But maybe that bird can find one solid branch. Chill there a minute, catch his breath.

Putting a game together takes time. A brother will be up and down, and find his ass in bullshit places. Some those places are real dangerous. But if a brother stays chill and smart, he will always find a safe place to maintain a minute. Maybe not perfect, but something alright. That's fine. Especially when streets dangerous all round.

Break on the five means:
Bird high up.
Crab asses whisper. "His female do it on the side."
Down the line shit shakes out.
Paid.

Bird found the highest branch in the highest tree in the whole damn park. Set up his nest. That might be a good look, but when a Player climbs that high up the game, he's all alone. Crab asses will find a Player way high up like that. Start whispering shit in his ear. Get him thinking that his homeboy is playing him. Or that his female doing it on the side. This type of static will trip a Player out and freeze his action. But bullshit like that clears up down the line. Player will shake off them crab asses, regroup with his homeboy or his female. Then it's all good.

Break at the top means:
Bird fly away.
Leave a feather.
Good look.

A True Player's run is over. He dies and fly up to The Heavens. Like birds flying south in winter.

Most birds flying in the city are dirty motherfuckers nobody want to touch. But some real nice birds pass through on their way south in winter. Sometimes they leave a feather on the ground. People walking in the park find that shit. Them feathers look motherfucking beautiful.

True Player who lived right leaves something beautiful behind him when he dies. Like them classic records brothers made back in the day. Real positive shit people still dance with today. Maybe the brothers who made them records died, but they left some beautiful shit behind. Helps people remember what's right in the world.

SLIM THING

An older brother sometimes marries a young SLIM THING. Or a married brother sets up SLIM THING and hits that shit on the side. Relations that ain't formal still have rules.

THE FEEL

The Slim Thing.
Trouble.
Not a good look at all.

SLIM THING down with a married brother have to know what's up. She ain't the main female here, and have to respect her place. If she try and make her man leave his wife, shit falls apart. Older brother hardly ever leave his wife. Divorce courts are real expensive. Even if he does bounce, that shit leaves a bad taste in people's mouth. Streets know SLIM THING is the bitch he was hitting on the side. SLIM THING knows her man cheat and lie. Brother be older now, so he worried he don't have all that dick SLIM THING need. Meanwhile, the wife is working overtime to fuck both them two sideways.

If a SLIM THING wants her own man, she have to find some brother who ain't married. But if she like them older married brothers who take care her right, baby girl have to be real with the set up. She ain't the main female here. Just ass on the side.

Same thing true for all relationships that ain't formal. When shit ain't written down and a brother ain't on paper with people, he best chill. If he putting in work for brothers who ain't pulled him in 100%, he have to maintain low key. He ain't really in. Just being used. That ain't always a problem. This type of set up puts some dollars in a brother's pocket. Help him make connects. Maybe develop into real business down the line. But right now, he don't have shit to say about the operation. He's just some brother on the side.

That don't mean he can't be down with these motherfuckers. Even if the scenario ain't 100% legit, people still have to be feeling each other. Respect and some friendly bullshit is good for business. Same for that SLIM THING with the married brother. Be a million swinging dicks on them streets. Should find one she likes. And there be X amount of SLIM THING working at them malls serving ice cream. Many them young girls real nice. Older brothers don't want to bring no difficult bitch into their world. People have to be feeling each other in these set-ups, or this shit don't work.

Brothers in the SLIM THING scenario with an organization should be chill and low key. Recognize where they stand in the reality of things. Play it like that, shit shakes out right.

THE LOOK

Wind blowing waves in the lake.
The look of Slim Thing.
True Player

**Is down with shit changing
and good when things end.**

When the wind blows on the lake in the park, there's little waves. Waves follow the wind. Same thing with the SLIM THING who links up with an older brother. Since he holding the property and power, she follows him. But every relationship takes left turns. People fight. When shit gets real tangled, them fights don't make sense. Shit starts out about burned toast, finish up with SLIM THING throwing dishes about something happened last year.

That's why a brother with the SLIM THING have to plan everything. He always have to think of the end scenario. Know where he want every situation to end, and direct shit to get there. Brother can't just drift with whatever SLIM THING is doing or feeling. SLIM THING herself don't know what she's doing or feeling. She's just a baby. So older brother have to lead 100% on everything.

Even just talking. Brother have to know the motherfucking objective before he open his mouth. Simple shit gets real complex, real fast with a SLIM THING. Plot shit out like a best seller. Never lose focus with the SLIM THING. Baby girl will wear a brother out.

THE BREAKS

**Break on the one means:
Slim Thing ass on the side.
Brother shot in the leg still walking.
Maintain. Good look.**

Rich people back in the day rolled different. When those women married a rich brother, they down with the fact that he hit shit all over town. When they saw their man being bored, the smart wife found the SLIM THING herself. Like quality control. Choose a young girl she can handle.

Before she hand that ass over, wife break it down for SLIM THING. Make sure baby girl know who's the main female in the situation. That might sound bananas to regular working mother-fuckers. But back in the day, rich women were good with the fact that powerful brothers chased pussy. So if they wanted all that money and status he got, them women had to roll with his reality.

When wife pick the SLIM THING, she's controlling that shit. Now she ain't wondering where her man is late at night. She knows exactly where he's at. Probably knows exactly how he's hitting it, too. Laugh with her girlfriends about that, playing cards and shit. Make her man buy some real expensive jewels for that ass pass she handed him. Happy to flash that ice. SLIM THING have her rent paid, she's happy. Brother in the situation real happy, too. Have that young ass for fun, plus a real woman running his household.

Families who roll like that stay powerful. Hold onto their money since they don't have no motherfucking divorce lawyers robbing them. Raise children who have both parents and a home. Them children inherit that money and grow more powerful. The whole house roll through history holding onto their loot.

That all said, situation like this really depend on the SLIM THING. She have to know her place. She's ass on the side. That ain't changing. If baby girl try and flip her status, the whole scenario take a hard left turn. Every motherfucker involved gets played bad.

Same style applies to a particular situation that might happen in the organization. Maybe Big Dog like some brother who don't hold status in the operation. This brother just funny, or good to bullshit with. So Big Dog make this brother his homeboy. Drink liquor with him. Play golf and shit.

That ain't a problem long as this brother don't forget his place. He's just a funny motherfucker Big Dog laugh with. If the brother starts fronting like he has status, motherfuckers holding real status will break it down. Shake him out the organization. So this brother have to maintain chill and friendly. He don't have no power, but that don't mean he ain't have no influence. Brother like that does positive shit just by being real for the Big Dog. Most motherfuckers are playing angles.

This brother have to roll like somebody been shot in the leg. Moves forward with a limp. That ain't no threat to other motherfuckers running the race. Good look.

Break on the two means:
Brother with one eye.
Maintain solo.
Alright.

This about a SLIM THING who ain't ass on the side. She married an older powerful brother. But she chose the wrong motherfucker. Man and wife should be like two eyes working together, seeing shit right. But this SLIM THING all alone, because her man out partying all the time. That breaks her heart, but she ain't let it break her spirit. Like a brother with one eye. He ain't look right, and don't see 100% correct, but he still peep enough to get by. Hard life, but rent's paid.

Break on the three means:
Slim Thing a slave.
Maintain like a whore.

Real ugly girl sometimes find a place if she give it up like crazy. She's that sister brothers call when they drunk late at night. Do her five at a time, laughing. Since nobody want homegirl for real, she's down for all types of porno shit.

That's like a brother who's a real freak. Into ill sex and all them drugs. Hires some fucked up individuals to do what he like in the bedroom. He hides that action. Always feels bad the next day. But he don't stop. It ain't important to judge this brother or add no warning. Every motherfucker knows where that lifestyle lead.

Break on the four means:
Slim Thing maintains right.
Married late in the game.

This SLIM THING real pure. Church girl, all that. She ain't trying to throw her ass around. Problem is, she ain't find a real brother, and her clock is ticking. All her girlfriends getting married. Still, this sister maintain. She know what's right. Knows what she want. Heaven loves a female like that. So she gets hooked up with a real responsible brother, filled with respect for her, who makes a loving father for her children. Just happens late in the game for SLIM THING.

Break on the five means:
Old Big Dog set up daughter's wedding.
She dress down.
Moon almost full. Getting there.
Maintain. Paid.

Back in the day with them rich powerful families, marriage had very little to do with love. Shit was about connections, power, dynasty, and politics. Ain't no SLIM THING back then have shit to say about who she marry. Her father decided. Rich motherfuckers especially. Big Dog back in the day found a brother who fit his business plans.

His daughters were all princesses. But sometimes Big Dog might marry them to some ordinary brother he had plans for. Woman was supposed to follow her husband in them days. So no matter how rich she was brought up, and how fine she dressed, Big Dog's daughter had to put all that behind her. She moved into this motherfucker's bullshit little house and did what he said. He was the man, she was the woman. If SLIM THING didn't respect that, her father looked bust ass for raising a female who didn't act right. Family lost face.

We ain't seeing that much today. But there will be times in a brother's life when he have to take a step down to find the way forward. Sometime that's extreme. Like if some motherfucking manager run off with all his finance. Maybe his wife wipe him out in divorce. Or the game flips ill, real fast. Player have to pull out with nothing but his dick in his hand, just to save his ass. Brother in that situation have to survive. Take whatever job he can find. Might be sweeping floors a minute. That ain't easy to do if he was running things before. But shit happens. Life break a brother down sometime.

Way to handle losing status is forget it was ever there. Smart brother don't bring none his uptown shit into downtown situations. Just do what the boss tell him. Follows them rules, no matter how bust ass they feel. Probably be crying real tears at night. But the scenario is worse if he fronts like he still hold status. Life changes. Have to deal with shit realistic. Brothers who flip with the script fastest are the ones who shake out best.

Break at the top means:
Slim Thing hold the basket with bust ass fruit.
Brother bring sheep from the butcher.
Bad look.

Way back in the day, when primitive motherfuckers married, they bring something to show respect for Heavens at the altar. SLIM THING show up with a basket of fruit. Brother bring some farm animal, then cut the throat with a motherfucking knife, right there.

This break here talking about disrespectful people who don't give a fuck. Like a wedding back in the day, where SLIM THING show up with some bullshit basket of half ass fruit. Brother so lazy he ain't even slaughter that animal himself. Bring some shit the butcher already killed. Both them people ain't believing in shit. Just rolling through the motions.

More than a few motherfuckers married like that today. They ain't really respect marriage. They don't think much of them vows. Still hitting shit on the side. Don't particularly care for the motherfucker they at the altar with. But since everybody doing it, they do too. That's a bad look. Heaven ain't give a fuck about disrespectful crab asses like that.

LEGENDARY

When a tight crew been maintaining forever, and their shit starts popping off, it gets LEGENDARY. This is a rare time that only happens when many pieces fall right the fuck in place. First, Big Dogs are breaking off large change for brothers, putting everybody paid. Next, True Player is in charge, running a crew of real brothers. Crab asses are in retreat, and streets loving what's positive. LEGENDARY runs ain't happen often and don't last long. History channels on TV call this shit a *renaissance*.

THE FEEL

Legendary. Paid.
Big Dog full of power.
Don't trip.
Shine like the sun.

Ain't just any motherfuckers who pop off LEGENDARY shit. Starts with a True Player backed by a righteous Big Dog. Player views life real large. Paints beautiful pictures in his mind. Shit other motherfuckers ain't have the power to think of. Then True Player bring them pictures to life. Has the moves to pull it off. Has a tight crew and they feeling him. Throw in 100% with serious skills. When Big Dog puts the weight behind them motherfuckers, shit gets LEGENDARY. Runs like this are real special. They don't last too long.

A True Player might trip on that. Get sad knowing that LEGENDARY brothers have to fall apart some time. But that's a bad look. Only a True Player who don't trip like that can pull off LEGENDARY runs. Whatever's next don't matter. When shit gets LEGENDARY, it's time to shine.

THE LOOK

Thunder and lightning
The look of Legendary.
True Player handle static
And break it down.

This Wrexagram is like Break It Down. But the look of Break It Down is lighting and thunder. LEGENDARY is thunder then lighting.

In Break It Down, brothers still organizing, so rules ain't all clear. When True Player break it down, he's teaching what's right and wrong. So he hits like lighting. Fast, hard, and real clear. Then Player roll away like thunder. Leaves brothers scared, so they don't want to fuck with him.

But a crew only gets LEGENDARY when their shit been running for some time. Them motherfuckers established. Rules are clear. Every brother know what's right and wrong. In established organizations, rules are like thunder rolling around. Reminds motherfuckers lighting will come down if they fuck with shit. If brothers hear that thunder and still decide to step out of line, True Player breaks it down fierce. Hits like lightning. Real shocking shit. Makes it clear to motherfuckers what happens if they don't mind the damn thunder.

THE BREAKS

Break on the one means:
Destiny bring brothers together.
They roll ten years,
Ain't no mistake.
Step up. Recognized.

LEGENDARY brothers need clear heads and real energy. If Fate brings two brothers like this together, they can't roll too long together, or do too much. LEGENDARY times ain't about being low key. Motherfuckers have to step up and shine. That way they be recognized.

Break on the two means:
Thick in the house.
No sun, stars out.
Step up and brothers hate.
Just be true.
Paid.

Only an established organization pops off LEGENDARY. Brothers who been rolling together for a long time, with real serious game. Established organizations have many motherfuckers in the operation. That leads to brothers fighting for power. Sometime this causes problems for a True Player when shit gets LEGENDARY. Light might be shining outside, but the organization is dark inside. Plays get shut down by all them brothers fighting for power.

Maybe one real brother wants to set things right. But he can't go at it hard. If he try and shake shit up, motherfuckers will hate on him. Shut him out. What this brother have to do is hold onto what's right. Just in his heart. Shit like that influences people. One low key, righteous brother can lean situations his way.

Break on the three means:
Eclipse.
Stars in the daytime.
Brother break his arm. No problem.

When the sun is blocked, there's an eclipse. Middle of the day goes dark. That's like a Big Dog too deep in his people. Has a large crew and maintains in the middle of them motherfuckers. Never looks out to see what's real on them streets. Loses touch with reality. Listens to crab ass bitches up in his face whispering shit.

When it's like that, True Player can't do shit. Don't matter if he's sitting right next to the man. When Big Dog is too deep in his people, nothing positive happening. Running plays would be like trying to play ball with a broken arm. But this ain't Player's fault. Just how shit shaking out.

Break on the four means:
Shit so thick it have to break.
Sun return.
Brothers down and link up.
Paid.

Darkness in the organization is passing. Pieces are falling into place. Smart heads are lining up with brothers who make shit happen. That's what it takes. Brothers who make shit happen don't pop off without people who do the thinking. And lots of smart motherfuckers making plans, without brothers who make shit happen, don't pop off neither. Both need the other to roll LEGENDARY.

Break on the five means:
Serious breaks on the way.
Fame and paid soon.
Good look.

Big Dog is down and real. Brothers with ideas have a chance to talk. Big Dog listens. These smart motherfuckers be on some next level shit. When Big Dog sets their plays rolling, shit pops off LEGENDARY. Makes brothers rich, famous, and real happy. That's a good look.

Break at the top means:
Rich house.
Scream at his family.
Look through the gate.
Nobody there.
Three years ain't see nobody.
Fucked.

This about a stupid motherfucker who gets the opposite of what he want. Brother's dreaming of a real fine house filled with his people. He builds a damn mansion and puts guards and maids all over. Shit feel like a museum. Ain't nobody want to kick it there. He's tripping about being the man of the house. Runs shit fierce, yelling at motherfuckers, breaking it down right and left. Nobody wants to deal with that. People fall off. His own family up and leave. Brother ends up in some big old house, all alone. Fucked.

WREXAGRAM 56
BOUNCING

BOUNCING brother is on the move. Sees strange motherfuckers and places he ain't ever been before.

THE FEEL

Bouncing. Paid on little plays.
Maintain.
Good look for a brother Bouncing.

BOUNCING brother rolls wherever he want. Pass through places he ain't have people. So a BOUNCING brother can't front and be hard. He don't sweat motherfuckers, neither. Since a BOUNCING brother all alone, he just rolls chill and low key. Lives correct, so he don't bring drama into his life. Protects himself by being real careful. He's alright that way.

BOUNCING brother ain't homeless. Just prefers to keep shit moving. Maybe have some job relocate his ass. Always lands in places that ain't familiar. So BOUNCING brother have to tone shit down. Can't roll with sketchy brothers or party sisters. Can't kick it in places ain't 100% right, like after hours parties or card games. BOUNCING brother don't know the players or the game where he land. So he lives life clean. That helps him hold onto his money, and stay out of drama.

THE LOOK

Liquor on fire:
The look of Bouncing.
True Player
Clear his head. Step slow when he break it down.
Don't mix up in court.

Some motherfuckers drink that real strong proof liquor. There's always a brother who splash that shit on the ground for laughs. Throw down matches, light that liquor up. Burns real fast, then it's out.

That's what justice should be like. When a brother's being set straight by the system, it should be a fast burn. Not no slow roast. That shit drag on too long, it breaks his spirit.

When a BOUNCING brother land in new places, he don't know how the game run. Might break some laws he ain't familiar with. Or cross some motherfuckers he don't know about. If shit flips legal, BOUNCING brother should try and pass through the system fast as possible. When a brother's from out of town, in somebody else's court, he should just pay the fine. Don't matter how bullshit the charge. If they bring a brother in for drinking apple juice on Tuesday, he should show respect and pay the fine. Tell them motherfuckers it won't ever happen again.

This ain't about being right. It's about being smart. A brother with no people and no connects, who fights motherfuckers in their own court, is done. Then he's caught in the system. Prison ain't no place a brother want to be. Many motherfuckers cooling out there for long bids, on real stupid shit. They tried to be right instead of being smart. End up there all day. Prison turns into home for them brothers. That's a real problem. When shit is running right, prisons are like a motherfucking hotel. Brothers check in, pay their bill, then leave. It's ill when brothers living in prisons like home. Nothing right about that. Bad for everybody.

THE BREAKS

Break on the one means:
Bouncing brother play with crab asses.
Play himself.

BOUNCING brother shouldn't bullshit too much. He don't want to be mixed up with silly motherfuckers and crab asses. Rolling professional maintains his reputation. BOUNCING brother dead wrong if he thinks laughing and acting like some fucking clown will put him in good. It won't. Brothers will just think he's bullshit.

Break on the two means:
Bouncing brother finds a hotel.
Has his money.
Finds a slim thing.

BOUNCING brother here is low key. He rolls correct, travels right, and finds a place to put down a minute. He's real with people in the neighborhood. They feel him, pull him into business. Help that brother find a job. Brother gets paid, puts down roots. Then he finds a sweet young slim thing. She takes care him right. That's beyond value. Love is priceless for a motherfucker with no people, just BOUNCING.

Break on the three means:
Bouncing brother evicted.
Lose his slim thing.
Bad look.

Some bullshit BOUNCING brother rolls into town. He don't act right. Puts himself in people's business. Talks politics and shit. Nobody like this motherfucker. Hotel tell him to check the hell out. Brother drinks liquor and takes it out on his slim thing. Tells baby girl she ain't shit. Slim thing walk right out the door. Now this motherfucker alone. That's a real bad look. When a strange brother is in a strange land, without no people, shit gets real dangerous.

Break on the four means:
Bouncing brother find a home.
Bank money, work job.
Heart ain't happy.

BOUNCING brother knows how to look low key, even though he's a player inside. That helps him find his place. Picks up a job, puts down money on a home, maintains. But he don't feel like he belongs. Never really gets in with the people living there. Feels like them motherfuckers trying to trip him up. So it ain't easy living. He always feels like the brother from out of town.

Break on the five means:
Perfect gift.
Bulls eye.
Good look. In on the game.

Traveling salesmen back in the day made it a point to show up in town with gifts for the Big Dog. Not just some shit they pick up on the way. Them motherfuckers did research to find the perfect gift for whatever Big Dog they about to meet. Put real money down. BOUNCING brothers like that were real smooth. Showed they know how to roll. Big Dogs liked that. Either bought some shit or pulled that brother into his crew.

Life throws different shit at a brother. Sometimes a motherfucker who ain't the BOUNCING type have to find a home in places he ain't ever been. If he rolls crisp, and plays that situation right, he might find some brothers who are down with him. Maybe even get in on the game there. Make some real money.

Break at the top means:
Bird nest burning.
Bouncing brother party and bullshit first,
Then sad and crying.
Lose his ride.
Bad look.

BOUNCING brother lost his shit. He let himself go, all party and bullshit, forgetting he's a motherfucker from out of town. When nobody knows a brother, he should roll low key and professional. If he gets stupid, that motherfucker will blow it. Lose his chance at finding work. Lose all his money. Have to sell his ride just to put food on the table. That's a bad look, yo.

LIGHT TOUCH

Some shit in life have to be handled with a LIGHT TOUCH.

Real ill shit that is crazy dark best handled with a LIGHT TOUCH. Like some little shorty who been fucked with. Little ones don't understand that shit. Get real damaged at deep levels. It takes soft words and a LIGHT TOUCH, for a real long time, before shorty feel right about the world. Some shit have to be put right like wind blowing clouds cross the sky. Real soft breeze, barely felt.

Ill motherfuckers can be beat back with a LIGHT TOUCH on the mental. If a Player thinks right, all the time, ain't no way into his game. Shit never gets hard and physical. His thoughts shut down ill motherfuckers with the LIGHT TOUCH.

True Players have a LIGHT TOUCH in the game. Be so real, they change the situation just by showing up. People see that True Player and remember what's good. Ill motherfuckers lose their grip and fall right the fuck off.

THE FEEL

Light Touch. Paid in small plays.
Good look to move.
Good look to say what up to Big Dog.

The LIGHT TOUCH works without being seen. Ain't no secret shit, just real low key. It don't stop working on a situation. Brothers who get over with a LIGHT TOUCH ain't dramatic. They don't blow right the fuck up out of nowhere. But they last longer, since their game been building forever.

Think on baseball. One motherfucker shoot himself up with steroids. Home run hero for a few seasons. Then he fall off. Put before the commission on drug charges. Done. Meanwhile, there's this other motherfucker playing for Cincinnati or some shit. He just bat singles but ain't ever miss. Have a twenty year career. That's the LIGHT TOUCH, right there.

A brother rolling with the LIGHT TOUCH needs clear goals. Since his game moves slow, it's easy to lose direction. Or just fall off. LIGHT TOUCH is a good look for brothers who ain't have much weight in the game. But it only really works if they down with some hard motherfucker who rolls deep. Always be situations where a brother have to break it down. LIGHT TOUCH don't do that.

THE LOOK

Wind ain't stop blowing.
The look of Light Touch.
True Player

Run the game all over.
Brothers roll for him.

Wind has power if it don't stop blowing. Wind just blow a minute, nothing happen. But if that wind blows for hours, it moves large clouds. Blow for years, it changes the landscape. Time is what makes wind powerful.

True Player with the LIGHT TOUCH only moves brothers by maintaining all the time. Shit done right from day one. No stopping. Time passes and motherfuckers start feeling him. Player starts running shit then. But if Player ain't real every day, for a long ass time, brothers won't recognize. Motherfuckers don't roll for a player like that.

THE BREAKS

Break on the one means:
Back and forth.
Maintain like military.

Brothers with the LIGHT TOUCH sometimes drift. Change their mind too much. Think shit won't work out. Don't trust their decisions. Brother in that situation have to check himself and stop tripping. Call the damn play and roll with it. Being hard like that is much better than drifting.

Break on the two means:
Ill brothers in the shadows.
Fight for the priests.
Paid. No problem.

Sometimes True Player don't see the enemy. He's fighting hardcore brothers hiding in dark places. These motherfuckers ain't ever show their face. Just whisper shit that moves through the game. Turn people that way. Sinister shit.

Player have to find out where these motherfuckers hiding. Learn what type of ill power they throwing. Then Player have to reach out for priests. Fighting ill dark shit like that is spiritual warfare. Real fierce powers that battle in the mental. But when them ill brothers are pulled into the light, they're done. Without a mask in the dark, bitches like that ain't shit. Bunch of corny motherfuckers, really.

Break on the three means:
Tripping on shit. Bust ass.

Brother should think shit through without tripping. When shit turn left, he puts his head around the problem. Decides the right play, then rolls on it. That's all. Brothers who trip on the problem for too long are fucked. Always find shit they think they missed. Or some part of the answer that don't seem 100% right. Motherfuckers like that show streets they don't handle business right. Makes them look bust ass. Bad look.

Break on the four means:
No problem.
Paid three times.

Player is real experienced, with status in the game. He rolls low-key but powerful. His style and skills put him paid three times more than anybody. Since Player is paid large, he moves it three different ways. First he shows respect to The Heavens. Throws money into the community. Maybe look out for them old people, or build a playground for the children, start some scholarships, help the churches, whatever. Next level of paper passed off to his people. Brothers who been down with him from day one. Motherfuckers who helped him get over. Player makes sure they cared for.

What's left goes his way. Sets himself up with nice real estate, lives fine. The Player paid large who moves it right is the height of success, yo.

Break on the five means:
Maintain. Paid.
No problem.
Everything work out.
Bad start, but it ends.
Before the jump, three days.
After the jump, three days.
Paid.

Shit Been Spoilt is when shit so fucked, brothers hit the reset. Don't need that here. In this situation, LIGHT TOUCH will set the situation straight. Handling the changes right is important. Player in charge maintains real crisp and sees shit clear. Before he decides how to roll, Player thinks up, down, and sideways on the motherfucker. Runs his plays then watches them like a hawk. Makes sure shit shake out right. Player mad careful like that puts his people paid.

Break at the top means:
Into the darkness.
Lost his money. Lost his mind.
Maintaining is a bad look.

Brother here understands things. Reads deep into the scenario, learns all the hidden shit fucking with brothers minds. Follows those ill powers to the darkness where they hide. But brother don't have the muscle to fight them shady motherfuckers wearing masks. Their darkness is too deep. If this brother rolls on them, he's done. First he loses his money, then he loses his mind. Some shit in this world just too damn ill. Step off, yo.

HAPPY

Sometimes a motherfucker just HAPPY. That's best handled low key. A brother should maintain his heart steady on the inside, and be chill on the outside when he's HAPPY.

THE FEEL

Happy. Paid.
Maintain.
Good look.

When Player's real HAPPY, his people feel that. Then they HAP-PY. That's a good look. Business rolls well for happy motherfuckers. Ain't nobody hand their money to brothers looking like they lost their teddy bear. But HAPPY brothers have to maintain. Otherwise them feelings bust out into party bullshit. Operations lose focus when people run around popping champagne.

When a True Player is real HAPPY, he holds his heart steady. That don't mean he's frowning. He just ain't throwing motherfucking confetti around. Heavens love a Player who maintains himself level.

Steady in the bad, steady in the good. Brothers feel that shit, too. Have respect and put in work for Player.

Hard motherfuckers run their operation different. Break it down all the time. Put fear in brothers. Make people jump. That works for a little while. It don't maintain for the long game. Brothers have a limit on that shit. One day they have enough. Tell that hard motherfucker to eat a dick. Or drag their heels in his operation, slow down business. Maybe wait for him in the parking lot one night. Boom.

But a HAPPY Player wins some motherfucking hearts. Brothers do extraordinary shit for them Players. History is filled with famous generals that soldiers loved. Brothers rolled out and died for them. That's the power of positivity. Nobody catch a bullet for some motherfucker they hate.

THE LOOK

Brews chilling together:
The look of Happy.
True Player down with his people.
Talk shit over. Share knowledge.

One brew ain't no party. That's a brother drinking alone. Bunch of brews chilling together brings people together. That's positive. Brothers together share shit they know. Knowledge lifts people up. Like a nice cold brew. Learning is best when brothers just kick shit around. Talking together, learning new tricks, throwing down stories, whatever. Brothers HAPPY when that's happening. Pick up moves for their game. Get excited. That ain't happen when some boring motherfucker stand there telling people what to think. That's bullshit. Brothers love to learn when knowledge is shared by motherfuckers having fun. That's when brothers just light the fuck up. HAPPY.

THE BREAKS

Break on the one means:
Brother Happy chilling.
Good look.

This brother is HAPPY with his damn self. He ain't need shit from the world. He's good with who he is, and what he has. Motherfucker HAPPY just chilling. He put his heart right. Have his HAPPY on the inside, where nobody can fuck with it. That's a good look.

Break on the two means:
Real.
Happy.
Good look.
No problem.

Sometimes a brother find himself where crab asses partying. Them motherfuckers ain't have responsibilities. Just smoke out, drink liquor, put their dick in whatever they want. True Player don't have time for that shit. He ain't really HAPPY doing it, neither. True Player needs real shit that means something. A brother who realizes this stops being tempted. Motherfuckers stop passing him shit, since he never pick up. Partying crab asses got no love for a brother who don't get stupid. Makes them fade off. That's a good look. Brother ain't have to deal with their bullshit no more.

Break on the three means:
Happy just roll up.
Bad look.

HAPPY have to be inside. If some empty brother tries to get HAPPY from the world, all sorts of motherfuckers show up. Wild brothers pulling jobs, heads with ill dust to smoke, freaky bitches with nasty pussies, whatever. Lots of brothers roll with that shit just because they bored. Motherfuckers with nothing real in their heart need to be entertained. Brothers like that always find a chance to party. Streets hear they a party motherfucker, so more party bullshit rolls up. Makes them party more. Then they're lost. Party motherfuckers ain't worth shit in the game. That's a bad look.

Break on the four means:
Deciding on Happy ain't right.
Check himself. Brother Happy now.

Many times, a brother find himself tripping on which way to roll. Party life is sexy. All that fat ass, drugs, good liquor and smoke looks good. Long as he's tripping on that shit—even if he ain't up in it—a brother is fucked in the head. But when a brother finally realize that heavy party have heavy payback, he's alright. After that decision, a brother feels much better. Just turns away from all that party shit. Don't trip on it no more. Then he's HAPPY.

Break on the five means:
Rolling with shady motherfuckers.
Danger.

Shady motherfuckers roll up on even the best brothers. If he let himself have anything to do with them, even slightly, their shady shit rubs off on him. And never for the positive. But if a brother recognizes these motherfuckers are straight up dangerous—-no matter how smooth they roll up—he shuts them out. His game stays crisp that way. No problem.

Break at the top means:
Carried away.

Silly motherfuckers always find shit to distract them. If a brother ain't real inside, party bullshit just carry him away. Ain't no question what happens next. When a brother stops maintaining, and starts partying, it's like letting go of the steering wheel in life. He ain't driving no more. Has no say in the direction shit takes. Whatever happens just happens. That ain't where a motherfucker wants to be in this world.

BREAK IT UP

When pressure make a brother tense, and he don't have no outlet, he have to BREAK IT UP. He do this with a light touch. BREAK IT UP ain't about smashing shit apart.

THE FEEL

Break It Up. Paid.
Old Big Dog went to church.
Good look to roll cross town.
Maintain and get over.

This Wrexagram looks like BRING IT TOGETHER, where True Player bringing together all the brothers and making the crew. But BREAK IT UP happens when the crew already been put together. There's static from egos here. Different heads think their way is the right way. Every motherfucker feel he's the smart one. That shit splits crews apart. Ain't a good look. Player have to step in and BREAK IT UP. That brings everybody together again, and puts shit back on track. It's best done with a light touch, yo.

Way back in the day, motherfuckers were mad religious. Few times a year, people in the village all come together for a real large ceremony. Everybody wearing robes, singing and dancing, playing them drums. They kill some goats together, light fires, all that. Joints like that brought brothers together on real deep levels. People forgot their personal shit and bonded with motherfuckers. When it finished, them feelings remained. People held that bond. Did business straight and minded the community. That's why Big Dogs back in the day ran them ceremonies like clockwork. It helped hold their people together.

Another way to bring brothers together is set a real high goal. Like when a nation go to war. Everybody throw in on that joint. Whole society become like a boat trying to cross the river. Every motherfucker put their back into it and row. Shit like that works in organizations, too. Brothers need goals. Real large goals that are hard to hit make motherfuckers pull together.

But only a True Player with the best interests of the whole organization can BREAK IT UP right. He don't do shit for his own advantage. He wants what's best for every motherfucker. If he run shit fair, and do shit right, Player will be able to BREAK IT UP correct. That stops the ego tripping, and keeps motherfuckers from drifting in different directions.

THE LOOK

Ice freeze and melt:
The look of Break It Up.
Old Big Dog killed a goat for the Gods.
Built fine churches.

In winter, park lakes freeze to ice. When spring come, that hard ice melts. It happens natural and easy.

Many brothers in the game get real hard and selfish. Pull back from people. Stop rolling with scenarios. Just trip on their ego. Think they the motherfucking man. Makes them mad isolated. They ain't flow with brothers no more.

That's why a True Player have to make brothers believe in something large. To pull off a real serious play, he have to reach motherfuckers' heart. Make them feel like they changing the world. Tell his people they on some legendary shit. Stakes that high will melt all them hard brothers, get them flowing together.

THE BREAKS

Break on the one means:
Move fast. Help.
Paid.

True Players crush static in a heartbeat. When storm clouds roll in, they BREAK IT UP before the lighting and thunder start. True Player tunes into situations at a deep level. He feels ill shit before it pops off. The minute brothers have static, Player moves fast. Pins down what's wrong between them motherfuckers and BREAK IT UP. He don't let shit build up. Or it blows up. That's a bad look.

Break on the two means:
Brother Break It Up.
Lean on the right things.
Good look.

When a brother been through x-amount of bullshit in the game, he sometimes turn hard. Starts feeling the world is shit, and everybody in it a motherfucker. That's a bad look. A True Player who starts feeling hate in his heart have to BREAK IT UP.

Starts by remembering all the good shit that happened in his life. Plays that got over. Brothers who looked out for him. Females who had love for him. Situations that shook out nice. Whatever good ever happened to him, Player remembers. That helps him realize shit ain't always fucked.

After that, Player shift focus to whatever he's hating on now, and stops tripping. Just BREAK IT UP. Player who checks himself like this will shake off the hate and roll right.

Break on the three means:
He Break It Up on himself.
No problem.

When shit is real ill, Player don't think of himself. To fix the situation, he might have to roll on plays that don't match what he wants in life. But they lead to good shit for his people. So Player takes all his hopes and dreams, and BREAK IT UP.

When a Player lets go of what he wants from life, he becomes real powerful. A brother like that is free. He sees shit straight, since he ain't looking for nothing. That lets him roll on real large moves for his people. But this only works in dramatic situations. Do or die, change the game type shit.

Break on the four means:
Break it up with his people.
Seriously paid.
Break It Up turns to pulling it in.
Regular brothers don't think this way.

When a Player's rolling on a real large play for the whole organization, he can't play favorites. Thinking of his homeboys first will fuck shit up. So Player have to forget his homeboys for a minute. Very few brothers are able to roll like this. Takes a real deep Player to let go of the motherfuckers right in front of him, to take hold of a larger piece, further down the line, for the whole crew.

Break on the five means:
Shout out. Sweat break the fever.
Break It Up. Player maintain.
No problem.

After a Player BREAK IT UP in the organization, shit is disorganized. Rolling on a large play fixes that. A big move works like a magnet pulling motherfuckers back together. Helps break up whatever was ill in the crew. Brothers be like: "Oh shit, that's a large play. We put paid with that." Forget their bullshit and throw in together.

Break at the top means:
Break It Up for blood.
Bouncing, backing off, rolling for them.
Good look.

BREAK IT UP for blood means heading off a beef before bullets start flying. And Player don't just look out for himself. He helps the motherfuckers who roll with him. Maybe he sees them in a hot area. Tells them to BREAK IT UP and bounce before shots start popping off. Or he hears some his people are dealing with shady brothers who run sideways game. Player tell them to BREAK IT UP and saves their money. Or maybe some of his homeboys are in a tight corner and need some muscle. Player rolls through to BREAK IT UP, helps them brothers out. That's a good look.

LIMITS

Large parks have lakes in them. Lakes have LIMITS. If water goes past the LIMITS, lake overflows. Fucks up the park.

Brothers need LIMITS in life. Lot of motherfuckers don't like LIMITS. But that shit is necessary. True Player LIMITS himself mentally. He's real about his abilities and the reality of other brothers. He knows the LIMITS of loyalty. He don't push people too hard. He don't roll for other motherfuckers on plays he ain't feeling, no matter who's running them. True Player also understands the LIMITS of being chill. He knows when to be low key about shit, and when a motherfucker has to break it down.

THE FEEL

Limits. Paid
Hardcore Limits ain't a good look.

Ain't nobody like LIMITS, but they help. If a brother LIMITS his spending when times are good, he ain't hungry when the game throws a lean stretch his way. LIMITS with cash save a brother from going bust ass, and keeps streets from talking shit about his business.

302

LIMITS run the world. Summer don't last forever. Winter don't, neither. Night and day have LIMITS, just like months and years. Shit is set up that way so time means something. Money works the same way. A smart brother puts LIMITS on cash flow. Makes a budget and stays with it. That holds his business together and keeps his people taken care of.

But LIMITS shouldn't be too hardcore. If a brother put real hard LIMITS on himself, it ain't healthy. He should throw money around and live some. Shit like that is good for a brother. Organizations shake out the same way. If Player puts real hard LIMITS on his people, they tell him to fuck off at some point. So there should be LIMITS on a motherfuckers LIMITS.

THE LOOK

Water in the lake.
The look of Limits.
True Player
Measure shit out,
Checks the essence. Comes correct.

A lake has LIMITS. But water don't. More water in the world than anybody know. That shit keep raining right the fuck down. But a lake only holds so much water. That's what makes it a motherfucking lake. If a lake don't know LIMITS, and try to hold more water, it turns into a swamp. Lake stays a lake by knowing the LIMITS.

Brothers the same way. A Player can't do everything in the world. Streets ain't seeing no brain surgeon NBA first draft pick race car driving lawyer hip hop movie star with a motherfucking muffin shop. Smart brothers put LIMITS on their game. They focus on one particular area and pop off there. Motherfucker without

LIMITS is all over the place. Real brothers respect their LIMITS. They know LIMITS help them focus. True Players stay free in their heart and mind, but put LIMITS on their actions. They decide what they want to do in life. Decide who they want to be. Then put LIMITS on whatever ain't part of that.

THE BREAKS

Break on the one means:
Not rolling on just whatever.
Nobody talk shit.

Many times, a brother who wants to make a real play in the game finds himself facing serious LIMITS. He just can't get past them. A smart brother knows when to stop. By understanding when to chill, he saves his power. He maintains where he's at, getting stronger, learning shit, looking for that opening. When it shows up, he pops off like a motherfucker. Pulls a strong, fast play and gets right the fuck over. That happens because he knew when to chill, instead of throwing himself at shit. Knowing when to roll and when to maintain are the most important parts of pulling off real plays in the game.

Old Big Dog break it down like this:

Problems start with words.
If the Big Dog talk shit he loses
Brothers from the streets who threw in with him.
If brothers from the street talk shit, they lose their job.
If shit just coming together isn't handled right,
Pulling it off ain't easy.
So a True Player don't talk much.
He don't just roll on whatever.

Break on the two means:
Not popping off.
Fucked.

It's smart to lay back when timing ain't right. But once LIMITS fall away, Players don't trip. They don't wonder and worry about shit. When it's time to roll, Players hit it. Nothing worse in life than missing that one chance to get over. Brothers don't really recover from that. Bring that shit to their grave.

Break on the three means:
Brother without Limits
Laugh now. Cry later.
No Problem.

If a brother just want to party and chase pussy, he forgets his LIMITS real easy. If he go all in on that shit, payback isn't pretty. Laugh now, cry later type shit. Brother like that can't be blaming others. When he realize his problems happened because he been acting like a stupid motherfucker, shit turns around. No problem, then.

Break on the four means:
Good with Limits. Paid.

LIMITS that make a brother too hard on himself ain't worth it. He waste time and energy trying to force LIMITS he ain't have the strength to respect. But LIMITS that feel more natural always work out right. If a brother wants to hit large ribs, extra chicken and a mess of brew one night, alright. He shouldn't ruin his life fighting what feels natural. But LIMITS that save his time and money always help. If he's good with LIMITS like that, a brother maintains without too much stress. Then he's ready for the jump when its time.

Break on the five means:
Nice Limits put a brother paid.
Maintaining. Good look.

LIMITS have to be played right. A brother is bullshit if he puts LIMITS on his crew without respecting those LIMITS himself. Motherfuckers will hate him, and hate the LIMITS he put on them. Start drama. But if the brother in charge puts LIMITS on himself first, and shows why, it's a good look. Brothers will see the LIMITS doing something positive, and fall in with that shit.

Like some brother who don't drink and play real ball. He ain't walk around telling motherfuckers not to drink liquor. He just play so crisp and real they start thinking "Damn, maybe if I chill out on this brew I play like that motherfucker there."

If Player set a good example by respecting LIMITS, brothers will pick up on that shit and fall in. People put paid.

Break at the top means:
Hard Limits.
Maintaining a bad look.
No more tripping.

If some motherfucker put real hard LIMITS on brothers, that shit don't last. The harder he come down with them LIMITS, the worse it get. At some point, brothers step up and break his ass down. Same shit with a brother's body. Try and live like a motherfucking monk, a brother's body send some fucked up messages his way. That said, sometimes a brother have to put real hard LIMITS down. When it comes to hard drugs, wrong shit in the bedroom, crime, or anything that make him feel real bad the next morning, a brother have to be ruthless on himself. Put them hard LIMITS down. That's the only way he saves himself from ill situations that wreck his life.

FOR REAL

A brother with heart is FOR REAL. He treats people lower down the chain right. He's solid with players high up the chain, too. Does what True Player says and handles shit right. People feel that. Say the brother's FOR REAL.

THE FEEL

For Real. Animals.
Paid.
Good look to roll cross town.
Maintain.

Animals don't understand words. But they understand what mother-fuckers be about. Animals feel shit. Dogs either down with a brother or bark at his ass. Nobody fools animals. They know who's FOR REAL.

Brothers who ain't smart, brothers who ain't right, and brothers real rough feel shit out like animals. They ain't use their head to listen to a player. Just feel from the heart. Motherfuckers like this see through all the fronting. Smooth words don't work on them. They don't fall for bullshit. Just know who's FOR REAL.

What matters to motherfuckers like that is being FOR REAL. That's it. The rest is details. If a Player want to lean this type of brother his way, he can't run game, talk nice, or bust out business plans. Just step up FOR REAL. Let motherfuckers sniff him out.

Once they decide Player's FOR REAL, that's a damn good look. Streets hear that shit. Be like: "You hear who threw in with Player? He must be FOR REAL, yo." Streets know fake motherfuckers never get love from those rough and simple brothers.

Being FOR REAL bonds brothers at deep levels. It's more than just business. Nothing special about motherfuckers feeling tight while they rolling on the same play. Murderers and criminals are down with each other on a job. Them feelings just based on business. Once business wraps, brothers peel off and forget. Even flip on each other. That shit happens because them motherfuckers had nothing holding them together that was FOR REAL. They was just in the same place, wanting the same shit. That's all.

But a player who's FOR REAL holds brothers together at deep levels. They believe in Player and feel him with their heart. That bond don't fall off when business wraps. Player who bonds FOR REAL with his people knows they down for whatever. If he have to roll on some motherfuckers cross town, they throw in FOR REAL.

THE LOOK

Waves in the lake.
The look of For Real.
True Player thinks through ill situations.
Holds off on breaking it down.

When wind blows some on the lake, it just makes ripples. But when wind blows real hard and deep into that lake, it makes waves. True Player who is FOR REAL handles problems in the crew like that. Before he break it down on a motherfucker, he move deep into that brother's heart. Player try real hard to see shit their way, and understand why that brother acted like he did. Player ain't just stay on the surface of things. He moves deep into the situation, so he feels it FOR REAL.

When Player fully understands why a brother dropped the ball, and decides not to break it down, he's running his crew with heart. That don't mean Player's weak. It means he sees clear, feels his people FOR REAL, and understands their problems. Motherfuckers love a Player like that. Brothers realize they dealing with a Player who respects them. It's real rare in life that a motherfucker feels somebody trying to understand him. Brothers show love for that. They don't want to drop the ball or fuck up no more. They roll for Player 100%.

THE BREAKS

Break on the one means:
Being ready makes a brother paid.
Shady plays trip a motherfucker out.

Bonds FOR REAL depend on a Player with a steady mind who's always ready. Whatever pops off, he makes the right play. His moves are FOR REAL because they come from the heart. He just act natural and shit falls into place. But a motherfucker who build bonds playing shady angles is fucked. That shit works against him. He ain't have no freedom, because he's depending on schemes and sideways game. The more he build that way, the more he trips out. Brother's always stressing if them shady bonds will hold when push comes to shove. He loses sleep, feels scattered. Can't be natural, because so much of his shit runs shady and sideways. Motherfuckers like that ain't FOR REAL.

Break on the two means:
Bird call out from the tree.
Baby bird answer.
Have some brews.
Let's drink some, yo.

Player moves brothers FOR REAL without trying. People just on the same vibe with him. Like a mama bird in the park calling out to her baby birds. Mama bird don't have to show itself and go looking. Just start singing and all them baby birds hear the song. Fly right the fuck over and be like: "Yo, what up." Player with positive vibes pulls brothers to him the same way. Brother like that never find himself alone. Motherfuckers just want to roll with him. They feel good with him.

Vibrations are real mysterious shit. Everybody have their own. People feel that shit at deep levels. When a Player who's FOR REAL have the right vibrations, they travel far and wide.

First, his vibe hits motherfuckers out there looking for something positive. Since they looking for what's good, their minds are open. When Player shows up, doing shit FOR REAL, these brothers be the first to throw in. Then word spreads. Other heads start leaning Player's way. But a brother can't force his vibes. Just have to live his life, and be who he is. Power from the heart is real mysterious. But it works FOR REAL.

Old Big Dog break it down like this:

True Player chills in his room.
He talk right, brothers one thousand miles away will hear him.
If True Player chilling in his room talking trash,

Motherfuckers one thousand miles away will hear that shit.
Break his ass down maybe.
Words go out a brother's mouth and influence motherfuckers.
Shit a brother does when he's alone affects people he ain't met yet.
Money and connects is what makes most motherfuckers powerful.
Words and action are what make a True Player powerful.
If he don't talk and act right, True Player falls off.
So True Player watch what he say, and watch what he do.
That shit moves in ways brothers don't understand.

Break on the three means:
Brother fall in love.
Now he throw a party, dancing and shit.
Now he crying. Now he singing again.

A brother who falls in love loses himself. He puts his happiness in the hands of that female. When she treat him right, he's laughing and singing. When she treat him bad, he's crying and shit. If a brother depends on other people for his feelings, he's fucked. Just goes up and down, heaven one day hell the next. Love is a trip. Whether that shit is bad or good a brother have to decide for himself.

Break on the four means:
Full moon near.
Straight ahead. Run that race.
Ain't nobody talking shit.

To make himself better, a brother should look up to somebody rolling right. That way he gets knowledge, like moon reflects light from the motherfucking sun. Brother don't front on the player he's trying to learn from. Always shows respect. Same with The Heavens. Brothers looking up for answers have to be respectful.

When a brother finds what he needs to learn, he should move forward. Nobody wins the race looking back over their shoulder.

Roll straight ahead. It don't matter how other brothers maintain. Player stays FOR REAL by focusing forward. That lets him move natural, through whatever bullshit popping off.

Break on the five means:
For real, holding it together.
No problem.

Big Dog here holds shit together with the force of personality. He's so FOR REAL, ain't ever have to break it down. Just shows up and shit leans his way. Since he's FOR REAL like that, Big Dog holds all the motherfuckers in his operation together. Without heart like that, brothers hold together for reasons that ain't strong. Fall apart when the first ill shit hits them.

Break at the top means:
Rooster sing to heaven.
Maintain. Bad look.

Roosters crow at dawn. That sound goes up in the sky. But roosters can't fly. A brother can talk shit, and motherfuckers will listen. Maybe even throw in a minute. But if all that brother have is words, his game ain't FOR REAL. Shit will fall apart when he needs it most. That's a bad look.

LITTLE PLAYS

Bullshit brother in a powerful position is a bad look. When a motherfucker who don't know shit is running things, True Players don't try large moves. Just runs LITTLE PLAYS.

THE FEEL

Little Plays. Paid.
Maintain.
Little Plays here and there. Nobody getting over.
Check that bird in the park.
Don't fly to the sun.
Alright flying low.
Paid large.

Low key brothers are always appreciated. But nobody likes a bitch. True Player maintains respect and handles situations right. Sometimes he rolls real low key. Other times he bring it up a notch. Make motherfuckers feel his weight.

When it's time for LITTLE PLAYS, large moves don't fly. Ain't the time to shoot for them motherfucking stars. Player just maintain his place. Thinks on them birds in the park. Birds don't try and fly to the sun. They chill lower in the sky. Stay nearby the nest. That's the feel of LITTLE PLAYS.

THE LOOK

Thunder in the office building.
The look of Little Plays.
True Player show respect when he roll.
Feels shit. Sad.
Mind that money.

Top floor in an office building is scary shit when storms hit. Wind shake that building. Lighting and thunder happen right out the motherfucking window. Player up there feels shit much deeper than brothers down in them streets.

True Player lives at a higher level. He sees, feels and hears shit much different from ordinary brothers. Like he's on the top floor in the storm, while they down in the streets. True Player tuned into shit much stronger than ordinary motherfuckers.

That's why he's more thoughtful than other brothers. He's deep about every move he makes. That sometimes looks fucked to other people. They don't know why he's so serious about shit. It also means True Player feels life hard. When his people drop or fall out the game, True Player is hit right through the heart. And because he's playing long game, with an eye to running shit, he's mad careful with his finance. Spends light, puts money into investments and shit.

Ordinary brothers will say he's a cheap motherfucker who don't know how to throw money around. Give him shit for not hanging out and whatever. Or that True Player think too much. Or that he care too much about motherfuckers and should lighten up. But really, True Player is living that way for them. His job is leading normal brothers through the world. That's why he feels deeper and rolls different.

THE BREAKS

Break on the one means:
Little bird gets fucked trying to fly.

Baby bird have to stay in the nest till it learns how to fly. Try and step out before them wings working, baby bird is fucked. But some situations are so ill, Player have to pull wild style moves. Like jumping out the motherfucking nest. But that's last resort, when nothing else working. In every situation, Player maintains business as usual for long as possible. If he flies off too fast, he burns out and don't make nothing happen.

Break on the two means:
Slim thing pass the father in church,
Say what up to mother.
Player don't reach Big Dog.
Meets brother up the chain.
No problem.

When a brother's knocking boots with some young slim thing, he ain't think of that girl as family. But when slim thing sees that brothers' moms in church or something, she should show respect. Just a proper *hello ma'am* is a good look. Normally, strangers say what up to the father, since he's the head of the home. But because she's just a slim thing, that wouldn't be right. Woman to woman is more respectful.

That's like a Player trying to get a meet with his Big Dog. If he can't pin Big Dog down for business, he don't force it. Just maintains. At some point, Big Dog will send somebody to check in on Player. Player just meets with that brother. No problem. Player don't start drama. Ain't a mistake to be real low key when dealing with powerful people.

Break on the three means:
If a brother ain't careful,
Motherfucker creep up behind and take him out.
Bad look.

When shit's ill, Players rolls real careful. Proud motherfuckers who play righteous get fucked. They all proud of being clean and feel like nothing will touch them. They ain't ready for that real ill shit brewing in dark corners. Be twisted brothers out there who break it down real hardcore. Proud righteous motherfuckers never understand that. Then they get hit. That's when they understand how ill shit can get. But it's too late.

If Player maintain his LITTLE PLAYS, ill shit misses him. When it's thick on them streets, and brothers are dropping, Player minds details. Nothing is too small to miss when it's dark out. If Player maintains like that, he won't be a target. Since he's minding shit tight, ill brothers won't creep up from behind.

Break on the four means:
No problem. Not fronting.
Stepping out is a problem. Watch it.
Chill. Maintain the mental.

Right here, we have a hard brother who tones down in an ill situation. Motherfuckers have to be real careful when shit's ill. Even hard brothers. Streets are unpredictable and dangerous. When it's thick like that, Players don't press forward. The best look is just maintaining the area. Player watches his motherfucking back, while keeping the mental focus on where he wants to be.

Break on the five means:
Dark clouds,
No rain.
Player pulls a nine and hits brother in the alley.

Sometimes dark clouds roll in, but it don't rain. That's like a True Player who has the power to set shit straight, but don't have no people. That Player have to find some real brothers. But when streets is ill, real brothers pull back. They hard to find. True Player have to ask around. Move low key through them streets, say what up without fronting, and find out who's real. He'll find his people that way, real simple. Like a clean shot down the alley, popping some motherfucker. Once True Player have a few real brothers to roll with, he'll put some plays in motion. Don't matter if shit's still ill on them streets. Player have people now.

Break at the top means:
He passes brothers in the street.
Flying bird don't stop.
Fucked.
Bad luck and trouble.

If a motherfuckers all busy, walking fast down the street, he might miss shit. Pass right by some down brother who wants to say what up. Rushing makes him miss connects.

If a little bird keeps on flying, and ain't ever go home to the nest, that bird gets tired. Tired birds who don't stop flying have bad luck. Fall out the sky, hit the street, get run over by a motherfucking bus or some shit.

When LITTLE PLAYS are all that's happening, but a player's still forcing large moves, he's fucked. If he keeps on trying to get over, trouble and bad luck find his ass. Fate don't give a damn about a motherfucker who don't read them streets right, and don't respect what time it is. Heaven have no love for that fool, neither. Brothers sure as hell don't give a damn. That's a real bad look.

AFTER SHIT FINISH

An ill situation played itself out, and shit is returning to normal. But right AFTER SHIT FINISH like this, a brother should be real careful. One bad move will flip shit ill again.

THE FEEL

After Shit Finish. Mind them details.
Maintain a good look.
Paid from the jump.
Down the line fucked.

AFTER SHIT FINISH, better things are starting to happen. Things are falling into place for a brother. But he have to mind them details. When a situation is falling into place by itself, a brother might relax. Let them details slide. Right there is how ill shit starts. Little things blow up down the line. Realistically, that's how most shit shakes out. When motherfuckers just been through some real ill scenarios, they don't start drama over details. But a True Player don't roll like that. It don't matter if he just been through World War Three. Player still maintain focus and handle details. Don't let nothing pass him by.

THE LOOK

Water on the burner.
The look of After Shit Finish.
After Shit Finish
True Player thinking on problems
And heading off ill shit.

When a brother's heating water on the stove, he have to keep his eye on that motherfucker. If not, that shit will boil right the fuck over and put out the burner. Or boil up into steam, so nothing's left.

Fire and water usually ain't have nothing to do with each other. But put water in a pot and light the fire, them motherfuckers work together fine. AFTER SHIT FINISH is about bringing different things together. A brother have to keep his eye on the situation. Watch the heat, make sure nothing boil over or burn away into nothing.

THE BREAKS

Break on the one means:
Pump them brakes.
Clipped crossing the street.
No problem.

After a major break, shit presses a brother forward. Phone starts ringing and motherfuckers show up with plans in they hands. But popping shit off all over ain't a good look. Trying too much, too fast, fucks a brother up. So True Player don't let himself get caught up with all them motherfuckers' plans.

But these situations have mad pressure. Getting over don't happen often. Brothers in the crew get real serious, saying: "Yo, this shit ain't last forever. Hit it now. Make money while you can." True Player might pump the brakes, but there's still lot of motherfuckers up in his face. He can't hold off everybody. So he'll get banged up some.

It's like running that yellow light at some intersection. Maybe a brother is driving fast and decides to just keep moving. His ride almost pulls through. Then some motherfucker clips his back fender. Ain't a large problem causing major damage. He didn't break no laws, neither. Shit was just rolling fast and it happened.

Break on the two means:
Sister lose her church hat.
Don't run for it.
Down the line it comes back.

When a real religious sister do church on Easter Sunday, she dress her best. Wear some real fine hat. But weather in spring is bananas. Strong wind might jump up out of nowhere, blow that hat off her head. Since she's dressed up nice, it would be a bad look for that sister running all wild down the street chasing her hat. Proper shit to do is let it go. Probably some brother down the street will see it blow by and pick it up for her. Or maybe some other sister from the congregation find it. Hand it to her when she shows up at church.

This is about a brother joined an organization that just got over. This brother ain't getting a good look from people up the chain. All them motherfuckers finally got a real piece broke off for themselves. Some them turn arrogant. Don't bother with bringing real brothers up in the business. Just ain't have time for that.

In this situation, brothers low in the crew sometimes start playing sideways game to be noticed. They start licking ass, or fronting

real loud to make brothers up the chain look their way. Run bull-
shit plays just to put their name out there. That ain't a good look.

True Player don't chase shit and throw himself away. If people ain't
having him, fuck them motherfuckers. Player just maintain his
game. Handles business and improves his personal shit without
stressing whether some bullshit brothers who just got over notice or
not. Times change. People will recognize a True Player sooner or
later. What a motherfucker owns, on a real deep level, can't be taken
from him. Shit might blow away a minute, but what's really his
comes back to a brother.

Like that sister step into church and somebody standing there
with her hat.

Break on the three means:
Old Big Dog
Put order in the game.
Three years for that shit.
Don't hire crab asses.

Old Big Dog was a True Player way back in the day when brothers
were all fighting each other. He stepped in and organized mother-
fuckers. That didn't happen simple. Real hard brothers never have
plans to join nobody. Wild motherfuckers from way out the area
weren't falling in, neither. But Old Big Dog had a plan to put peo-
ple paid. He realized if brothers stopped fighting, and the game
was organized, shit would shake out real nice for all them mother-
fuckers. He had the power to break it down. He had the vision to
pull it off. He stopped the wars and put brothers paid, all over the
area.

This break is about bringing order to a situation. When a Player
rises up and gets power, he usually try to expand his operation.
That means war. Brothers don't take new ground just by asking for

it. Taking turf is a real hard battle. Pulling property from mother-fuckers is the worst war to fight. Brothers fight to the death. That's their land, yo. Pry that shit out their cold dead hands. It ain't going any other way.

Since turf is so hard to win, Players have to hold that shit real tight when they finally take it. But many times, a Player will send crab asses to manage the new property. That shit is far away. And since them crab ass motherfuckers bother him, it gets them out his face. That's a real bad look. It fucks shit up permanently. No chance a new area will pop off with crab asses running things.

This shit is true in situations large and small. Not just war. Business rolls the same. Every motherfucker coming up wants to expand his shit. But taking new territory has its own set of problems. Putting a crab ass at the wheel shouldn't be one of them.

Break on the four means:
Fine clothes turn to rags.
Be careful all day.

When a crew just gets over, they become the new power. Their game starts expanding. During this time, fucked up things might happen. Hidden shit in the organization might come to light and shock brothers. Since they rolling strong, ain't no problem to hide it from them streets. Brothers pull a cover-up, forget whatever happened, and keep shit moving.

But a True Player don't forget what happened. He looks at it like a sign of what ain't right in the organization. When other brothers roll on, Player stops to handle this shit. By minding things real close, he heads off problems. Otherwise, this shit will pop up down the line. Fuck the whole organization real bad.

Break on the five means:
Brother building hospitals on the east side. Nothing there.
West side brother dropping dimes in the basket. Happy.

AFTER SHIT FINISH, and everything finally come together for a brother, he sometimes handle The Heavens different. His large status makes him puts on shows. He throws down big money, real loud, for charities. Or starts building hospitals with his name on them. Writes checks for museums and them fashionable foundations. But none of this has heart. Brother really ain't thinking about what The Heavens want. He's just putting on shows to look like a righteous motherfucker.

People only see what's in front of their eyes. But The Heavens see what's in a brothers' heart. Maybe a broke brother with real respect for The Heavens drops just a few dimes in the church basket. That will bless him better than some hospital a fake motherfucker built. Large shows with no heart don't mean shit to The Heavens.

Break at the top means:
Drown in the water.
Fucked.

AFTER SHIT FINISH, when a brother pulled himself through real rough waters, he shouldn't look back. The only play is moving forward. But many brothers who live through ill shit trip out on it. Feel real fascinated they made it through. Start thinking what a wonderful motherfucking human being they are. But standing there, looking back AFTER SHIT FINISH leads to problems. Only a brother who moves forward, never looks back, and forgets them rough waters really makes it through, 100%.

RIGHT AROUND THE CORNER

This is when shit starts changing from being fucked up to running right. Like when springtime RIGHT AROUND THE CORNER. Flowers ain't out yet, but that motherfucking winter is ending. Even before it happens, streets feeling better. That's a good look to finish *Yo Ching*.

THE FEEL

Right Around The Corner. Paid.
But if the old man
Gets clipped by a bus,
Nothing positive happening.

This is a real large job with major responsibilities. It's about leading streets out of bullshit and back to order. But this play should shake out. A movement this large will pull together motherfuckers who normally work in different directions. Since this job is so important, Player have to be real careful at the jump. Like an old man crossing the street uptown.

Old man crossing the street is legendary shit uptown. They choose real careful when they pick the corner to cross from. Look both ways about fifty times. They listening too, trying to hear shit their eyes missed. Stand there through three lights changing, just to have the timing down. Only then they roll. Streets ain't no joke for them old motherfuckers. Shorties different. They fast and ain't have shit to worry about. Just run right cross the street laughing, between them cars and everything. But the old man moves slow. Have to be real careful. Even then, sometimes one them old folks gets clipped by a motherfucking bus. Then all that looking around they did didn't matter none.

When good shit's RIGHT AROUND THE CORNER, being slow and real careful sets a brother up to be paid.

THE LOOK

Water under the stove:
The look of Right Around The Corner.
True Player mind the pieces,
Find the right places.

If a motherfucker put a pot of water under the stove, it don't boil. Shit have to be in the right place for things to happen. So a brother have to understand where shit supposed to be. To learn that, he have to look into all the parts of a situation. Have to understand all the forces involved. Have to know what goes where. If a brother puts the pieces in the right place, shit runs right. But to put the pieces together, a brother have to put himself together first. Only somebody who sees shit right will run things right.

THE BREAKS

Break on the one means:
Clipped by a bus.
Bust ass.

Shit hasn't come together yet. Everything is all over the place. Brothers want to push forward, just to see results. But rolling like that leads to bullshit, since timing ain't right. So a brother here check himself. Chilling a minute will save him from popping off into bust ass bullshit.

Break on the two means:
Hit them brakes.
Maintain. Paid.

Time ain't right to roll yet. That don't mean a brother just sit sipping liquor and chilling. His game falls off that way. True Player builds strength while he's waiting. Reads books, lifts weights, maintains focus on his goals. Then he's ready when the door opens. If a brother stays strong like that, and remembers where he wants to get to—even when he ain't moving forward—shit will shake out for him.

Break on the three means:
When shit's Right Around The Corner, popping off is a bad
look.
Large play shakes out.

Time to set a situation straight, but Player don't have the weight to pull it off. If he tried to roll anyway, ill motherfuckers would break it down for him. So Player have to find himself a crew. Reach out for real brothers who are down. Then they all throw in together, roll on shit, and set the situation straight.

Break on the four means:
Maintain. Paid.
Stop tripping.
No joke breaking down ill shit.
Three years paid out for real.

Heavy fight here. Player is facing the illest type of bullshit, but this fight have to happen. Player got to be real strong in his heart and mind. Have that mental game. Decide he's winning this mother-fucker. No doubts. A battle this fucked leaves no time for tripping. Player is fighting forces that just don't give a fuck. Maybe that's ill brothers in business. Maybe that's ill parts of his own damn self. Either way, shit that don't give a fuck don't go down easy. Player needs all his power to win. The fight will be long and hard. But winning will have a solid pay out. When a Player finally gets over on all the ill shit he's facing, he finds a real foundation in the world. The fight teaches Player how to find the power in himself, and how to handle that power right. That's a damn good look.

Break on the five means:
Maintain. Paid.
No problem.
True Player shine.
Good look.

The fight is finished. What's real came out on top. All the shit a brother used to trip out on while he was coming up don't matter no more. Winning proves that he handled shit right. He's shining now, a True Player. Real brothers throw in with him. Money rolls in. Damn good times. And just like the sun feels better after it's been raining forever, shit here feels real nice after the bullshit before.

Break at the top means:
Drinking brews and party
Feeling fine.

No problem.
Party brother
Loses it for real.

When times are changing for the better, brothers feel good. Bullshit is finished. Everybody down with each other. The new plan is being worked out, and good things are RIGHT AROUND THE CORNER. While details are settling, brothers have time on their hands. Share some brews, party some, just kick it. That ain't a problem. But a brother should stay chill with this. If he party like a motherfucker and let himself go, he lose his place in the new situation.

WORD

Yo Ching Glossary

Producer's Note: Vast grammatical liberties are taken throughout *Yo Ching* in order to reflect the vision of True Player most accurately. As this endeavor is rooted in colloquial discourse, I trust any lack of authenticity or clarity shall be pardoned by—or at very least explained by—the regrettable limits of my own talents. In effort to transcend these limits, I fashioned the following glossary while working with True Player. It shall provide an indispensable key for readers striving to understand the words, terms, and meaning of *Yo Ching* to fullest measure.

—H. G.

Angle: *(noun)* field of endeavor within a crew, organization, or the game.

Area: *(n)* one's neighborhood or immediate vicinity of personal influence in business.

Beef: *(n)* dispute between two persons or parties.

Big Dog: *(n)* established, esteemed, land holding and power wielding member of the community. Whether CEO, business mogul, pop star, syndicate head, or royal prince, the Big Dog holds indisputable influence and status. They operate within the bounds of society, but possess the capacity for full and unrestrained expressions of power to secure desired results. Big Dogs are employers of men, builders of empire, judges of disputes, and dealers of favors. The nature and character of Big Dogs spans the moral spectrum, from enlightened to regrettable.

Blahzay: *(adjective)* an attitude of indifference or disinterest.

Born Wrong: *(adj)* an individual with defects from birth that impair his ability to conform with accepted societal standards of moral behavior.

Break It Down: *(verb)* enforce justice or rules with punitive measures which are delivered verbally or violently, depending on the severity of offense.

Break Off A Piece: *(colloquial)* dispense and distribute wealth, gains, property, or favorable aspects of profitable business to worthy individuals. (*True Player ran his angle tight. When that organization got over, Big Dog broke off a piece for him.*)

Brew: *(n)* beer, an intoxicating beverage.

Brother: *(n)* any race, creed, or type of man.

Bullshit: *(n)* instances, events, or people devoid of merit, substance, or positive attributes.

Bust Ass: *(adj)* derogatory term denoting a person of ill kept appearance, poor business acumen, meager or no financial holdings and very low social status.

Crab Ass: *(n)* reprehensible human possessing deplorable character. Sloth, greed, ineptitude, theft, dishonesty, delusions of grandeur, cowardice, manipulation and selfishness prevail in the lamentable crab ass. Crab ass individuals ruin organizations, efforts, and relationships through mere participation. Many crab asses develop particular Machiavellian skill sets which enable them to achieve position, status, and merit in the eyes of others. This is rarely earned, and very seldom benefits their organization or area.

Crew: *(n)* close knit group of people held together by shared bonds, working towards collective goals.

Deep: *(adj)* situations or individuals with substantial depth of meaning or character, often producing penetrating reflection within others.

Down: *(adj)* describes amenable people of straight forward character who participate in activities without producing antagonism.

Down The Line: *(prepositional phrase)* in the future.

Down With: *(v)* to be in accord or agreement with an individual, institution, or group. (*He had a beef with that motherfucker but Big Dog cleared shit up. Now they* down with *each other.*)

Drop The Ball: *(v)* commit an error or make a mistake; usually not of grave nature.

Fall Off: *(v)* reversal of fortune or cessation of efforts that result in the rapid decline and often ultimate termination of a professional career, personal reputation, place of business, partnership, friendship or relationship.

Fucked: *(adj)* an entirely negative position with no advantages whatsoever.

The Game: *(n)* the highly competitive field of endeavor which pits individuals and/or institutions in opposition to win material gains, financial resources, social power, status, desirable females, business advantage and/or valued property within an area, organization, operation, or territory.

Getting Over: *(v)* achievement of indisputable success which results in the attainment of prized and thoroughly consolidated positions of power for individual, crew, and/or organization.

The Heavens: *(n)* the animating power behind all of nature. An omniscient, omnipotent, highly moral force that transcends human awareness and creates all nature of order, activity, matter, time, and space within our universe. The Heavens may be petitioned by man for favor, and also offended by man's activities and/or attitude.

Ill: *(adj)* possessing highly negative characteristics.

Ill Brothers: *(n)* criminally minded men prone to violence. Ill Brothers are dynamically negative, always dangerous, and routinely participating in detrimental and illegal pursuits from routine theft to mass murder.

Ill Shit: *(n)* negative situations or events.

Joint: *(n)* 1.) a man's penis. 2.) a collective effort in business.

Knocking Boots: *(v)* the act of sexual intercourse. *(That motherfucker was knocking boots with his slim thing. Now they all got a shorty.)*

La: *(n)* marijuana rolled and smoked in the fashion of cigarettes to produce pleasing narcotic effects upon the user.

Left Turn: *(n)* negative development within an individual's life/crew/organization that produces detrimental effects.

Losing Weight: *(v)* significant but not terminal decline in fortune that results in the loss of material possessions, social status, or market power for an individual or organization.

Maintain: *(v)* holding one's position through ceaseless engagement in consistent activity towards desired outcomes.

Motherfucker(s): *(n)* generic, inoffensive title for men. May be modified towards negative or positive connotations through the application of predicate syntax. *(Stay away from them crab ass <u>motherfuckers.</u> Or: Don't stress. I know that <u>motherfucker</u> from around the way. He's alright.)*

Nine: *(n)* nine millimeter handgun, a popular and efficient weapon.

Old Big Dog *(n)*: historical figure of unknown era, with origins in ancient China. Regarded as the world's first True Player, Old Big Dog is either sole or contributing author of the original *Yo Ching* material.

Operation: *(n)* system of efforts within a crew or organization that result in specific outcomes.

Organization: *(n)* large group of people, often composed of several crews, held together through established leadership and the pursuit of mutual aims, usually financial or imperial in nature.

Party Motherfucker: *(n)* shallow individual who pursues social diversions and hedonistic pleasures to the detriment of personal development.

Play: *(n)* any strategized action intended to benefit an individual, his crew, or an organization.

Player: *(n)* 1. benevolent, ambitious, talented, dependable individual who rises in the game through natural leadership, harmonious relationships, and the responsible management of effective angles. 2. abbreviated title for a True Player.

Pop Off: *(v)* visible commencement of robust activity.

Pound: *(n)* heartfelt greeting involving a brief physical embrace.

Put Paid: *(colloquial)* to receive compensation for efforts; a variation of *get paid*.

Real: *(adj)* possessing the valued attributes of authenticity, integrity, honesty, dependability and an entire lack of pretense. While often used to describe people, enterprises and experiences can also be referred to as real. (*Last night I was reading my Yo Ching. That shit is _real_.*)

Recognize: *(v)* acknowledge the merit, ability, status, or skills of another.

Roll: *(v)* commence an activity towards desired results.

Rolling On Motherfuckers Cross Town: *(colloquial)* any highly dangerous enterprise that holds the potential for real and significant losses, including but not limited to: personal injury, extensive and grievous liability, financial ruin, and/or death for the participating individuals.

Shake(s) Out: *(prep)* the end result of efforts. (*Let's pop off and see where this joint _shakes out_ down the line.*)

Shit: *(n)* elastic and all encompassing term which refers without negative connotations towards many sundry instances, objects, events, and activities. The meaning of *shit* is discerned through context, as well as the absence or presence of modifying syntax. (*In business, a brother should handle his _shit_. Or: Them ill brothers pulled some fucked up _shit_.*)

Shorty: *(n)* child or minor under the age of personal agency as recognized legally by the community.

Sister: *(n)* any race, creed, or type of woman.

Slim Thing: *(n)* nubile, highly desirable young woman possessing alluring physical maturity that often precedes her mental development.

Step Up: *(v)* challenge the words or actions of another, usually in a confrontational manner.

Streets: *(n)* the public at large, where the populace participates in market trade, shared leisure time, and forms general consensus.

Throw In: *(v)* the act of joining or professing allegiance to an individual, crew, or organization.

Tight: *(adj)* well managed and fastidiously maintained endeavor or activity.

Trip: *(v)* excessive mental speculation that results in distorted perception.

True Player: *(n)* highly evolved leader of men with advanced mental, physical, visionary, organizational, and spiritual capacity. Achieving an elevated understanding of reality, True Players demonstrate that understanding through powerfully maintained excellence in their chosen field of endeavor. Rising from Player status, True Players transcend personal interest to work for the benefit of all. Recognized as masters, flowing in harmony with The Heavens, True Players reflect the highest values held by humanity.

ABOUT THE AUTHOR

True Player been round.

ABOUT THE PRODUCER

Hugh Gallagher has written for established and emerging brands in New York, Los Angeles, Bangkok, Taipei, and Portland. His journalism has been featured in *Rolling Stone*, *Wired*, *Harper's* and *Newsweek*, where he covered the 2014 *coup d'état* in Thailand. Hugh has written scripts for Daft Punk videos and commercials directed by Spike Jonze. He is the author of the novel *Teeth*, and his famous *College Application Essay* is an internet comedy classic. Hugh is a graduate of New York University. For more information, visit www.hughgallagher.net.

Made in the USA
Columbia, SC
22 June 2018